HOT AND BOTHERED

LeBron James, the Miami Heat, and Modern-day Mythmaking

LeBron James, the Miami Heat, and Modern-day Mythmaking

Hot and Bothered: LeBron James, the Miami Heat, and Modern-day Mythmaking

Chip Maude

Published by Chip Maude, 2024.

To my teachers growing up who always encouraged my writing and love of sports: my mother, Cheri, Miss Dea and Mr. Carpenter.

I don't know truly when this journey began. I figured with how culturally relevant the 2010s Heat was that there would be not one, not two, not three books written about the traveling circus.

Okay, if you made it past the obviously low-hanging fruit of a joke right there, I applaud you.

Years after LeBron James' "I'm coming home" exit from Miami, numerous books and documentaries chronicled his journey. Dwyane Wade released a photo autobiography near his retirement, while TV specials covered *The Decision*, Wade's final season, and Chris Bosh's sudden blood clot diagnosis that ended his career. LeBron occasionally discussed Miami, more so in segments of his HBO show and an ESPN+ mini-series. Several works detailed his stirring championship run in Cleveland right after the Heatles era. Brian Windhorst even penned a standout book on LeBron's business savvy and growing empire.

But as far as I could see, no one had pierced the veil on documenting 2010 to 2014 of the Miami Heat. And I honestly felt that there was a void.

Maybe it was how suddenly LeBron left the Heat, coupled with how quickly he led another franchise back to championship prominence in his home state. Maybe it was fatigue from wall-to-wall 24/7 coverage of Miami (which, admittedly, slowed down and became less absurdist at the end). Perhaps it was that the principal reporting boots on the ground moved on, but had the blueprints in storage for down the road. A real possibility is that only two years after LeBron ended a ten-year dynasty (at least according to Pat Riley), Kevin Durant made a shocking decision much in the same vein as LeBron made, joining the 73-win Warriors and many of the same talking points, real or imagined, resurfaced and much was played out again.

Who knows? All I do know is that, for better or for worse, I wanted to do this project. I wanted to selfishly take the ride again, this time from a slightly removed 35,000-foot view.

This began as almost encyclopedic, which you may still pick up on at times. I felt ultimately that that wasn't interesting enough. There are Wikipedia pages and ten-year anniversary pieces for that. The four-year run was anything but linear. I wanted to take a stroll down memory lane, attempt to repaint the fishbowl the Heat was in, and, to a certain degree, all basketball fans were in with them. I wanted to address the media coverage, which as I mentioned above, surely got fatiguing even for the harshest of haters. And then, to tie it all together, I wanted to write on the narratives (nails on the chalkboard) that not only consumed the coverage of the Heat during those years, but seemingly have prevailed to this day.

Society at large has moved on from *The Decision* as they have from thinking players exercising free agency is the thermal exhaust port of the NBA Death Star, exposed and ready to be obliterated. Player empowerment became a lexicon, as did "taking my talents to..." and the aforementioned "not two, not three, not four, not five, not six, not seven" schtick.

Being so many years removed, there are details and moments that have slipped through the cracks, even for the closest observer of those years. Some details and moments, to many, will be quasi–Mandela Effects.

There are moments I do not cover, whether by omission or commission. Not *everything* in the four years was necessary or even interesting. For example, the 2011 MVP award that Derrick Rose eventually won wasn't very controversial at the time, became so after LeBron's dominating performance defending him in the playoffs, then over time became a complete revisionist history on why Rose won and that no, no there definitely *wasn't* voter fatigue or fear of voting for the unliked guy. I just did not see that angle as being interesting. The MVP process in general started a slippery slope years after, but the seeds were already being planted for the most toxic and boring award discourse in sports.

I hope you notice that I also intentionally try to avoid hypotheticals. I address a few in terms of media coverage, but in general I don't think they're worth anyone's time. You as the reader don't deserve to be dragged through an alternate universe. Someone else can tackle that, and much better than I ever could.

I touch upon it at the end of this book, but ultimately the Heat did not ruin the NBA, as so many lamented when the Big 3 formed. In fact, many feel the NBA has never been able to recapture the magic it had in those four years, despite their best efforts at recreating the furor of free agency and player movement. It could easily be said that the NBA kowtowing to the players since *The Decision*, and more specifically under Adam Silver's leadership, has disengaged the average fan much more than the Big 3 ever did.

The main thing about the Heat was there was no apathy. No one said, "Oh the Heat? They're neither here nor there for me." For whatever of a multitude of reasons, which I hope I cover adequately in these pages, people loved or hated the Heat. All three members of the Big 3 were likable, popular, successful players on their own before teaming up in Miami. The fact that a free agent union would draw so many people to loathe them likely was a perfect storm, as trite and unimaginative as it sounds. To begin with, only maybe five teams in the league had a chance at landing one of the Big 3 in free agency, let alone two. So, 25 fan bases were already going to feel less than and rage against *the man*. Miami being heartily booed in Salt Lake City or Portland or Memphis made no sense, but it was the world in which they existed. And yet, people booing and hating meant *they watched.* The Heat played to sellout crowds virtually every single night of those four years. They were on national TV the most by an insane margin.

The Heat was, bear with me for the overused term, trailblazers in a real way. But more adequately, they were modern Dienekes. As mentioned above, the Warriors signing Durant a couple years removed from the disbanding of the Big 3 was criticized, but all the arguments and bad faith talking points had already been aired out years before. While the Warriors were on TV a lot, they never captured the ire, love, or hand wringing about *legacy* and *built not bought* that Miami endured. Or the eyeballs. LeBron and the Heat cleared the path.

As of this writing, the Denver Nuggets are hoisting the 2023 NBA Finals trophy, Wade is set for summer enshrinement in the Naismith Memorial Basketball Hall of Fame, and LeBron has, genuinely or not, hinted at retirement for the first time. The page has fully been turned on the Heat. Hopefully this volume at least keeps a bookmark in for those four years.

Thank you for taking this journey with me.

Vamos.

Chapter 1 - Kingmakers

If you close your eyes and someone says *The Decision*, it's pretty likely we all think one of the same couple of things: LeBron James, in a purple checkered button-down, muttering the cringey, rehearsed line of "I'm taking my talents to South Beach" or he, Chris Bosh, and Dwyane Wade, in crisp white Miami Heat uniforms, dancing in smoke and lasers at a pep rally.

The Decision, both the actual decisions LeBron, Bosh, and Wade were going to make in the summer of 2010 and *The Decision*, the TV special LeBron used to announce his, captured the nation.

You know the story by now: three of the most sought-after free agents ever, all free agents at the same time, oh and by the way the glitziest of NBA markets were all prepared to make them offers from New York to Chicago to Los Angeles to Miami.

If you happen to not know the story, here it is as quickly as possible:

LeBron James, anointed on the hallowed cover of *Sports Illustrated* in 2002 as *The Chosen One*, had just won his second straight NBA MVP and led a mediocre Cleveland Cavaliers roster to its second straight 60-win season, but also second straight disappointing playoff exit. Born and raised in nearby (sort of) Akron, it was assumed LeBron, who many considered one of, if not the best, player in the league, would most likely stay in Cleveland.

Dwyane Wade was a slippery combo guard who burst onto the national scene as a junior at Marquette, leading the Golden Eagles on an unexpected Final Four run. He followed that up by winning a championship (and NBA Finals MVP) with the Miami Heat in just his third season. While LeBron and Lakers guard Kobe Bryant typically got top billing as the best player in the league, many on the periphery felt Wade was neck and neck. He had overcome roster turnover and injuries following the championship run to re-establish himself as a nightmare two-way player. But, burdened by another mediocre roster, Wade hadn't gotten out of the first round of the playoffs since that Finals win, four years earlier. From Chicago, it was good odds that the two teams in the running with the best chances were the hometown Bulls and the Heat.

And then there was Chris Bosh, a long, rangy, skilled big man on the Toronto Raptors. Bosh was a college professor trapped in a perfect NBA body; in his free time, he read books with titles like "A History of the World in 6 Glasses" and was a hardcore computer coder. "I always wanted to be a graphic designer," he said. "I wanted to get into web design and multimedia. I still get intrigued when I look at different websites and wonder what kind of code they put in. I'm into all kinds of technology. When I was in school my favorite subject was math. I took algebra, calculus. I just loved breaking the codes and solving problems." Bosh would later pen an op-ed for wired.com titled "Here's Why You Should Learn to Code".

Also fluent in Spanish, Bosh wasn't just a nerd; some of his promo videos on YouTube to drum up All-Star votes featured him dressed as a fast-talking cowboy used car salesman trying to convince folks to vote via paper ballot.

He had been trying to break the code of postseason success. While he was the only NBA player in 2009-10 to average over 24 points and 10 rebounds, he, unlike Wade or LeBron, had never been out of the first round of the playoffs, and even then, had only been to the postseason a pair of times in his first seven years in the league. Though Bosh liked Toronto, him staying put seemed like an impossibly long shot.

All three players were drafted in the first five picks of the 2003 NBA Draft, and all had been teammates on the 2008 USA Olympic team that won gold in Beijing, China. All three also signed shorter second NBA contracts, opting for three-year deals as opposed to the four- or five-year standard, as to become free agents earlier, and congruently, all in the same summer (gasp!).

ESPN debuted a LeBron Tracker in 2010, updating sometimes multiple times a day with leanings or whisperings about his free agency intentions. All three were asked daily, usually in multiple ways, about their status. Theories were hatched, also seemingly on a daily basis.

On his radio show on June 28, days before teams could officially meet with free agents, national personality Stephen A. Smith said, "You're only as good as your sources, as a journalist, and from what I'm being told, after hearing what everybody has to say, LeBron James will agree to team with Dwyane Wade, he's going to South Beach. LeBron James and Chris Bosh are going to South Beach; they are going to play for the Miami Heat."

"My guess at the time: Smith got word that Miami was in the lead, took it and ran with it, then hoped he was right," wrote Bill Simmons. "If he was right, he became the big winner of the summer of 2010. If he was wrong, he could always claim that he WAS right, but that something got screwed up and things changed."

The long shots were just that: long shots. Los Angeles, New Jersey (soon to be Brooklyn), even Dallas and Houston.

Everyone figured it came down to Cleveland, Miami, New York, and Chicago for the services of LeBron, Bosh, or Wade, or some combination of two. The three players had meetings, sometimes at the same times in the same buildings, alternating who they were listening to.

Bosh tweeted out, "It's been an exciting first couple of hrs. Got some interesting visits and presentations from Houston, Toronto, Chicago and Miami. We'll see who else will come out tomorrow."

"I've never seen Pat Riley so nervous," Wade told his agent Henry Thomas after the meeting with the Heat representation. Riley, of course, was the godfather Miami Heat powerbroker, formerly championship head coach turned team president.

After pitching Bosh and Wade, the Miami contingent of Riley, owner Mickey Arison, and head coach Erik Spoelstra turned their focus to Cleveland and pitching the belle of the free agency ball, LeBron.

As the Miami group flew to Cleveland for their meeting with LeBron, Wade instructed Thomas to arrange another meeting with Chicago. Immediately, optimism abounded in the Bulls organization. How could they not be in a favorable position if Wade was asking for another meeting only hours after their original meeting?

Near the end of the meeting with LeBron, Riley reached under the table and pulled up a velvet bag and slid it across the table to James.

"How bad do you want this?"

James pulled the drawstrings apart. His eyes grew wider.

Inside were twenty-one championship rings, three different versions in platinum, silver, and gold, of the seven championship rings Riley had won as a player, assistant, and head coach.

Riley continued to talk about sacrifice and James' ultimate goal, but the point had already been made. Riley finished, leaving James with one word to stew on: dynasty.

What he had pitched to James he, and the organization, believed would be the modern-day dynasty, one to rival the dynasties of the 1980s Celtics and Lakers and the 1990s Bulls.

ESPN reported:

At 1:50 p.m., the Heat's representatives paraded through the lobby of the IMG building without saying a word. Before getting in their cars, they passed the Los Angeles Clippers' two-man contingent of acting general manager Neil Olshey and executive Andy Roeser.

Olshey then joked that Riley went into overtime with James.

"Is Coach going to get fined for going over his allotted time?" Olshey asked a person who works for James. "Don't worry, we'll be short."

The Clippers wrapped up their meeting with James in about an hour.

James would host both the Bulls and the Cavs the next day. Cleveland would be armed with a fresh face in their pitch to James: recently hired head coach Byron Scott, who had played for Riley with the Lakers in the 1980s, was introduced as James was meeting with Miami.

"I think at the end of the day, he's going to make the right decision, and he'll be here in Cleveland for the rest of his career," added Scott. "His legacy of winning championships in his hometown will be like nothing he's seen in his life. There's nothing like winning at home. I won three titles in my hometown, and there's not a better feeling."

Word had already begun to leak that Wade was leaning towards committing to Chicago, which also spun the idea that James' final decision would come by July 5, supposedly giving him time over the weekend after the final two pitches concluded.

The Cavaliers had an 11 am meeting with James. It was not planned to be extensive or time intensive like Miami's. Their pitch was simple: stay home.

ESPN reported that the Cavs wanted to "tug on James' heart strings" as they organized a "fan tunnel" down East 9th Street to welcome him. Hundreds of fans lined the sidewalks outside the IMG Building, and when James pulled into the parking garage, fans held up signs that simply said "Home" while others tossed white powder in the air, paying homage to his popular pregame ritual.

Cleveland planned to keep their presentation short and colorful, playing to James' light-hearted personality. Cavs owner Dan Gilbert had commissioned a Family Guy-type cartoon to keep the mood light, playing off James' affinity for the popular TV show. The Cavs also hinted at James' community involvement and his attachment to the region.

As the pitch wound down, Cavs general manager Chris Grant asked James if he would be willing to recruit Bosh to accept a sign-and-trade deal with Toronto to team up with James in Cleveland.

As Brian Windhorst of ESPN wrote, "James replied that he didn't know Bosh well and didn't know his plans... Bosh had no interest in playing in Cleveland."

Wade, Bosh, and LeBron had a short phone call before LeBron arrived at the University of Akron for his high school basketball camp. He was mum.

Chicago had hoped for a commitment from Wade after multiple meetings, but their front office was getting increasingly nervous as the hours passed with no word from him.

Those in NBA circles were catching wind that Wade and Bosh were a package deal and that Wade had likely convinced Bosh to join him in Miami.

James was still undecided.

And this is where it all gets murky. Stephen A. Smith had reported a week prior it was a done deal. Who his source was would never be known, and it's now assumed that more likely than not he wanted to stake a claim, right or wrong, before anyone else.

Brian Windhorst would claim years later that he had received the LeBron to Miami scoop and rejected it because of the absurdity.

"I got tipped off that LeBron was going to go to Miami, and I rejected it because I said, no, they can't make the cap space, and those guys aren't taking less," Windhorst said. "I pushed it right out. I could have really followed up on it, like, ten days out because I didn't respect that, yes, they could make the cap space, and yes, those guys would consider taking less."

Wade has since claimed they were all originally headed to Chicago, contingent upon the Bulls trading homegrown swingman Luol Deng. "It was us trying to put together our dream team in a sense," he said. "Chicago was very tempting from a standpoint of what they had on the roster when it came to the young talent. But when it came to the point Miami was able to get three players, that changed the whole dynamic of the summer. It would be a different story (if the Bulls were). We thought about it. That didn't happen. It was something they (Bulls) talked about. They were very open with us with what they were trying to do. They heard the news of Miami being able to bring three players in. But it never happened. So, we never had to think that far. They (Miami) came with the idea that they can get three players. We never thought it was possible. I was shocked when I heard it could happen. But I know LeBron's eyes were here (Chicago). I know my eyes were here. I know Chris' eyes were kind of everywhere because he was in Toronto, so he was just happy that people knew who he was. Toronto was a little different than it is today."

"If the Bulls were able to trade Luol Deng to the Clippers, which they had talks about doing, that Big 3 would've been in Chicago," long-time Chicago sportswriter K.C. Johnson said later. "Trust me on that one."

Wade, according to Windhorst, was the one who pitched the idea to Chicago. People inside the Bulls told Nick Friedell that Bosh had committed to them. "Chris Bosh, according to more than one person in the organization, said that, 'I'm coming to play for the Bulls'", said Friedell. "Straight up. He said, 'I'm coming to play for the Bulls. This is where I'm going to be.'"

Bosh would later say that the Bulls *wanted* him to commit. "They said, 'If you come, Dwyane or LeBron is going to come. So, you need to make a decision.' That was my pressure."

Wade seemingly verified that story: "The Bulls, the Knicks, every team that was in the runnings in 2010 could only bring in two star players. So, in Chicago, it was gonna be a race to either it's Chris and me or Chris and LeBron; it wasn't going to be all three of us. So, Miami was the only team that made sure to put themself in a position that all three of us can come in."

"What should LeBron do? Pick Chicago," Bill Simmons wrote. "That's where the rings are. The fact that he didn't say to Bosh, 'Come to Chicago with me, we'll play with Rose and Noah and win six titles together' was the single most disappointing outcome of the summer. That team would have been a true juggernaut with pieces that actually complemented each other, unlike this pickup-basketball situation that's brewing in Miami. Even with Boozer there in Bosh's place—and I think he's a great fit for them, with or without LeBron—it could still translate to multiple titles, because Rose could have been the best second banana since Kobe in 2001.

"Just know that Kobe would have caught a whiff of those rings and gone to Chicago. Same with Jordan. Same with Magic and Bird... How can you care about winning and NOT go to Chicago?"

How it all came together is still in question. It's like a game of telephone, the further we get from the genesis, the more convoluted it becomes. The subjects themselves can never seem to get the story straight.

Wade said in his autobiography that he and LeBron had already discussed playing together before they got word the Heat would have cap space cleared for three max contract free agents.

"'Well, who is that third guy?' LeBron and I were both like, 'Chris Bosh.'"

"I remember Chris looking at us back and forth and not saying anything," Wade wrote. "Then he finally breaks his silence.

"'Wait...this is for real?'"

Wade offered that no decision had been made until after all three had completed their meetings. He claims he went underneath a rental house in South Carolina on the Fourth of July to get on a three-way call with Bosh and LeBron.

"So wassup? What y'all feeling," he wrote. "I jumped in first. 'Honestly, to me, out of my options, the best spot for me is either Chicago or Miami.' Everyone said the teams they were considering. Then the question was do we want to play together in Miami.

"'I'm in,' I said.

"'I'm in,' Bron said a few seconds later."

"Fuck it," he says Bosh said. "I'm in!"

The simplistic approach that Wade relays surely is missing an immense amount of details. But "that's my story. And, dammit, I'm sticking to it," he wrote, very tongue in cheek.

"Many around the league assumed the playing-together plan had been predetermined for months, if not years," wrote Brian Windhorst. "To this day, all three players maintain that nothing was decided until that call."

Adrian Wojnarowski spun a tale of the three players colluding during the 2008 Beijing Olympics "about the summer of 2010, about the chance of a lifetime to chase championships and roll like a touring rock band."

He continued on that the Heat had cleared the requisite cap space on draft night in June and "from then on, (LeBron confidant and NBA power broker William) Wesley had two words about LeBron and the Heat for the closest of associates: done deal."

The plot grew thicker, in the world according to Wojnarowski. Wesley and LeBron's business manager, Maverick

Carter, got entangled in a feud over who was able to say what and to whom. He also told of secret meetings between the NBA Finals and free agency between Wade and LeBron's inner circle. Woj's story and Wade's diverge both on specific details and some generalities. Woj maintained that the three had a call on July 6th, Bosh committing to Wade and Miami and LeBron still non-committal. As per Wade's version of events, that call took place on July 4th with all three coming to the aforementioned agreement. In Woj's version, Wade and Bosh announced their intentions to play together and then only after that, got word from LeBron he was coming. But Wade said after their July 4th call, LeBron went AWOL and he and Bosh were nervous of LeBron backing out to return to Cleveland.

Another version of events from ESPN writers Chris Broussard and Marc Stein was that the Big 3, as they would come to be known, met in *Miami* the week before free agency began.

Local reporter Jorge Sedano refuted the report, posting Wade's itinerary of the week in question which did not have him in Miami.

Tim Reynolds, also a Miami reporter with sources all in and around the Heat organization, tweeted: "2nd person: Summit in Miami 'absolutely' did not happen."

The two ESPN writers then doubled down! "A modified version of the ballyhooed free-agent summit that was initially suggested and then downplayed by Dwyane Wade has indeed taken place, ESPN.com has learned.

"Sources close to the situation said Monday night that three of the biggest names in basketball — Wade, Chris Bosh and LeBron James — met over the weekend in Miami to seriously discuss their futures, with a focus on the increasingly plausible possibility of those three teaming up with Wade's Heat."

In yet another version, Ian Thomsen *of Sports Illustrated* alleged that at All-Star *2006,* LeBron, Wade, and Bosh "started talking about forming an alliance that would change the NBA for years to come".

"We're not that smart," Bosh said years later, shooting down the tall tales of the long-ago formed alliance.

Bill Simmons floated that "Someone Who Knows Things told me" that an actual pact had been made after the 2008 Olympics between LeBron, Wade, Bosh, and Chris Paul that they would all play together!

The thread pulling seemed more and more absurd the more the thread was tugged upon.

Adding to the intrigue, legendary NBA enforcer Charles Oakley asserted that LeBron told him in 2009, *in Miami,* that he was leaning to joining the Heat in free agency.

"I had dinner with him, gone out, we had a good time," Oakley recalled to JJ Redick years later. "He said, 'I'm thinking about going to Miami.' I called Pat, told him I need a couple of tickets for the game. At halftime, he has that special suite he goes to. I was talking to him and I said, 'I talked to someone who said they might be coming here next year.' He said 'Really?' I said, 'Yeah, you might be playing against him tonight.'"

Eric Reid, the Heat TV play-by-play announcer, was skeptical. "Nobody in their right mind going into that thought the Heat was coming out of it with LeBron James, Chris Bosh, and Dwyane Wade."

All these years later, it is possible that the only true version of events is the one captured by a film crew following Bosh for a documentary on the free agency process that ultimately would never be made.

"Bosh recorded everything. He recorded his conversations with Wade, his conversations with James, his meetings with Pat Riley and just about everything else you could imagine," wrote Arash Markazi of ESPN, "even though some teams he met with asked him to stop recording during their meetings."

The footage has never been seen, mostly because Bosh's team, while they had over 80 hours of footage, soon realized that around 800 hours was necessary for a full documentary.

Wade asserted he and Bosh didn't know LeBron was planning to do *The Decision*. That may have been true (ESPN only announced *The Decision* on July 7), but the concept had been in the works to varying degrees for almost a month, since game two of the NBA Finals. The brainchild of a sports fan named Drew Wagner via an email to Bill Simmons' mailbag, the idea grew, landing at the feet of LeBron's manager, Maverick Carter, who was all onboard and convinced LeBron.

It was confirmed that after whatever happened earlier in the week with regards to a three-way decision, LeBron went conspicuously quiet.

"Bron went radio silent on me... it was like three days I didn't hear from him at all... nothin'," said Wade.

"Everyone was excited, but LeBron had gone dark. And that made us all worry a little bit," said David Fizdale, a Heat assistant coach. "Even Dwyane wasn't totally sure."

Whatever LeBron's decision was going to be, it would be broadcast live in primetime on ESPN.

And this is where you likely remember a clearly uncomfortable LeBron ("he looked uneasy," his business manager Randy Mims recalled), wearing that purple checkered button-down ("terrible shirt choice - why'd he pick that," laughed Wade), fidgeting around a dull and uninspiring barrage of questions from Jim Gray. Half the country had heard the news from Smith, Broussard and company, and then probably a quarter of the country were in denial of the news they had heard, and yet another quarter had no knowledge and would find out live.

By the time LeBron answered "the question everybody wants to know" with some of the most famous string of words in NBA history, America was ready to blow a lid.

You already know what those words were. But in the off chance you may have forgotten:

> *This fall, man, this is very tough. This fall I'm going to take my talents to South Beach and join the Miami Heat.*

Wade and Fizdale jumped up from their private dinner table at Prime 112 in elation.

LeBron insisted he had been flip-flopping and only decided earlier that day. He also said very few people knew of the decision ("pilots for his private plane had filed a flight plan to Miami, and rooms were booked for James and his friends alongside Bosh's group at the W," reported Windhorst).

"I don't think LeBron was 1000% sure," Wade admitted.

LeBron hoped the Cleveland fans would understand his team choice, a longshot and more than slightly tone deaf. No matter what *The Decision* was or was not, one thing was for sure: using a nationally televised prime time slot to jilt one franchise and its fans at the altar wasn't going to get golf claps and the polite *thatta boys.*

Cleveland had a right to be furious and the burning jersey spectacle that played out, while extreme, was a fair reaction to what Cavs fans felt was destiny. LeBron was *him,* long before *him* was a thing said every few seconds by teenagers. He was the manna from the heavens delivered to a downtrodden franchise in a downtrodden economy in a downtrodden sports town. That he became a two-time MVP and took the Cavs further than they ever had only seemed to be the prophecy marching towards inevitable fulfillment. It was understandable, then, that LeBron, *their* LeBron, giving them the proverbial *going in a different direction* felt so much like the Red Wedding.

"Cleveland does not own LeBron James," wrote John Krolick. "LeBron James was born in Akron. He was drafted by his hometown Cavaliers, who signed him to a contract. He played at a high enough level to make his contract a relative bargain. He then signed an extension with the Cavaliers. Again, he played at a high enough level to more than justify the money he was given by the Cavaliers.

"LeBron does not owe the Cavaliers any more than he has given them. LeBron has never needed to pay off some cosmic debt to Cleveland. He's done all he can to bring a title to the city, but it was never about anybody forcing LeBron to win a title for the Cavaliers. He tried to win Cleveland a title because he wanted to. Cavs fans just got to watch.

"We are not LeBron James, and LeBron James is not us."

The Decision as a television product, a lesson on journalistic integrity, and the concept in general were all ridiculed far and wide.

"Unusual and poorly-executed," was about as kind of a review, from Chris Fedor, that there was.

"Narcissistic, self-promotional program – that was thinly veiled under the premise of philanthropy," opined Cory Stewart.

"TV's equivalent to waterboarding," LeBron biographer Buzz Bissinger called it.

"Some found ESPN guilty of violating a key ethical journalistic tenet—paying for news," wrote ombudsman Don Ohlmeyer. "Others disdained the network's perceived pandering to a superstar, a trait causing them to ponder the network's biases. Still others decried a simple announcement being manufactured into the suspense of a 'second coming.' The monstrous hype that led up to the special was a calculated and constructed spotlight that media far beyond ESPN helped feed. To many, the aggregate was an affront to humility, loyalty, moderation and instead became a celebration of greed, ego and excess."

It was hard to argue the production was well thought out, from staging Boys and Girls Club kids as a mix between an audience and hostage victims, to Gray's boorish questions, and multiple commercial breaks before the actual announcement. In theory, the idea of announcing an unprecedented free agency choice on live national television was good enough. In practice, at least in the actual execution of *The Decision*, it missed the mark woefully.

But, as Michael Smith pointed out, "His brand is not about whether you like him or not, it's about paying attention to him. He did this because he can. He's the king, and he rubbed it in everybody's face. It's a different day and age."

Dan Le Batard agreed: "That television show signaled LeBron James owning the decade."

TV logistics aside, what grabbed hold immediately, far and wide, was the idea that LeBron (and basically only LeBron) had taken the easy way out, joined his rivals and could never be looked upon again as one of, if not the best, players in the world, let alone *the chosen one* (gasp!).

The low-brow logic was everywhere all at once.

"I think it's a cop-out," Bill Simmons penned. "Any super-competitive person would rather beat Dwyane Wade than play with him. Don't you want to find the Ali to your Frazier and have that rival pull the greatness out of you? That's what Jordan would have done. Hell, that's what Kobe would have done."

It was great prose, almost as if the same man hadn't penned: "Just know that Kobe would have caught a whiff of those rings and gone to Chicago. Same with Jordan. Same with Magic and Bird. How can you care about winning and NOT go to Chicago?"

Jordan would have never joined his rivals, he would have kept trying to beat them HIMSELF!

Magic and Bird would have never joined up!

Kobe wants to kill you, he's not going to invite you to play with him!

The hypotheticals quickly went off the rails. Putting aside the cold hard facts that Jordan's Bulls were on the ascent and drafted one Scottie Pippen, coinciding with both the Celtics and Pistons aging out, earlier in Jordan's career arc than LeBron now stood, who was to know? Reports had long circulated that Jordan, and maybe to a greater extent, the Bulls front office, were interested in various trades shipping Pippen out in the mid-90s.

Just because he never exercised his free agent rights to go play for another team in his 20s didn't mean he wouldn't have. It didn't mean he would have either. It was a hypothetical projection, that's all.

Of course, Magic and Bird would have never joined up, putting aside that both were drafted to well-stocked teams, Magic being the #1 overall pick, drafted to a 47-win team via a now-obsolete free agent trade rule. He joined a 5-time MVP who had been an MVP in his rookie season, Kareem Abdul-Jabbar, future Hall of Famers in Spencer Haywood and Jamal Wilkes, and blossoming young players Michael Cooper and Norm Nixon, who would make multiple all Defensive teams and all-star teams, respectively. Not to mention adding such future Hall of Famers as James Worthy and Bob McAdoo and an All-Rookie team performer in Byron Scott. Adding 37-year-old Shaquille O'Neal and 33-year-old Antawn Jamison, as the Cavs had done in 2009, this was not.

Bird also, in a hypothetical world, would have had little incentive to change teams. Though his Celtics weren't in the same admirable position as the Lakers, they had drafted Bird a year before he graduated and plugged him into a roster featuring a trio of future Hall of Famers in Tiny Archibald, Dave Cowens, and Pete Maravich, and a young Cedric Maxwell, no slouch of his own, who would win a Finals MVP the year after Bird's rookie season.

Now swept under the rug and mostly forgotten, Kobe had virtually been the conduit for O'Neal's trade from the Lakers (to the Heat, leading to the 2006 title with Wade), then pouted and demanded a trade. When the Lakers came to him with a proposed trade to Detroit he balked, only wanting to go to

Chicago, which would have been a cents on the dollar trade for Los Angeles. Wisely, they did not acquiesce to his request, but added All-Stars Ron Artest and Pau Gasol as the Lakers got a second championship wind, winning the 2009 and 2010 titles.

So, while the hypotheticals could never be known, none of the respected legends faced the same circumstances as LeBron or Wade or Bosh. When other Hall of Famers turned talking heads who, in fact, *had* quote unquote joined up, the train was off the tracks.

Charles Barkley said, "If I was 25, I would want to make sure I was The Guy ... LeBron is never going to be the Guy." He called *The Decision* a "punk move" and a "dumb idea". The criticism didn't end with that. Barkley continued, "That was torture. I want that hour back in my life."

The last part was admittedly true. The first part may have been as well... in another hypothetical world. Barkley had attempted to tank his draft stock, but ended up on a Philadelphia 76ers team only a season removed from a championship of their own, and also with a trio of future Hall of Famers, guys known by a singular name like Dr. J, Moses, and Mo. By the time Barkley was 25, he was the guy, and the Sixers were progressively getting worse, much worse than the Cavs in the final years with LeBron. So much so, Barkley demanded a trade to a loaded Suns team. And then four years later was again traded to a team only a couple years removed from a title and boasting future Hall of Famers, this time in Houston.

"With this move, LeBron can no longer be in the conversation with Jordan, Magic, Larry Legend, and Kobe for the greatest ever," wrote a Lakers blogger, Josh Tucker. "The greatest individual players in the history of the game have met the ultimate challenge head on, willingly, and overcome it. They have relished the competition, rather than seeking to diminish it, or stack the deck against it. They arrived in town, embraced the challenge of delivering victory for that town, and stuck it out until they delivered. The greatest players have been the undisputed leaders and best players of their teams, the unquestionable MVPs of championship squads, and they never considered taking the easy way out.

"Simply put, the greatest players in the history of the game were also its greatest competitors, and LeBron clearly does not fit into that category."

Matt Moore, then with NBC Sports, was much more measured, as he tended to be, in scouting the landscape.

> *James' decision brought about a rash of comparisons to, who else, Michel Jordan. The ghost that hangs over every great player in this league cast its shadow over LeBron tonight because Jordan would never defer to another superstar. He would never openly admit that he needed help. No, instead Jordan would rise up and take the team on his back, carrying them across the sky and into the sun, stealing its light to bring back and light his bedroom to read by. He would vanquish the Jabberwocky with his ballpoint pen that he signs his lucrative checks with and would never take a step out of the spotlight so he could share it with someone else.*

> *Jordan. The crown that gives us scoliosis.*

> *What James has done, outside of the Cleveland context and the ridiculousness of the television special, is agree*

Hypotheticals aside, it was really, *really* hard to argue that the decision to leave Cleveland wasn't the best *basketball* move for LeBron. If true legends were graded on championships and Cleveland was inching further and further away from that tier, how could joining a tandem of All-NBA caliber players in Wade and Bosh *not* be the best route?

"Don't knock us for trying to win championships, that's what y'all made the point of the game is," Wade said. "I sat with him face to face and I seen it wasn't about scoring titles no more for him, it wasn't about all the things, the commercials, and the MVPs and all the things he had. He had that but he was still empty inside and he wanted and needed something else for his career."

"We're actually showing that winning is more important above everything else," Bosh added. "It doesn't matter about ego, shots, attention, individual accolades, it doesn't matter."

Henry Abbott, one of the most thoughtful and beautiful NBA writers ever, tried to wrap his head around the walls closing in on LeBron from the general public:

What is James' crime, exactly? I have been hashing out this issue with e-mailers over the last few hours. Most accept that he had the right to choose whatever team he wanted. Most accept that Cleveland was not the best team. Most accept that he played hard for the Cavaliers and—this year's playoff disappointment notwithstanding—got better results than could have been expected.

Pretty much it boils down to the fact that he put himself on TV to make this decision, which sends the twin messages that he has an overblown view of his own role in the world, and that he's insensitive to how the whole thing would play in Ohio.

And OK, fair enough. Quibble with his media philosophies if you'd like.

But realize, if you're bitter, you're bitter about the format of his expression. Not the contents of his soul. And absent evidence he has done something actually wretched, it's a little extreme to call him nasty names on the Internet, isn't it?

In this world of ours, you will find some truly terrible people. There are murderers. There are rapists. There are abusers, bullies, polluters, dictators and everything else.

And this is the guy you need to single out?

Even in the NBA's own pantheon, you will find Magic Johnson who once got a coach fired, Kobe Bryant who stood in a parking lot on hidden camera cursing his own team and coaches, Michael Jordan who fought with and bullied teammates. The list goes on and on. The point is, if you're in the mood to be charitable, you can love just about anybody. If you're in the mood to hate, you can hate just about anybody.

Why is it that so many are in the mood to hate LeBron James?

A theory: It's because he stepped out of place. Players play. That's how it was. They are quiet and sweaty craftsmen who ought not to be heard from except to call out plays and say "yessir" to the coach. The way sports used to be, owners did things like make billion-dollar decisions and general managers and agents did things like agonize over personnel.

But that was always a myth. The owners, GMs and agents may have seemed like they held all the cards, but that's only because players weren't great at wielding the power they had. The players always drove the value, because they are what motivated the fans who paid for everything. It has taken decades, but eventually a player—this player—figured out how to really put himself in the driver's seat, with billionaire owners lining up, one by one, attempting to earn his valuable affections.

He took the power of free agency and instead of just quietly using it to slip out the back door, he milked it. He played it out. He built his own roster. He played kingmaker.

The Kingmaker, despite having just made the biggest decision of his life and in theory setting himself up to compete for championships for the foreseeable future, was despondent.

Chris Broussard suggested LeBron could have changed his mind on the flight while guys were still working to get him to the Knicks and the Cavs were holding out hope for an about-face.

"Some on the plane said there was no party," Broussard said. "There were tears. They knew it would be negative, but to the level which it went just shocked them."

"Our flight to Miami was one of the quietest flights, no, not one of 'em, *the* quietest flight I've ever taken," said Rich Paul, LeBron's friend and agent. "I could be on the plane by myself, and it wouldn't be as quiet."

Many speculated that LeBron may have gone back on his decision after seeing the vitriol and the anger. That is, until *the letter.*

Incensed and emotional Cavs owner Dan Gilbert took it upon himself to take on the loss of LeBron and continue to stoke the hatred emanating from Cleveland fans. In a ridiculously long letter, ironically posted in Comic Sans font, Gilbert unloaded, calling the move a "cowardly betrayal", callous and heartless, shameful display of selfishness, and tagged LeBron with a dreaded spell and bad karma.

"I want to make one statement to you tonight:

"I PERSONALLY GUARANTEE THAT THE CLEVELAND CAVALIERS WILL WIN AN NBA CHAMPIONSHIP BEFORE THE SELF-TITLED FORMER 'KING' WINS ONE

"You can take it to the bank."

It was understandable that Gilbert would be fired up at not only LeBron leaving, but the way in which he did, and that Gilbert felt LeBron had taken the Cavs organization along for a dog and pony show without ever having the intent to stay. All understandable. But to shoot off the letter in such a timely fashion, one that bordered on racist and personal attacks, was not.

There was no turning back now.

"It really stung hard with them," Pat Riley said.

LeBron's plane landed in Miami in the wee hours of July 9th.

Riley told Ian Thomsen of meeting LeBron on the tarmac:

"That night at three in the morning we met him at the airport," he said. "He had two private charters come in, and I brought a lot of people down, family and everything. They got off the plane, and I remember walking right up to LeBron. He was worn-out. He was just worn-out. He almost had tears in his eyes.

"LeBron just gave me a big hug and he slumped. And I just remember how heavy this was for all of them. It wasn't like they were smiling and happy to be in Miami. They had just broken the chain of his life in Akron, and it took tremendous guts to do that. I hear it from players all the time: 'I'm a grown-ass man, treat me as such.' Well, he made a grown-ass decision by doing that."

"When we got there, whatever time it was, I was like FUCK, what the hell just happened," remembers LeBron.

Bosh asserted he didn't know the outcry of LeBron's decision nationally because of the intense excitement in Miami. "We're at Mr. Chow in South Beach ... we partied all night," he laughed.

As much as *The Decision* was derided, and as much as the sports public hated the move, and as many hypotheticals were created in one night, it may all have likely blown over if LeBron was neither seen nor heard from for a few months, maybe right up until media day.

But no. The cherry on top of the Miami Heat Big 3 formation happened the next night on July 9th.

Originally scheduled to be a party for Miami fans to celebrate Wade returning to the Heat was now a welcome party for the entire Big 3. Because of a concert the night before, staging was already set up and would become an introduction of sorts for Bosh and LeBron and an appreciation for Wade.

Or so it was assumed.

The plan was for the players to sign their contracts in the bowels of the American Airlines Arena, take a few questions from the assembled media, then get on to the party upstairs and thousands of salivating Heat fans.

One problem: the original paperwork for the contracts was going to be obsolete; Udonis Haslem was on his way to the arena to inform the Heat he would be going elsewhere, either Dallas or Denver.

"I was about to get the fuck up out of here," Haslem remembers.

En route, Haslem took a call from his agent. Wade had convinced Bosh and LeBron to take slightly less money on their contracts to keep Haslem. He agreed in his car and ran in to celebrate with the personnel he was about to say goodbye to. He would be reunited with his University of Florida teammate, Mike Miller, a tier or two below the likes of LeBron, Bosh, and

Wade as a free agent but coveted nonetheless, and one who voiced to Miami his desire to play with his college buddy.

"I ain't comin if it's going to take UD out of here," said Miller.

Miller was well liked across the league, a do-it-all guy with as smooth of a shooting stroke as there was in the league.

"I wanted to find out if I had it or not," he explained. "I wanted to see if I'd puke on the big stage or if I'd make shots."

Miller hadn't been to the playoffs in four seasons and had never been out of the first round.

The contracts had to be ripped up and started again. By the time Wade, Bosh, and LeBron had signed on the dotted lines, taken the requisite photos of them holding their fresh white Heat jerseys, and taken the standard questions, it was time to scurry into those jerseys and join the party upstairs.

They were literally being instructed to what was in front of them as it happened. Waiting in a corridor underneath the court, an ops manager told them, "There's going to be a staging area, I'm going to load the three of you on the lift."

"The Heat's always organized, but this was sort of this open-ended thing: when are they coming out, what are we going to do?" said Eric Reid, who emceed the event. "It was not a tightly scripted event."

"Nobody told us what they were doing, they didn't tell us they were planning anything until right before!" says Bosh.

Some fans caught the first glimpses of the Big 3 walking from the tunnel to the staging area. They were then lifted up and emerged to smoke and lasers, backs turned.

"They had the pyrotechnics and the lifter thing, I'm like yo, Rick Flair did the same thing," Bosh explained. "I know how to work a crowd. I've been waiting for this my whole life."

When the three turned around and witnessed what beheld them, Wade giggled. They walked down the stage, high-fiving fans just as a performer would have done on the same stage.

LeBron and Bosh were taken aback at the party, an arena full of fans celebrating mere free agent signings. LeBron folded his arms and nodded; Bosh let out a primal roar.

"Bron and D, they were trying to act like they were cool... I was like, man I waited my whole life for this," said Bosh.

But the event wasn't just a runway show; the three took up stools and got peppered with softball questions from Eric Reid.

A meatball question that seemed innocuous and in the spirit of the event soon became national headlines and a part of NBA lore forever.

"We know you three kings came down here to win championships," said Reid, leading LeBron to the well. "Not one championships, LeBron, tell us about that!"

LeBron took the bait, throwing down the alley to Reid's oop. "Not two, not three, not four, not five, not six," he said as the crowd got increasingly unhinged and Bosh and Wade started laughing at the absurdity. "Not seven," he punctuated.

The joke wouldn't be just reserved for the Heat faithful in the building; the soundbite made its way everywhere, yet another example of LeBron's perceived narcissism and short-cutting. But the problem was, it wasn't interpreted far and wide as a joke, but rather a guarantee. The tone and setting got completely lost in the race to burn the Big 3 at the stake.

"I was the fool that asked LeBron the question, I teed it up for him," Reid sheepishly admitted later.

"I didn't take it serious," Wade said rhetorically. "Anybody out there who took that serious, come on guys...you know how put a little salsa on your story...that salsa became, oh we gonna hold him to it."

"We were oblivious to the fact of how it would be perceived," Bosh said. "We were just having fun...didn't really think about it."

What also was lost was a comment from LeBron that seemed to indicate the players were aware of what was ahead but were committed to the work required to get to the mountain top. "We gonna challenge each other in practice," he said. "The way we gonna challenge each other to get better in practice, once the games start, I mean, it's going to be easy."

Those that did get ahold of the comment only put it in the bucket of the shortcut, easy-way bucket, even though it was hearkening back to a famous Michael Jordan quote: "I practiced harder than I played ... by the time the game came, all I had to do was react to what my body was already accustomed to doing."

(Congruently, Heat assistant David Fizdale would say, "Practices should be a war. Practices should be harder than the games.")

"They injected fuck you from Miami to the United States," laughs Dan Le Batard. "It was very Miami."

The Heat, really more so LeBron, had hit the grand slam in the public's eyes: signing with his constituents, spurning the Cavs in such public fashion for a glitzy, shallow market like Miami, doing it unrepentantly on primetime national TV, and then the smoke show pep rally.

"We didn't plan that," Bosh said laughing, "walked right into that one."

ESPN would soon lead the charge of around the clock Miami Heat coverage.

ESPN in general was becoming the Penrose stairs of media, beginning with *The Decision*. The primetime hour of air on their network was pimped out to LeBron's group, giving them the exclusive rights to the top news story not only of the summer of 2010, but likely the entire year. In return, ESPN, by securing the literal breaking news, tied down content on their other platforms and networks in perpetuity. They were Rapunzel, spinning their own gold out of their own straw.

This, of course, would not be slowed down at any cost. ESPN launched *Heat Index*, a bastardized version of their attempts at having multiple reporters covering multiple sports in multiple metropolises (LA, Chicago, Dallas, etc.). Bastardized in the sense that ESPN didn't summon multiple reporters to cover multiple sports. No, no. They summoned four writers to cover one *team* in one sport in a midsize market. The goal was simple: churn out as much daily content about the Heat as possible. It was mocked on many hands, but one thing was unmistakable: the journalism and writing were exceptional.

Heat Index would be headed by Kevin Arnovitz, a revolutionary in his own right who virtually pioneered X's and O's blogs with video spliced in. He was a true five-tool hitter who could explain complex schematics in the simplest of terms while also having incredible writing chops to dissect business and organizational aspects of the NBA.

"Kevin Arnovitz is a fuckin legend," said Wosny Lambre. "If you want to talk about somebody who is foundational to the way the NBA is covered...Kevin Arnovitz pioneered that shit."

"Coming away from 'The Decision,' I believe some people had false impressions of what our site would be," said Arnovitz.

"Our goal has not changed. We strive to deliver a package every day, multiple times a day, which is informative, compelling and provocative. We want to interact with Heat fans and be the source of record for Miami Heat coverage."

Brian Windhorst would be brought in from Ohio where he had been a Cavs beat writer and had known LeBron (by way of his mother who taught LeBron at St. Vincent - St. Mary's) for over a decade. "It's impossible to listen to Windhorst and not glean something smart and nuanced about the league we cover," wrote Arnovitz.

Windy, as he was begrudgingly known, was the only member of the *Heat Index* with any real prior access to LeBron or his group, having also known Rich Paul, Maverick Carter, and Randy Mims from his time in Ohio.

But he quickly learned that past access didn't equal future access. As he would later say, LeBron and his group harbored resentment with ESPN for their coverage of *The Decision* and so Windhorst took the hit as LeBron saw him as a company man and complicit in the negative coverage.

Michael Wallace wasn't coming in from anywhere; he had been covering the Heat for the *Miami Herald* since 2006 and had painstakingly earned the trust of Riley, Wade, and Udonis Haslem.

"Mike Wallace understands something so few of us do: The inscrutable nature of Miami's sports culture," Arnovitz said. "(He) is going to be our tour guide."

"Shortly, we will announce the final member of our team—one of the brightest young basketball writers in the business," Arnovitz said on October 11.

And the brightest young basketball writers turned out to be rookie Tom Haberstroh, *the stats guy*.

"I got a call from Kevin Arnovitz after I wrote a few articles and he was like, would you consider moving down to Miami to cover LeBron James?" Haberstroh recalled. "I'm in a shitty little apartment in Wethersfield, Connecticut and you're going to pay me?! I would pay you large sums of money to cover that team!"

Arnovitz tasked the young Haberstroh with covering the Heat in a completely new and unprecedented way. "Tom, I just want you to explain the basketball experiment," he remembered Arnovitz instructing him. "Try to capture this in numbers and in words what's happening."

By creating *Heat Index*, ESPN was paying for coverage of the Heat, to then in turn cover the coverage, usually at an exhausting rate. But it was hard to argue that a) the strategy wasn't sound and b) that it didn't work! What also could not be impugned was the exceptional journalism. Arnovitz was Austin, Texas: he was at ESPN but he was not *of* ESPN. He valued integrity and storytelling and was not going to encourage or really condone knee jerk reaction journalism.

His treatise on the origins of the *Heat Index* and what the vision would be was tinged with remorse that the landscape was already so ripe with non-storyline storylines: "We've found an insatiable appetite for news about the Heat among basketball fans," he wrote. "Even after the initial firestorm over LeBron James subsided, readers stayed with the story of the Heat all summer and into the fall."

But what should have made every reader's pulse rise with excitement was the level Arnovitz wanted to detail this circus.

> *This social and cultural terrain is rich, but there are also the equally tantalizing basketball possibilities the unprecedented assembly of talent in Miami offers us. It's incredible fodder for junkies. To boil it down to its essence:*
>
> *How is this going to work?*
>
> *What happens when you place the game's two most efficient wing players, both in their prime, at the shooting guard and small forward spots on the floor? Is it antiquated to even consider position as a factor when both guys transcend the traditional skill sets associated with their respective positions? Do the Heat need a point guard? A prototypical center? Can they do it with an iffy bench? What brand of half-court offense should head coach Erik Spoelstra craft for this team? Should he resist the temptation for structure and rely on the otherworldly instincts of his superstars, or should he parlay their one-on-one dominance by designing orderly sets that get his guys the ball precisely where they're most dangerous?*

As earnest as Arnovitz was and the *Heat Index* turned out to be, it was not received well nationally, mostly by other media constituents. "It's not even a matter of degrees — ESPN's '*Heat Index*' is off-the-charts silly" was the headline in the Los Angeles Times, before any content had been offered.

"The Revolution Will Not Be Televised, But ESPN's Got The Apocalypse Covered," bemoaned another blowhard that seemingly couldn't grasp supply and demand or media at large, Andrew Sharp.

"It was justified, I think ten writers would've been justified," Haberstroh said.

Thomas Galicia, of *Bleacher Report*, was much more pragmatic of the *Heat Index* announcement, which, of course, coincided with him being much less of a blowhard than a majority of his colleagues.

"Good businesses listen to their customers, all this tells me is, ESPN is listening," he wrote. "If you're tired of the Heat coverage on any website, don't watch the games, don't read the articles. But will you do that? Of course not!

"Right now, the demand is for the Heat, not just from Heat fans, but from Heat haters too. Sometimes though I think maybe they aren't really 'haters,' because they seem to show this team so much love by reading about them and talking about them."

"There was this idea that ESPN.com was a public trust," Haberstroh told Bryan Curtis of the Ringer a decade later. "Kevin always talked about this. He was like, 'This ain't no public trust. This is supply and demand.'"

It was immediately strange that ESPN could allocate good resources, great even, to the *Heat Index* and get so much blowback, but allocating very low brow resources, like their morning blowhard shows, to not even coverage but rather 'loud declarations and gesticulations, was totally fine.

"I often went into work feeling like I had a target on my back," said Haberstroh.

The fellow sportswriters and journalists who couldn't grasp the *Heat Index* were seeing the ground tremble before the earthquake of how covering sports was changing in real time.

"The best way to understand these charges is that the writers were seeing a vision of the future of NBA writing," wrote Curtis. "In the broad sense, The *Heat Index* showed the media how to cover an NBA season minute-by-minute. At first, the very idea of such coverage seemed like a stunt."

Optics aside, most pundits figured the championship was over in July.

"Get back to me when LeBron is 31 because for the next 5 years it's over," wrote NBA bettor Haralabos Voulgaris.

"The Heat's schedule is one worth noting though because of just how realistic 72 wins can be," John Friend opined for *Bleacher Report*.

Jeff Van Gundy of ESPN threw gas on that fire, not only open to the idea, but predicting that the Heat would break all wins records. "They will break the single-season win record [of 72]," he said. "And I think they have a legit shot at the Lakers' 33-game [winning] streak [in 1971-72], as well. And only the Lakers have even a remote shot at beating them in a playoff series. They will never lose two games in a row this year."

The season couldn't come soon enough.

Almost two weeks after the pep rally, Bosh still hadn't bought a house in Miami, but was planning on starting to look with his girlfriend and soon-to-be wife Adrienne.

LeBron bought a breathtaking home on the water south of Miami, but his family would not be along to christen the new digs; Savannah, his long-time girlfriend, told *Harper's Bazaar* that she didn't want to uproot her two boys yet, especially with the oldest ready to begin kindergarten.

"She admits it took her some time to warm to the idea of life in South Beach," wrote Lola Ogunnuike. "'Personally, Miami was not my favorite place. Vacationing there is great: You go for three days and get some sun, and it's time to go home,' she explains. But the weather helped win her over. 'When they told me it doesn't get any colder than 50 degrees, that sold me. We get below-zero weather in Cleveland...I can't wait to have a sunny Christmas,' she says. 'It will definitely be an adjustment, but we'll make it. We're not complaining.'"

"On the ground every day, it was me and LeBron," said Randy Mims, LeBron's chief of staff.

But Mims would also have adjusting to do: where he had had free roam in Cleveland to tend to LeBron's affairs, no such access would be given in Miami.

"I got a phone call from our agent at the time and he's like, 'you know you're not going to be able to work with the team,'" he remembers. "We're just going to have to figure things out.

"I kind of took it like almost being fired. With the Cavaliers, I was executive administrator of player programs and personnel. I would work along with the coaching staff to help with any communication with the team. It was supposed to be a smooth transition over."

It became quickly apparent the transition would be anything but smooth for LeBron and his management group.

"The transition to move to Miami was a bit overwhelming because it was in this new city which is way different than where we're from," says Maverick Carter. "We realized we had to be even closer."

"I spent the first 18 years of my life growing up in Akron, Ohio," LeBron said. "I get drafted to a place that's 30 miles away. When you spend 25 years of your life in one place, I know every street, every block, I know every highway, I know every back road, I know every place. So, the move to Miami, not only was it a difficult challenge for me playing for a different franchise and different team, it was a whole new lifestyle...it was a drastic change... You're not only learning yourself on the fly, you also now have to learn a whole new culture."

It was announced by the Heat in the middle of September that the newly formed squad would hold training camp at Hurlburt Field and Eglin Air Force Base in Fort Walton Beach, Florida, a small panhandle military town more than 600 miles away from Miami.

"This is a terrific opportunity for our team," said Coach Erik Spoelstra. "The base will provide the ideal setting for us to focus on basketball and building camaraderie with limited distractions. It also presents us a unique and fantastic opportunity to spend time with the Airmen who defend our freedom."

Players expecting a chill, South Beach camp were in for a rude awakening. Practicing in small high school-type gyms with a few rows of bleachers and cinder block walls, the Heat would begin old school: with a two-a-days session on their very first day.

Brian Windhorst reported that "They didn't shoot in practice for the first three days, it was all defensive and conditioning drills. For each full workout during the season, everyone wore knee pads and mouthguards. It was full contact. If you were caught grabbing your shorts out of fatigue, you were told to stand up."

Spoelstra didn't mince words when asked what the emphasis of camp would be: "Defense and intensity." The tone was set right away when Spoelstra put James and Wade on opposite teams in the first defensive drills, installing what he hoped would be a top-flight defense.

Wade and James were already known as very good defenders who could switch to defend different positions, disrupt passing lanes with their quickness, and wreak havoc after turnovers in the open floor. Bosh was considered an average defender, never being featured on top-end defensive units in Toronto. But Spoelstra was bullish on Bosh's ability to switch on defense, mostly onto smaller guards at the top of the floor while also being the vocal backline defender in the general scheme.

The Heat got after it. Wade called the camp practices "the most competitive practices in a Miami Heat uniform that I've ever had".

In between sessions, the team watched officers exhibit their firepower in a range setting, shooting machine guns, launching grenades, and blasting the bejesus out of water barrel targets.

Spoelstra wanted the team to feel the intensity right out of the gate, which he wanted them to play with, but also the intensity that would be required for a team so heavily watched and scrutinized.

Chapter 2 - Trouble in Paradise

Just two days after returning to Miami, the Heat would face the Detroit Pistons in the first preseason game, normally a sleepy affair with the goal to get "game legs" under players and tinker with lineups, albeit in small doses. This, however, was not normal.

"There are eight NBA preseason games today, but there's really only one," a local TV sports segment began. The eyes of not just the basketball world but the sporting world at large would be on Miami. Despite the heist of top-level free agent talent, there were questions as to how Miami would fit together as a basketball team. Wade and James had played their entire careers as the main facilitators, "with the ball in their hands" in basketball parlance. Bosh hadn't been the main facilitator per se but had been the number one option for most of the previous five years with the offense going through him at his preferred spot from the left block. How the three would or could coexist was going to be monitored closely.

But much of that speculation would have to be put on hold when just over three minutes into the game, Wade was defending a down screen on the baseline and came up clutching his right hamstring. He wouldn't play again in the preseason.

Another injury blow would happen not long after when Mike Miller tore thumb ligaments during practice, an injury that would sideline him for up to two months.

Bosh summed up the disappointment: "We're just now coming together, and we have a little bit longer of a road to get better."

The Heat knew the preseason was not their ultimate goal, and finished it with a 3-4 record. Wade would be back for the most anticipated opening night game in NBA history, a Tuesday nighter against the defending Eastern Conference champion Boston Celtics.

Before the Heat boarded their charter on October 25 for Boston, Spoelstra called an impromptu team meeting. The message: the big picture. He had dusted off the Larry O'Brien championship the Heat had won in 2006 to send home the meaning of the big picture, that it was to hold another one of the O'Brien trophies at the end of the season.

"I don't need to see the trophy to be motivated," James told the throng of reporters before departing. "I know what I'm here for and I know what it takes."

Wade was set to return to the floor for the first time since his hamstring injury in the first quarter of the first preseason game. When asked about potential rust and lack of chemistry, he said, "I'll be fine, I've got a bunch of guys around me that are pretty good themselves. They don't necessarily need me at 1000%."

The game itself needed no additional fanfare. Boston won the Eastern Conference the previous year only to lose the championship to Kobe Bryant and the rival Lakers in seven excruciating games. They were a heady group of proud veterans who did not take lightly to the hoopla surrounding Miami's newly assembled cast. "I'm pretty sure Boston's getting tired of hearing about the Heat," veteran forward Juwan Howard presumed.

Most prognosticators did not see Boston as a proper match for Miami's firepower, however there was no loss of respect amongst the Heat players, many who had been shut down by

Boston in the playoffs before, including both James and Wade in 2010.

"All there's been so far is talk, but we know that we have to go through the battle, we have to go through the journey," Spoelstra said.

TNT Sports would broadcast the game in Boston which would be the first game of the NBA season. "We know that the first game of the season will be like a playoff-type intensity and we know their crowd is going to be ready," Howard predicted.

"I remember the sheer shock of that first game in Boston," says Kevin Arnovitz, witnessing the first regular season game of the *Heat Index* era.

"How many people are here?" Brian Windhorst asked NBA league operations head Tim Frank.

"More than a Finals game," he grumbled.

TNT got what it wanted.

The arena was packed well before tip-off, green everywhere. The fans were on their feet before the ball went in the air and let out a huge sigh when new Boston center Shaquille O'Neal missed a short layup on the first play of the game but would get right back into the raucous mood when Wade was called for an offensive foul a few seconds later.

On the ensuing possession, a series of actions got the ball to Heat center Joel Anthony double teamed in the paint with only three seconds left on the shot clock. He alertly found James on the wing. Before he could even get a one dribble pull up over Pierce off, the Boston faithful serenaded him with boos. Those were quieted when the shot fell, and James had made his first basket as a member of the Heat.

The game got off to a clunky start with easy misses, tight whistles, turnovers, and stagnant offense on both sides. Boston settled in first, generating dunks for O'Neal and a Pierce corner three. By the first media timeout over six and a half minutes into the game, Miami had three turnovers and trailed 11-6. It wouldn't get much better.

"This is a tough watch," an NBA scout muttered.

"They just had no idea," said legendary NBA bettor and purveyor Haralabos Voulgaris. "You could see they were just passing the ball back and forth, and it would be okay if Dwyane Wade had the ball in isolation. Then, on the next possession, they'd give it to LeBron, and he would do something in isolation."

"There was no order to what the Heat were doing on offense," laughed NBA presence Wosny Lambre.

The Heat trailed by as many as 15 points deep into the third quarter before starting to come alive, featuring a lineup of James and four bench players (Zydranus Ilgauskas, James Jones, Eddie House and Udonis Haslem). James hit an angle three in front of the Boston bench, a deep two at the top of the circle and then found House for an angle three on the opposite side of the floor. James ended the quarter cutting Boston's lead to six with a twisting layup after he split a high pick and roll with Ilgauskas. Soon enough that Boston lead had ballooned back to 13 with just over four minutes to go. Wade and James both hit threes and James hit a running layup high off the glass to somehow cut the lead to three with 1:10 left.

But all five defenders lost Boston sharpshooter Ray Allen on the next possession to ice the game. Ultimately, the final score was 88-80, which did not adequately portray how thoroughly

Boston had outplayed Miami, especially for large portions of the game when Miami couldn't generate points.

James carried the scoring burden with 31 points, but committed 8 turnovers. Wade and Bosh combined to shoot a paltry 7/27 from the floor and Wade had a six turnover night as well.

It was obvious the team had missed Wade and the opportunity to gel, but the team did not seem to wear much disappointment from the loss.

The Heat had exhibited their new public relations brainstorm: to have LeBron and Wade speak together at the podium to avoid any chance of the two being painted as off-message. Not only that, but the Heat would also make LeBron available to talk to the media at practice, at shootaround, before the game, and then on the podium after every game with Wade.

"It's a feel-out process," James said.

"This is one of 82," added Wade. "Sorry if everyone thought we were going to go 82-0. It just ain't happening."

"It was a big game. It was a fun game," Boston coach Doc Rivers said. "They're going to be a lot better when we see them again. And, hopefully, we are as well."

Miami wouldn't have much time to lick their proverbial wounds as they played in Philadelphia the next night against a plucky 76ers team. James again struggled with turnovers, 9 in total, but a huge third quarter elevated the Heat to their first win of the season, 97-87.

"We're not at our peak; we're not even close," Wade said after his 30-point night and looking much more comfortable than the night before. "Eventually, when it's time to be there, we will."

The Heat was anxious to play two of their next three games at home and show Orlando and their general manager Otis Smith what they thought about his comments from the summer.

After *The Decision*, Smith had said of LeBron, "I was surprised that he went. I thought he was, I guess, more of a competitor."

Miami once again used a massive third quarter to propel them to victory over the Magic who many considered to be a prime threat to Miami with their combination of a dominant big man in Dwight Howard surrounded by capable shooters. James and Wade made three threes over a two minute stretch right out of halftime to turn a six point game into a laugher, 97-70, the fewest points Orlando had scored in a game in over five years.

James addressed Smith's comments afterwards. "We heard everything Orlando had to say about us in the offseason," he said. It's not like it's satisfying. I'm not relieved because it's a long season. But they know we're here for the long haul."

"It was really exciting—I mean, really exciting," Bosh said. "The fans of Miami have been anticipating this game for a really long time, ever since July."

"It's a good win," Spoelstra said, "but we can't get carried away."

They would not.

Two nights later in Newark, New Jersey to face the Nets for the first of three regular season meetings, Miami picked up right where it left off with a scorching 29-18 first quarter en route to another laugher.

Bosh, James, and Wade combined for 55 points and aside from James, the Miami starters committed only two turnovers. "The balance is what we are here together for," Wade said, "to have an opportunity to make the game easy on everyone and we're doing it. We're playing great team basketball and we're still not where we want to be, but we're making sure everyone gets an opportunity."

"On the way to the game, I even mentioned it to Chris, just saying, 'This is a point where we could have ended up at,'" James said. "But at the end of the day, we're the Miami Heat team, we're the Miami Heat franchise and we have a goal."

The third quarter was quickly becoming Miami's trump card as they mashed the Minnesota Timberwolves two nights later behind a 29-17 third quarter advantage to win their fourth game in a row.

Wade was fantastic with 26 points in 24 minutes and Miami got 9 three pointers from their bench duo of James Jones and Eddie House.

"We have a lot of young guys on our team," Minnesota coach Kurt Rambis said after the 129-97 bludgeoning. "They got a taste of guarding some of the elite players in our league. Our team got a taste of just how powerful a team can be."

James hit 6 of 8 shots in the dominant third quarter before sitting out the fourth.

The Heat seemed to have found their stride and found it quickly. It had only been a week since the loss in Boston to start the season and what had followed was all-world defense and a balanced attack in the following four games.

But Miami had not had to come back from any early deficits since that opening night in the Garden. They trailed by seven only four minutes into their road affair in New Orleans, eventually finding themselves down 12 by the end of the first stanza. The rest of the game was spent playing catch up, as Bosh hit a crucial 3 and Wade made two free throws with seven seconds left, but Eddie House's game winner would not fall as Miami suffered their first loss since Boston.

"One thing we have to continue to learn, that every time we step out on the basketball court, no matter who we're going against, we can't just show up, you know, because we have this uniform on, because we have who we have on the court," James succinctly said. "We have to play and it's not about Xs and Os, it's about the energy level. We know we can still make a comeback because of the talent that we have, but teams are always going to be excited to play us. If we don't match that effort early, then it's always an uphill battle throughout the whole game and that's what it was."

The focus shifted to what would be a much-needed six game homestand and seven out of eight in Miami overall. They smacked the hapless Nets again, 101-89, before playing the meat of the homestand against two contenders, one from each conference: Utah and a rematch with Boston. How far had Miami come and how much progress had been made since opening night?

It appeared early on that Miami was getting its footing and imposing their identity. The Heat jumped out to a 51-32 halftime lead and seemed poised to coast into their matchup with Boston two nights later.

But then something strange happened. The team predisposed to defend at a nightmarishly high level couldn't get stops and the lead evaporated. The Heat regained its composure and stood tall, regaining the lead 88-81 after a Wade cutting dunk with just over four minutes to go.

Utah called a timeout with 37 seconds left down 98-90 and Heat fans headed to the exits trying to beat the nightmare traffic on Biscayne Boulevard. Out of the timeout, Jazz power forward Paul Millsap drilled only the third three of his career to cut the deficit to 5. After quickly putting Heat starting point guard Carlos Arroyo on the free throw line, the Jazz went to their Olympic and All-Star guard Deron Williams to knock down a three to cut the lead down even more, now to just 3 points with a tick under 22 seconds left.

Arroyo was fouled again, making both free throws. Then the unthinkable happened with Millsap hitting the fourth three pointer of his career with 12 seconds left.

And then the fifth.

And then after Wade split a pair at the line, Millsap found the rebound of an off-balance three-point attempt from CJ Miles to put it in at the buzzer to force overtime.

The remaining fans in the American Airlines Arena were in stunned silence. So was the team.

The Heat regained its composure and led quickly in overtime, 111-107 after a Wade dunk. But Utah, as it did in the fourth quarter, refused to fold. The fragile four-point lead became a one point deficit in under a minute when Millsap knocked down two free throws and Andrei Kirilenko, a 29% three point shooter the year before, nailed a three. After a series of turnovers and misses, Wade, also a poor three-point marksman, knocked one down to tie the game at 114-114. He would then foul Utah center Francisco Elson just before the buzzer. Elson connected on both free throws to close the door on what had seemed like an easy win only 45 minutes earlier.

"At some point in the year, unfortunately, we have to go through something like this," Spoelstra said.

"I think we panicked a little bit as a group," Wade added.

After holding Utah to a paltry 32 first half points, Miami allowed 72 in the third and fourth quarters. "They didn't play great defensively there at the end, but their offense is a lot bigger issue," a scout assigned to the game mumbled.

There was also little time to correct the issues; Boston was coming to town two nights later for a rematch of opening night.

The Celtics, and Ray Allen in particular, had no issues with Miami, coasting to an easy 112-107 win that looked over at 22-10 in the first quarter.

"No one's happy about it right now," Spoelstra said. "But it's only us that can make it get better."

"You get to a point where you say you try to rush it, you try to rush the process," James elaborated. "And we just can't do that. We're talented enough, we're going to win some games, we're going to win a lot of games. But we have to accept this process and understand that it's going to be one."

Miami stood at 5-4, "the best 5-4 team in the league," as Wade put it, but the team was sluggish and the effects of the letdowns versus Utah and New Orleans seemed to be at the back of their minds.

"There's no need to be frustrated," Bosh said. "We're nine games into the season and we can't play perfect basketball right off the bat. We're up against a lot. We just have to keep working...When it's all said and done, I think we'll be where we want to be."

Taking advantage of a soft close to the homestead, the Heat beat lowly Toronto, Phoenix, and Charlotte, playing stronger on both ends of the floor. All the equity built up by beating up on the weaker teams in the league was erased when they couldn't close out Memphis on the road and lost on a tough Rudy Gay buzzer beater over James.

"I don't care if James Naismith was guarding me, which would be scary because he's dead," Gay boasted. "I really don't care who's guarding me to be honest with you."

James defended the play well, as Gay was falling to his right along the baseline. "Have to give Rudy Gay credit, he had a very difficult shot," Spoelstra told the postgame scrum of reporters.

The loss wasn't the only sour spot on the night: Haslem sprained his foot to add to Wade's injury status (sprained wrist).

Wade returned two nights later at home to face the Indiana Pacers, but he might as well not have as he suffered the worst shooting performance of his career, making one shot, which subsequently matched the output from Miami's bench in a disappointing 93-77 loss where the Heat failed to score over 20 points in two separate quarters.

"We came into their building knowing how good they're supposed to be," Pacers guard Brandon Rush said. "And they just had a bad night."

The bad nights were becoming all too familiar, even early in the season. "They don't have any go-to plays when they have to have a basket, it's way too stagnant," an NBA scout observed.

"We're in a position where we're going to get everybody's best and we haven't gelled as a team," Bosh said. "This is what we asked for coming into it, and we just have to keep going."

The team hoped it would start to gel up the road in Orlando versus one of the Eastern Conference favorites Magic. With Floyd Mayweather, Jr. sitting courtside, the Magic dealt a quasi-knockout in the first quarter as they led 26-18 and never looked back, winning 104-95.

The losses were piling up for the Heat, as were the injuries. Bosh left the game briefly in the first quarter with back spasms and never looked the same; Haslem's season was in jeopardy after surgery to repair the torn ligament in his left foot; Mike Miller wasn't expected back until after Christmas because of a broken thumb and ligament damage; Wade was playing through a sprained left wrist; James had been dealing with a shin problem for a couple weeks; and Juwan Howard was playing with a broken nose. The rash of injuries to the Heat's big men necessitated the release of little used Jerry Stackhouse and the signing of veteran Erick Dampier. No one used the injuries as an excuse, but it was hard to ignore that the team seemed battered not only physically, but mentally.

"It will eventually" turn around, Wade said. "Right now, it's not. I wish I had the answer to it."

Even President Barack Obama had said before the game in an interview with ABC that it "takes some time for the team to come together."

Two nights later back in Miami, the Heat doused Philly, 99-90 behind 61 points from Bosh, James, and Wade. "Not the prettiest game for us all the way through," Spoelstra said. "But it was an important game to bounce back, and just remember what it was like to win."

Would the bounce back be permanent? One month into the season, Miami sat at 9-7. The proclamations of the ease of winning seemed a thing of the past, but the slow start, despite being well below expectations both internally and externally, was not disastrous. Injuries had affected a third of the team, beginning with Wade's injury in the first preseason game. The time required to gel simply was not being afforded; the casual sports fan likely assumes that NBA teams practice on non game days. That could not be further from the truth. Miami was practicing virtually only in the middle of three consecutive days off. Otherwise, they would have light shootarounds on game days and watch film as a team on off days between games.

Scouts around the league were more optimistic about the team than most. "They have three of the best guys in the league, they'll sort it out," a scout analyzed.

It would be difficult to "sort it out" on the road in Dallas. The Mavericks were 11-4 and had won four straight. Center Dirk Nowitzki was playing some of the best ball of his MVP career and the veteran-laden team was tough and smart.

Bucking the weeks-long trend of slow starts, Miami trailed by just two at halftime. But the third quarter was an abject disaster: the Heat missed its first ten shots out of the break and a Nowitzki fadeaway to get the lead to ten in the third was all Spoelstra needed to see to call a timeout. LeBron and the rest of the players sauntered to the sideline, Spoelstra muttering something in disgust. As LeBron retreated to the bench, he and the coach theatrically bumped shoulders. Which, of course, was immediately interpreted as *something*.

"The bump was absolutely a message," said Brian Windhorst. "LeBron doesn't do that without sending a message."

The Heat would lose the game, getting the deficit to five in the fourth quarter but never closer. The record was now 9-8, replete with good games immediately followed up with poor games. There was a plethora of reasons one could come up with for the inconsistency and frankly the underperforming relative to the top talent on the roster.

The players held the first of the rote and ridiculous tradition of players-only meetings. "Everybody had an opportunity to get off what they had on their chest or what they had in their head about us figuring things out," LeBron said. "Right now, we are a 9-8 team, and we have to own up to that."

LeBron, Bosh, and Wade met with Riley the day after the loss. Everyone was understandably frustrated and Riley, they thought, was the appropriate sounding board.

"They just said, 'We're not feeling it,' or something like that," Riley told Ian Thomsen. "We talked about the typical things that we have to do, have patience and all of that stuff.

"And I remember LeBron looking at me, and he said, 'Don't you ever get the itch?' I said, 'The itch for what?' He said, 'The itch to coach again?' I said, 'No, I don't have the itch.' He didn't ask any more questions, and I didn't offer any more answers. But I know what it meant, and I always go back and wonder about what he was thinking at that time. He walked out scratching his leg like it was itching."

The story quickly devolved into LeBron openly wanting Spoelstra fired, which Riley himself refuted. "Not from him to me, ever," Riley said. "As far as that goes, no, he never, ever walked in and said anything."

"LeBron couldn't nuke his coach," Le Batard said. "He (Spoelstra) had quite the support system."

"In Miami, there is one man in charge and that is Pat Riley, and everyone falls into line from there," explained Zydrunas Ilgauskas. "It's very simplified for you. There is one way to do things: his way."

"Frankly, we gave Spo a tough time – which is normal, and I'm sure he had hell trying to figure out how to coach a team full of superstars and NBA legends," remembered Bosh. "That's a lot of pressure, and everyone always thinks they have the best opinion of how things should go."

Spo, as he was universally known, was in his third season as head coach of the Heat. He had famously worked his way up from being a summer video coordinator in 1995.

"I had no background in video," Spo confessed. "He (Riley) asked me if I could do the job, so I said, 'Oh absolutely, I'm your guy' not knowing at all what the job entailed."

"He's like Batman," Wade said. "He goes into his cave. Nobody sees him."

He made enough of an impression to stick on with the organization and later become Riley's right-hand man and win the championship alongside him in 2006. "There's a commanding presence about him," Riley noted.

When the waters got bumpy in the two immediate seasons after the title, Riley handpicked Spo to succeed him. Riley liked to tell the story that he got so distraught with his own performance in the 2007-08 season, in which the Heat finished a dismal 15-67, that during a vacation with his wife, Chris, in Los Angeles, he actually peered over a 19th floor railing and contemplated jumping. "Honey, don't do it, it's not worth it," he remembers Chris telling him sarcastically.

"It was like a godfather scene," Spo remembers of Riley finally passing the baton to him after the disastrous season. "He brought me in on a Saturday. The lights were down, I sat on the other side of the desk. I could barely make out his face, but he could see me, and he said, 'Hey, I'm done. You knew this day was coming, and you're ready for it.'"

"He's a man that was born to coach," Riley said at the press conference to introduce the boyish-looking, 37-year-old Phillipino.

Taking over a team devoid of top tier talent outside of Wade, Spo led the team to a season over season improvement of 28 games and back to the playoffs. At that juncture, he wouldn't be confused for an innovator on either side of the ball, but his team had an identity: they were tough, played hard (honestly a rarity in the NBA oftentimes), punched above their weight, and knew the pecking order: Wade, Wade, and more Wade. And Wade trusted Spo fully: Spo had helped him fine tune his jump shot after a meteoric rookie season that ended in a dismal showing at the 2004 Olympics.

Spo was a basketball junkie, a competition-holic, Jorge Sedano termed him. Summer leaguers and players at the end of bench marveled how off-day shooting at the facility could turn into the hardest, most mentally challenging endeavors they'd ever encountered, as soon as Spo showed up.

He wasn't a task master in the sense that he didn't delegate and then stand around looking on. "One thing that he does that a lot of coaches don't do is that he's hands on with the players," Haslem appreciated. "He's in the drills, he's pushing you off pick and rolls, he's boxing you out, he's bumping around with you."

But make no mistake, Spo may have had a softer demeanor than his predecessor, but he was not a pushover. "He's very detailed, very organized, very specific, and he wants to see things done a certain way," assistant coach David Fizdale explained. Practices may not have been the three-hour wars of attrition that

Riley favored, but basketball was a job and you were expected to *work.*

Even though Spo had both Riley and Wade's blessing and endorsement, LeBron bristled early on. It was the worst kept secret that LeBron was accustomed to getting what he wanted in Cleveland and that coaches were generally afraid to criticize him or tell him no.

Spo was not. And LeBron didn't like that.

Well-placed "sources" (thought to be Maverick Carter) spoke to ESPN's Chris Broussard about the displeasure in Miami, pointedly with Spo:

> *In contrast to the popular view that Spoelstra has been hesitant to jump on Wade, LeBron James and Chris Bosh, sources say the Heat coach has shown no fear in criticizing them.*
>
> *Exhibit A was a recent shootaround in which Spoelstra told James that he had to get more serious. The source said Spoelstra called James out in front of the entire team, telling him, "I can't tell when you're serious."*
>
> *"He's jumping on them," one source said. "If anything, he's been too tough on them. Everybody knows LeBron is playful and likes to joke around, but Spoelstra told him in front of the whole team that he has to get more serious. The players couldn't believe it. They feel like Spoelstra's not letting them be themselves."*

Spo, like Riley before him, relished confrontation, believing it to be a covalent bond to team unity and trust down the road in the moments that would matter.

"The Heat are fine with discomfort because they force confrontation, and they put cards on the table," explained David Thorpe. "They have a 'FUCK YOU' culture."

If LeBron believed he could strong-arm Riley to punt on his protege and return to the sideline at the whim of his best player's behest, he was severely misguided on so many fronts. "He probably gets more resolve when people are getting all crazy and trying to force him to do something," Spo would say of Riley. "That's when he's going to dig his feet in even more."

Riley strongly believed in process, in trial and error, in failure. "This stuff is hard, and you've got to stay together if you've got the guts," he would famously say four years later. "And you don't find the first door and run out of it."

While Riley was painted in the public sphere as a loyalist above all else, that loyalty in earnest only stretched to non-players in the organization. He had also been around the NBA long enough (40 years at that point) to know what worked and what didn't work. And he knew that kicking a young, respected coach to the curb at the first sign of turbulence did *not* work.

If LeBron was hoping that Riley would take the reins and be less demanding and more accommodating, he was creating his own pipe dream. If there were two things Riley wasn't, it was accommodating and facile. He was legendary for the aforementioned hours-long practices and micro-managing every facet of the organization he could, from the color of towels in the hotels to the handwriting on the locker room whiteboard.

Shaquille O'Neal had said nearly ten years earlier that he couldn't foresee himself playing for Riley because "those five-hour practices he puts his teams through… I think Riley burns out his teams. All those suicide drills, where you run and run. It just takes too much out of you."

Wade had to have known what was behind the Riley door, having played for him and been in his orbit for seven years. Surely, he would have talked some sense into his friend, LeBron?

"Now is when the organization — be it president Pat Riley himself or Spoelstra in one of their series of meetings or perhaps both — need to tell James that they won't completely accommodate him," Brian Windhorst wrote. "Spoelstra will remain the coach and the team is going to stay the course. That means James, whether he likes it or not, will to continue to be asked to sacrifice parts of his game. It may be hard in the short term but this course of action will make a difference over the long haul."

Many presumed, and it was widely expected, that even if not Riley, someone else would soon helm the Heat.

"I remember coming in on Monday, wondering how Erik Spoelstra was going to react to a lot of speculation about his job status," recalls Windhorst, "and Erik being absolutely as confident as I had ever seen him that entire season.

"That was a huge moment because, while he was certainly projecting it to the media and therefore the public, he was also projecting it to the players."

"You respect that," said LeBron. "When your general doesn't panic, no matter what the situation is, then the rest of the soldiers don't panic either."

According to Kevin Arnovitz, Riley had told Spo not to lose touch with his players. "When things got rough, I told him, 'Make sure you don't lose contact with the players,' Riley said. Regardless of what's being said or who's being blamed, don't lose contact with them because they're your allies. Your greatest allies are your best players, and their greatest ally is their head coach."

"It was tough," Wade said. "We were into the unknown. It looks great on paper, but then it becomes real, and tough to make all this work. There was frustration—from LeBron, from Chris, from Coach, from me. Then we got together and we said, 'This is a decision we all made. We all want to be together. This is our head coach. He's not going anywhere and we're not going anywhere. Let's figure out a way to make sure this works for the betterment of us and our careers.'"

Spo, with Riley's undaunted blessing, steadied the ship. The Heat regrouped and was 11-8 by December 2.

Oh, December 2.

It had been circled on every Clevelander's calendar since the schedule was released.

"I will never forget that day, December second, 2010," said LeBron. "It was nuts."

"It was all just one big fuck you towards me," he added. "Everything was aligned for that to be that type of moment, just for everyone to let out that fury."

Chapter 3 - The Return

~~LeBron haters~~ Cleveland fans packed Quicken Loans Arena as soon as the doors opened at 5:30 pm local. It was a Thursday night, but that had little bearing on who was going to be at work Friday.

Cleveland officials (likely to the chagrin of Dan Gilbert) had attempted to put protocols in place, undoubtedly having gauged the same feelings that Skolnick had. Drinks would only be served in plastic cups, a protective enclosure was put over the Heat tunnel to the locker room, signs were supposedly vetted. Those measures could only contain the now five months of pent-up anger, frustration, sadness, hate, contempt, you name it.

What Wade felt was hatred: "Have you ever seen hate up close and personal?" he asked, disturbed.

TNT, undoubtedly giddy to have gotten the game on their network, could only capture so much and still broadcast a game. They showed the Heat run onto the floor for their final layup lines, nearly every fan simultaneously filming and booing. "A night unlike any other," coined TNT host Ernie Johnson.

"This feels like the NBA Finals right now," Kenny Smith declared, before the ball had even tipped. "Like a game 7," Charles Barkley interjected.

"The energy was so crazy," Rich Paul said, exasperated.

LeBron would first touch the ball 12 seconds into the game near the Heat bench. The boos intensified tenfold as soon as the leather hit his hands. A minute later he would score his first basket, facing up on the baseline, letting the crowd unleash more deep booing, then hitting the jumper. The crowd went eerily silent. Typically, there would be a smattering of cheers for the road team. Not tonight.

"He's gotta be nervous out here," Steve Kerr said on the telecast.

But LeBron never looked nor played nervous.

"My mindset going into that game was 'I'm going to tear they ass up,'" said LeBron.

The decibel level of the booing every time he touched the ball dropped as Miami stifled an early Cleveland run and open up a ten-point lead towards the end of the first quarter. But while the general boos may have decreased, the isolated venom did not.

"It was awful words," Wade remembers.

"Get these people some help," assistant Ron Rothstein thought.

"The vitriol was so ugly I couldn't have been more uncomfortable," Doris Burke said.

"It was a mob scene," Wosny Lambre said, "they wanted to kill him."

Reggie Miller unsurprisingly was appalled that LeBron would dare mix it up with former teammates on the bench. *Pouring gasoline*, he said. Yes, because LeBron talking to folks inside the lines, folks he had been around intimately for years prior, was a bad look juxtaposed against the crowd that Miller certainly had to have heard.

Early in the third quarter, LeBron pushed the ball up the court after a rare Cleveland make, only to be trapped on the wing right in front of the Cleveland bench. The ball would ultimately go off a Cavs player to remain Miami ball, but the sight of LeBron in trouble and losing balance along the sideline elicited the loudest cheers of the night (the Cavs were down by 21).

"This crowd is just desperate to get back in it," Kerr noted. "The perfect play for Cavs fans to get excited about."

As Miami inbounded the ball the "ASSHOLE ASSHOLE ASSHOLE" chants began. James drilled a long fading away two pointer to silence the crowd yet again.

LeBron was scoring so quickly in the third quarter, on catch and shoot threes, lobs in transition and runaway locomotive layups, that the fans didn't even have time to unleash the boos. To finish the quarter, LeBron stuck a tough fadeaway in the corner right in front of the Cleveland bench and turned to let them know about it. "This is not fair now," Miller declared.

As the game ended, LeBron rose from the bench to dap up former teammate Jawad Williams before being rushed off the floor by Heat head of security David Holcombe.

Traditionally, the networks did post-game interviews with the star of the game on the court. Once again, tonight was not traditional. Tonight, Craig Sager would do the interview in the hallway in front of the Miami locker room. "The thing you'll never see again probably is that a postgame interview was done in the hallway after the game instead of on the court," said LeBron. "There will never be another moment like that in sports."

"That was the most ugly game I've ever been a part of," Wade would say of that night.

"It's crazy, they were so bad to him on returning to Cleveland," Le Batard noted.

"I have never seen anything like that, I coached for 50 years...I have never seen people react the way they did... it was frightening, it was scary... people just weren't rational," Rothstein said. "Never seen anything like that in my life."

Aside from Miller's odd comments about fraternization, LeBron had handled himself extremely well under the circumstances. Even though he dodged Sager's question with canned lines, there was no humanly way he wasn't relieved. He was gracious in the interview ("I have the utmost respect for these fans") and seemed contemplative without ultimately apologizing for the decision or *The Decision*.

It is astounding that the Cleveland fans' behavior wasn't heavily criticized outside of those who experienced it.

"It was a vile time and I thought one of the worst behaviors I've ever seen by a fan base," said Eric Reid.

As the years would pass, players would be enabled by the league to have fans ejected for far less than LeBron heard en masse on December 2.

Why the silence? Why was the line drawn in the sand for fan behavior much more liberal for that game? Because a player left a team via his free agency rights and did so in a clunky, tone-deaf manner justification to treat him that way? And not feel repercussions? It didn't make sense then and it makes less sense now. Surely fans were pissed. Undoubtedly fans were angry. No doubt they were hoping for a crushing environment for LeBron and the Heat and an embarrassing performance leading to a Cavaliers win. But when does empathy become enabling? Where does humanity end and hatred begin?

The Heat coaches and players all said the right things and to a man took the high road. The same could not be said of Cleveland on December 2, who not only acted like buffoons but resorted to throwing batteries at the Miami bench.

Media coverage would start to change following the win, and for one very painful reason: the Heat began to win. And win *a lot*.

Chapter 4 - Uh Oh

Miami won six straight games by double digits to extend their winning streak to nine games before hosting Cleveland in Miami. A six-point win kept the Heat from becoming the fourth team ever to win ten games in a row by at least ten points.

"I've never won 10 games in a row," Bosh said. "So, I'm happy."

The Heat would win three of four following the second Cleveland win, setting up a much-anticipated Christmas Day game on the road versus the defending champion Lakers.

Los Angeles was gunning for a three-peat, the first in the NBA since they themselves had done it from 2000 to 2002. They were seeking their fourth straight Finals appearance, something that hadn't been done since the mid-80s Boston Celtics. The Lakers were playing well for a team with a lot of tread on the tires; they were 21-8 heading into the Christmas matchup. And truth be told they were a tough matchup for most of the league. Kobe Bryant was a Jordan clone who was virtually impossible to guard one on one, the Lakers started two behemoths in the feathery Pau Gasol and the slithery southpaw Lamar Odom, flanked by the bruising bull Ron Artest, he of Malice at the Palace infamy.

Bryant had texted LeBron after *The Decision*: "Go ahead and get another MVP, if you want. And find the city you want to live in. But we're going to win the championship. Don't worry about it."

The game itself would lack much drama outside of LeBron and Kobe jawing up the floor after the latter committed a reckless offensive foul in the fourth quarter. "I wish I had a translator," Jeff Van Gundy marveled on the telecast.

Miami had almost no problem disposing of the champs, 96-80. LeBron had a triple double and Wade and Bosh combined for 42 points. In what should have served as a yellow warning light to the rest of the league, the Heat team also seemed to show leaps and bounds they had made on the offensive end since opening night in Boston. Back in October the offensive was rudderless, disjointed, and full of complex off-ball screens and cuts that inevitably led to contested one on one shots late in the shot clock. Christmas was very different, against a very good Los Angeles defense. Much of the unnecessary off-ball action had seemingly been scrapped, allowing the Heat to play downhill with much more force. While there was still a your turn/my turn aspect, both Wade and James tortured the LA defense by hitting catch and shoot jumpers, most initiated by the other. James hadn't hit more than three three pointers in a game all season, and wouldn't the rest of the regular season, but splashed in five in LA.

Miami would win seven more consecutively after the Christmas Day shellacking, bringing their record to 30-9 after an incredible comeback overtime win in Portland. A back and forth, seesaw game saw the Heat trail by seven with just under two minutes remaining. A LeBron pull up three cut the lead immediately to four, Wade shook Patty Mills with a vintage crossover and finished in the lane 30 seconds later, and LeBron knocked down two free throws with 24.6 seconds left to send the game to overtime.

Booed on every touch, Wade and James were surgical in the extra period. With Portland down four and under 20 seconds left, the Blazers sent a double team to LeBron on the wing in front of coach Nate McMillan. LeBron simply rose up over both defenders and buried a 3. "Ballgame," muttered Blazers play-by-play announcer Mike Barrett.

McMillan called a fruitless timeout as LeBron strutted across the court, both hands raised, egging on the booing Blazers faithful.

Three nights later in Los Angeles, this time to face the upstart Clippers, Miami was blitzed 44-26 in the opening quarter and could never recover. The Big 3 combined for 84 of the 105 points, a theme that would become all too prevalent.

LeBron would miss the next night in Denver, a 130-102 domination by the Nuggets, setting up yet another highly anticipated matchup, this time with a team that at one point thought *they* had secured the Big 3: the Chicago Bulls.

But with the Big 3 down to a Big 2 as LeBron sat out with an ankle injury sustained in LA, the Heat and Bulls traded quarterly punches, with Chicago prevailing 99-96.

Miami would suffer an OT loss to Atlanta in LeBron's return, then reel off 12 wins out of 14 games. But an 85-82 loss at the hands of the Celtics in Boston soured everything, the Heat's third loss in three tries to the defending conference champs. Horrendous quarter-long stretches continued to plague Miami, as did unimpactful bench play with the reserves mustering 8 total points.

"They're going to be a different team in March and April, the more important months, when we'll probably have to see them again," acknowledged Paul Pierce.

The losses to the teams in the East seemed to be dark clouds on the horizon; the Heat could handle any team on any given night, and their stifling defense made mincemeat of weaker teams. But the 2-5 record versus Boston, Orlando, and Chicago did not impress anyone, least of all themselves. They followed the loss with a little three game win streak, highlighted by an insane Wade 92-foot football throw to LeBron for an alley oop layup in Indiana. Next up was a tough stretch of games that would seemingly make or break the season: Chicago twice, Orlando, New York, and San Antonio all in a ten-day stretch.

Chapter 5 - Don't Let Go of the Rope

The Chicago Bulls were firmly in the race for the best record in the Eastern Conference heading into the matchup on a Thursday night in the United Center, which, due to the roaring success of the team, had been rebranded as the Madhouse on Madison.

Physical and tough, they took on the identity of their new head coach, Tom Thibodeau, an NBA lifer who first cut his chops with the expansion Minnesota Timberwolves back in 1989. Tibs, as he was affably known, had spent years with coaching royalty Jerry Tarkanian, John Lucas, Jeff Van Gundy, and was the de facto defensive coordinator of the Boston Celtics with Doc Rivers that won the championship in 2008 and come oh so close again in 2010.

Tibs' offense would never be confused for Paul Westhead or Mike D'Antoni. It was a grind it out, drawn out, halfcourt affair. His defense, however, would widely be viewed as changing the landscape in the NBA. It was fine-tuned during his Boston days, soon after the NBA had reinstituted the legality of the zone defense. One of the key aspects to Tibs' defense wasn't a true zone, per se, but rather "zoning" behind the ball. In essence, bringing the defenders that weren't guarding the ball closer to the paint. It colloquially became known as "shrinking the floor" because with more defenders closer to the paint and, by default, closer to the basket, the space to drive seemed (and was) much more compact.

Beckley Mason wrote on ESPN.com:

He is often credited with being the first coach to fully leverage the abolition of illegal defense by loading up

His pick and roll defense was almost the polar opposite of Spo and Miami's trapping philosophy. The defender guarding the screener would drop below the screen, several feet off the ball handler, in order to not give the ball handler a runway to the hoop while also allowing the main defender to recover and not give up a pass to the roller. It became commonplace to hear Chicago's screen defenders, usually Carlos Boozer or Joakim Noah, screaming *"ICE! ICE!"* to communicate to the main defender what to expect behind him.

The Bulls had been an up-and-coming team for a couple years and still featured original draft picks Luol Deng (2004), Joakim Noah (2007), and of course the enigmatic Derrick Rose (2008). They had also assembled a deep team behind their core, raiding three starters from the perennially successful Utah Jazz teams: power forward Carlos Boozer, and wings Kyle Korver and Ronnie Brewer. Tibs had seamlessly married his defensive scheme to a deep, strong team.

Miami would struggle offensively out of the gate before two LeBron fast break dunks after four minutes of play, one a two-handed reverse, the other a one hand swinging tomahawk. He would add a fastbreak layup on the next possession, going one on three to score. A chorus of boos followed him every time he touched the ball, even dribbling the ball in the backcourt.

Wade and LeBron would combine for 63 points, but a brutal 1-for-18 shooting performance by Bosh (the worst in the NBA in 34 years) coupled with two meager bench points saw the Heat trailing 89-84 with a minute to go. Wade got a friendly bounce on a tough baseline jumper to cut the Bulls lead to three. Following a timeout, Miami deployed a secret weapon: LeBron defending Rose. Insane on its face due to the height and weight differential, LeBron had the superior length and could match Rose's quickness one on one. LeBron spent nearly ten seconds denying the ball at the top of the key before Rose finally broke free and missed a free throw line jumper. LeBron steamrolled in transition to a tough and-one banker, being fouled by Rose to miraculously tie the game.

Running 1-4 flat, an NBA staple isolation set with Rose at the top of the key guarded again by LeBron, the Bulls generated virtually a wide-open corner three for Deng as Wade committed the cardinal sin of helping off the strong side corner when the rest of the Heat defense was in good position. A make by Rose would have been doable, but tough. Instead, Deng sunk what would be the game winner. "Derrick has been making great plays all year," Deng said. "I just knew he was going to make the right play. D-Wade was so concerned with helping LeBron."

LeBron forced a three on the other end and the Heat fell 93-89.

"It makes it frustrating just knowing that if I would have made two or three of them in a close game like that it would have made a difference," Bosh said.

While the Heat would rebound the next night against Washington with a 121-113 win behind 41 from Wade, issues that arose versus some of the better teams in the league were also arising versus bottom dwellers like the Wizards. The bench was wholly unproductive, the center rotation was woefully weak on both ends, and the rotating cast of point guards couldn't defend much or seem to hit shots. Against the Wizards, Dampier and Ilgauskas were thoroughly destroyed on the boards by Javale McGee and Spo only played one true point guard, Chalmers, for 33 minutes.

On most nights it honestly didn't matter. The Big 3 was so good and could figure out how to put points on the board that even an opposing team's best shot was usually going to fall short. Nick Young registered the second highest scoring output of his season with 38 points, and yet Wade, Bosh, and LeBron combined for 81.

Going back to the first month of the season with the Paul Millsap flame thrower game and the Rudy Gay game winner in Memphis, the Heat players knew they were getting the best of each opponent every night. The fact that the Heat team itself showed up to answer the bell was as remarkable as it was exhausting.

The Knicks were coming to town with a deceiving record and an intriguing roster. Having also lost out on the summer sweepstakes, New York signed Amare Stoudemire, a physical but diminishing power forward, and had just traded for All-Star Carmelo Anthony nearly a week earlier.

Miami's crowd was put into a frenzy early and often, after a LeBron over the head flip to Dampier for a wide-open dunk and then a minute later when LeBron caught an alley oop thrown behind him with his left hand and threw it down. A long Bosh two pointer put the Heat up 15 a few minutes before halftime.

But in a stunning swing, the Heat went into the break down by one after a flurry of jumpers was punctuated by a Bill Walker heave at the horn. Rebounding from the Knicks' counter punch in the second half, LeBron scored a twisting layup with four minutes to go to give Miami a six-point lead, 82-76.

Once again, the Knicks responded with a flurry to snatch the lead back, 85-84 when Mr. Big Shot Chauncey Billups stuck a deep wing 3 over Wade with a minute to go. "It's a shot that I like to shoot," Billups said. "It's kind of a far shot, but it's in my range and I knocked it down."

With 11 seconds to go, LeBron would get a head of steam from the top of the arc one on one versus Anthony, who jumped in front of a mini crossover to get a good contest on LeBron's off balance shot. The extra effort allowed Stoudemire to come help over off of Bosh and block the shot into the waiting hands of the Knicks.

"I felt like I got enough room around Melo," LeBron said after the game.

"I watched it the whole way," Stoudemire said. "I knew what he was going to do."

LeBron would get another chance to tie the game with nearly the identical play that was run against Chicago three days before, with LeBron running to the ball and catching it going to his right, only to reverse course and shoot a three going left. While the result wasn't as poor as in Chicago, it nonetheless did not go in.

"We just didn't execute down the stretch," Bosh adequately summarized. The Heat scored a paltry four points in the last four minutes and had seemingly been incapable of getting a stop on defense.

"There's a reason we keep losing these close games," Wade said. "So, we've got to figure it out." His 12 points on 15 shots surely didn't help the cause much.

"We will have our breakthrough," Spo proclaimed. "And as painful as this is right now, there will be a time that we break through and we're able to execute and win a game like this against a quality opponent going down the stretch. What you hope is that the pain of a game like this resonates enough to make a change."

But when would that breakthrough be? The Heat had to that point amassed the best record in the East (tied with the Bulls), but went through far too many anemic stretches offensively, nearly every game. Eleven of their 17 losses had been by five points or fewer and they only had five wins in such scenarios. Two losses in three games would not break this team, not after the insanity that had surrounded them in November. But alas, this string of games were supposed to be barometer games, versus teams they would likely face in April and May. And 0-2 did not breathe much confidence.

A full three days off before Orlando came to town would hopefully serve as a much-needed rest, recover, and regroup time.

They would need to regroup all right.

A baseline dunk put the Heat up 73-49 a little over three minutes into the third quarter.

Gilbert Arenas hit a three pointer about 12 minutes of game time later to tie the game, 82-82.

Miami somehow dusted themselves off the mat to get yet *another* chance to tie a game they trailed by three.

With eight seconds left, Spo drew up a play to have LeBron and Wade cross on the baseline and Mike Bibby, who had been signed the day before, set a screen for a loitering Bosh at the top of the key. His three was lightly contested by a much smaller Jameer Nelson, and still missed long. In one motion, Mike Miller grabbed the rebound in the middle of the lane and kicked out to a wide-open LeBron in front of the Orlando bench. His attempt fell harmlessly short. "Got a good look," James said. "Just didn't go in."

And the hand wringing would begin all over again.

"We've blown a lot of games where we were in full control," Bosh said. "And we have to do something."

"The urgency is there," Wade added. "Just got to finish it."

"We continue to get big leads and we continue to falter," James said. "Hopefully we can figure it out soon."

Blowing a big lead wouldn't be a problem the next night in San Antonio. The Spurs blitzed out to a 36-12 first quarter lead and never looked back, winning by 30.

"We're still a confident bunch," James said, optimistically. "We know it's a tough stretch for us right now. We lost three games in a row, but I feel like all it takes is one win."

The collective resolve was certainly being tested. How could it not be? An NBA team doesn't think one loss is going to lead to three. Or that two close losses are going to lead to a 30-point blowout. And besides, this particular team would not be graded on the regular season. Regardless of the seed, the expectation was a championship. But the championship couldn't conceivably seem further away. Were close losses (aside from the Spurs debacle) to good teams worse, even in a micro sense, than losing to bad teams that got up for one night to play the Heatles? It was all ultimately semantics. Miami wouldn't be able to quiet any critics in the regular season aside from a record setting campaign, and the hopes of that went out the window before Thanksgiving.

Being back at home to host Chicago would be welcome. It's generally accepted, whether statistically proven or not, that role players perform better at home. Comfort, sightlines, what have you. And Miami needed role players to give them something. Anything. Because Bosh surely wouldn't shoot 1-for-18 again and Miami could more than likely bank on the Big 3 having their typical performance. The role players would need to take advantage of their chances.

Anyone who had the TV turned on between Friday night and Sunday night had most likely seen some graphic showing the Heat's struggle vs teams .500 or better (15-25) and their scoring drop off vs those teams and those under .500 (6 points worse). If there ever was a must-win game, it was this.

Or was it?

Was there really a must-win game in the regular season for a team that had already secured a playoff spot, and was jostling for actual top seeding? It made for good pregame coverage and talking points, but the championship trophy was not actually being hoisted on Sunday in Miami regardless of record vs teams above .500 or a blowout victory. It just wasn't.

Bosh certainly did not shoot 1-for-18 again. He was aggressive looking for his shots and finished 9-for-14. Yet another sluggish third quarter kept the game close. Late in the fourth quarter down 3, Wade passed to LeBron out of a double team in the short corner. LeBron whipped a cross court pass to a wide-open Mario Chalmers in front of the Bulls bench who hit a game tying three pointer with no hesitation. After Kyler Korver was off on a three pointer, LeBron flawlessly read the Bulls' pick and roll coverage at the top of the arc, catching Joakim Noah dropping too low tagging the roll man, Bosh. LeBron swung it once again to Chalmers who sensed Noah closing out and attacked, driving around him for an uncontested layup. Maybe the late game woes had organically solved themselves?

But no sooner had Chalmers scored five points to give the Heat the lead, he fouled Luol Deng, sending him to the stripe with a chance to tie.

Deng hit the first before missing the second off the back rim. Erik Dampier had been subbed in by Spo for rebounding purposes. But neither he nor LeBron could keep Noah from tipping the rebound alive back to Deng, who was fouled again. This time, he sank both free throws.

And here the Heat was again: down very late to a good team with a chance to tie or take the lead.

While the creativity had been mediocre at best in the last week of end of game situations, the shots had been good looks by LeBron and Bosh in those situations.

Out of the timeout, the Heat ran a token pick and roll with the sole purpose of getting Noah switched off Bosh and onto LeBron at the top of the key with a head of steam. Noah, in a stance, was positioned to keep LeBron from getting to his right hand. LeBron got a slight step on Noah off a hesitation dribble to get deep in the paint, but Noah, a future Defensive Player of the Year, recovered magnificently to get his right arm up and force LeBron into a wild left-handed layup that bounced high off the glass.

Wade came out of a scrum with the ball on the baseline but short rimmed a fall away.

"The Miami Heat don't close *again*!" proclaimed Mike Tirico on the ESPN telecast.

"We have guys who can close," Bulls coach Tom Thibodeau said smugly after the game.

The loss was another gut punch, a reality that no one could have seen coming back in July during the pep rally. Or even during the period of four total losses in December and January combined.

The wolves were circling. Everyone internally knew it and externally expected it.

"The Miami Heat are exactly what everyone wanted, losing games," Wade summarized after the game. "The world is better now since the Heat is losing."

The world of Heat haters and critics would get even more of what they wanted, and this time from an unlikely source: Spo.

"There are a couple of guys crying in the locker room right now," he bizarrely said in his postgame press availability.

Spo was generally curt with the media, which he viewed as an overall annoyance. He was respectful, but rarely gave them anything of substance. This seemed to be a massive slip-up. This wasn't the first week of the season when the waters of the Heatles hadn't been waded in sufficiently. This was one month left in the season, likely the most covered and scrutinized season in the history of the NBA.

Inevitably, the hand wringing in the media over who the crying players were had begun before the papers even hit the presses.

Spo said Pat Riley, sensing the coming onslaught, did what he rarely did and stepped in, but in an unusual way.

"I walked in there, and there was a bottle of wine and two glasses," Spoelstra told *Newsday*'s Barbara Barker. "He said, 'Come in here and share this with me.' And the first 20 to 30 minutes, we just sipped the wine and didn't say one word. That's what I really needed at the time. He just has a feel."

Spo attempted to downplay the entire episode the following day during media availability, walking back his initial assertion by saying he wasn't entirely sure he saw literal tears. "This is a classic example of sensationalism, looking for a headline," he added. That sounded trite at best. He had made the headline with his comment. There really was no other way to parse it.

The Heat players had clearly received PR training before they appeared before the media.

"Spo is the captain of this ship and we're behind whatever Spo says," LeBron said. "It doesn't matter. Spo can go out there and say whatever he wants about the team, and we're going to stand behind him." The genuineness of that comment would be unknown, but it sounded like a literal copy and paste from a PR staffer.

Maybe the most prescient comment regarding the entire CryGate, as it absurdly became known, was from Kobe Bryant on a radio show in LA: "Everybody responds differently. If guys are crying in the locker room, guys are crying in the locker room. That doesn't mean they're chumps. That doesn't mean they're soft. It doesn't mean anything."

It doesn't mean anything.

To any normal team, yes. To the Heat, sadly that wasn't reality.

Of course, four straight losses signaled to the media the end of it all. "They can't beat the Celtics, and they know it," proclaimed J.A. Adande. "The Bulls have moved ahead of them, and Orlando has an even shot to beat them."

"The three stars certainly don't give you the impression that they're looking for the nearest foxhole to climb into together and fight their way out of this," added blowhard Marc Stein. "Leadership? Unity? Show us some, Heat. You three are supposed to close."

You could tell a lot by a media member by how they covered the germane, and certainly many lost their footing in the daily overreactions that became the norm. A season wasn't defined in Boston in October any more than it was in Miami in March. Certain few in the media seemed to grasp that reality, something about seeing the forest from the trees...

The Heat would get a chance to face Kobe and the defending champs again four nights later and following their fifth loss in a row, this time to Portland, 105-96. Wade and LeBron were spectacular, combining for 69 points, while Bosh and the bench combined for a measly 15.

"I have to be more aggressive and demanding it (the ball) in my comfort zone," Bosh said after his paltry performance. "I need to be assertive ... I have to be my normal self."

Spo did not make the lede this time, instead saying one of the most prescient things of the season: "The only thing we can do is to keep on grinding and. Not. Let. Go. Of. The Rope."

Bosh was everything he said he needed to be, notching 24 points and nine rebounds and generally having no problem with Lakers defenders, whether inside or out on the perimeter.

A close game throughout looked like it may follow the same script as all the others the past two weeks. Bryant answered a Wade layup with a three pointer from the wing to tie the game,

88-88 with just under two and a half minutes to go. When Bynum blocked Bosh on the next possession, the resigned sighs could be heard around the country. *Here they go again.*

Late game execution, not just on offense but defense as well, had doomed the Heat during their streak of futility. That would change. Wade stripped Bryant and pitched ahead for a LeBron dunk to go up by two. Wade would then block a Bryant corner three and then promptly cross Bryant to the ground before scooting around Gasol for a layup to extend the lead to four. A missed straightaway 30-footer by Bryant virtually sealed it.

The streak was mercifully over.

Chapter 6 - The Other 9

Miami played like a team with a monkey off its collective back. They bludgeoned two West playoff teams, including exacting revenge on the top seed Spurs, following the big Thursday night win over the Lakers. They would also get 30+ points and 10+ rebounds from each of the Big 3 in 125-119 win over the Rockets, the first time since 1961 that a trio of teammates accomplished those lofty stat lines (Oscar Robertson, Jack Twyman and Wayne Embry of the vaunted '61 Cincinnati Royals being the last to do it in a non-overtime game). "I didn't realize it until the end of the game," said Bosh.

Along the way, a much less anticipated rematch in Cleveland resulted in a loss. The buildup would never surpass the prequel. "I expect the worst," LeBron said. "But worse than last time, Dec. 2? No." But the Cavs celebrated as if it was a playoff game.

"Not in our garage!!" tweeted the ever excitable Dan Gilbert.

Cleveland could celebrate a virtually meaningless regular season game at the tail end of March. Miami had their sights on the playoffs, and so did the basketball world at large. The pep rally had been poorly received, the 9-8 start had been a premature grave dance, and the five-game skid had probably been a red herring in the macro.

It was unknown how much could be made of a 100-77 drubbing of Boston to virtually secure the two seed and a potential second round rematch. The Celtics had boasted a 3-0 season series edge on the Heat, and it was the final week of the season. Neither team made much of it, rightfully so.

"We proved we can beat them tonight," Spo said. "That's about it, in my mind."

All told, they would win seven out of eight games versus playoff teams following the LA win, five by double digits. Some of the questions about Miami had been answered; others still lingered. The center position was still a bur in the saddle. Ilgauskas had good chemistry with LeBron and was a grizzled vet, but after a myriad of career injuries he was also a slow-footed behemoth that routinely got torched guarding smaller, quicker players and almost always got exposed on the boards (he had double digit rebounds once in a game after New Years). Dampier was a more brutish defender but was also aging and couldn't bring the same shooting Ilgauskas could. Miami's hands were tied at that position.

Point guard was equally questionable. Arroyo had been jettisoned to make way for free agent Mike Bibby in the middle of the losing streak. The latter seemed like a great fit, another heady vet with a good shot and defensive instincts. But his shot had faltered at the tail end of the season, leaving question marks where only Mario Chalmers remained.

Chalmers was a college hero at Kansas with confidence approximately the same size as the state. He was long armed with a good stroke from distance. He wasn't running the offense, but he wouldn't really need to with LeBron and Wade.

The other blinking red light was the Heat bench, which wasn't so much an island of misfit toys as it was an island of toys that either couldn't play or were maddeningly inconsistent. Mike Miller, the free agent coup, had been riddled with injuries. James Jones would get spot duty, but was a lousy defender. Eddie House, also a lousy defender with a picture-perfect jumper, would also get occasional burn, but was neither a traditional point guard nor a real 2 guard. Sadly, he was just ahead of his time, a tweener. Dexter Pittman, Jamal Magloire, and Dampier were unplayable bigs. Juwan Howard, the wily Fab Five veteran, could be a stop gap but couldn't be depended on for big minutes or to hold water defensively. That left the still-injured Udonis Haslem and Joel Anthony, an undersized big who not only had learned how to play basketball from a book but couldn't shoot either. He was nimble enough to defend at a good level and had proven his mettle late in the season.

Miami had answered the bell at the beginning of the season and in the dog days. A team that appeared so destined for implosion had not only rebounded but had the full attention of the entire league. While there were shortcomings and questions, there were also undeniable truths. The Heat was a *sumbitch* on defense where their ultra-aggressive scheme married to their quickness and speed turned solid NBA offenses into mush. They had veterans, this wasn't a team of young men venturing into their first playoffs with expectations. And above all, they had three of the best players on one team. All three in their own ways were nightmares to defend. Wade with his slithery quickness, creating space and angles where neither previously appeared. LeBron with his brute strength mixed with his unselfishness and playmaking. And Bosh who had successfully united his post game with a catch and shoot game. It was still somewhat of a secret to the basketball public at large, but Bosh was an incredible defender, long enough to make up for his slighter frame, quick enough to run interference on smaller bigs. He was surprisingly agile for a man of his size, meaning he could switch and defend wings and guards as good or better than any other big man in the league.

The services of all three would be necessary to make the deep run they had promised, and the world had been awaiting.

Philadelphia served as a first round sacrificial lamb. The Heat rolled relatively effortlessly, 4-1. "They're not good enough," Steve Kerr said succinctly about the 76ers.

And then, almost as if preordained, loomed Boston, the team the Heat had been assembled to beat. "It just always felt like at some point we would have to go through Boston," LeBron said.

The crown of the Eastern Conference since Garnett and Allen had been traded in the summer of 2007, the Celtics were the "anti-Heat".

Although Miami had explicitly been built to win championships, and by default, to beat the Celtics, there was no unanimity in the basketball media. Five of twelve ESPN "experts" picked Boston to win the series, even without home court advantage.

"These three guys think they can beat us 12 and until they start playing with the other 9, they can't beat us," proclaimed Boston coach Doc Rivers to his team.

It was a white out for game 1 in American Airlines Arena, and Wade put on a show as the Heat jumped out to a 15-point halftime lead. James Jones made four three pointers and two technical free throws in the second quarter. "JJ probably had the best game of anybody," James said, understatedly.

"Someone had to step up," Jones said. "I got some good looks. All of our playmakers got me good looks and I was able to knock them down with confidence because these guys trust me in the big moments."

Paul Pierce got into multiple skirmishes with Wade, LeBron, and Jones, and would be ejected, seemingly a failed attempt at intimidation.

Miami brushed aside Rivers politicking in his postgame presser, lobbying that flagrant fouls should have been called on multiple Heat players. "Very interesting that Doc said that," Wade coyly responded.

But one game, a series does not make. And Miami knew that. "Ultimately, what we're trying to do is beat the Boston Celtics in basketball, the game of basketball, four times," Spo said. "We have one of them right now."

Game 2 wouldn't follow the same exact script as its predecessor, but an equally impressive win. Miami's defense held Allen, Pierce, and Garnett to 36 total points, while LeBron tallied 35 himself, 13 in the fourth quarter.

"LeBron was transcendent," Boston sportswriter Jackie MacMullan said. "He was exactly the player everybody thought he would be."

The highlight of the night was a toss up between LeBron putting Rondo on the ground in a transition spin move leading to a two hand dunk, or Wade euro-stepping around a confused Garnett for an and-one layup.

The Celtics were unshaken. As the saying goes in the NBA, a series doesn't start until the road team wins a game. Back in Boston for two straight, they would be met by a raucous crowd — one that had toppled many opponents who couldn't match the home team's energy.

"Now the mental discipline begins," Spo said. "This thing is just getting started."

"It's gonna be a hostile environment and this is still a team that's dangerous," summed up LeBron.

In front of their hostile crowd, the dangerous Celtics presented an energy and a toughness that Miami couldn't match. "They came out and played extremely hard. They played harder than us and they played more efficiently than us," Spo said in disappointment after the loss.

Adding to the intensity levels in the building, Rondo returned from a gruesome dislocated elbow he suffered after getting tangled with Wade. He had a pick six steal and layup, starting the sequence by poking the ball away from LeBron with his injured left arm.

Bosh was horrendously quiet, going a paltry 1-for-6 from the floor with five rebounds. He wasn't the only one as Iglauskas and Bibby combined for two points and Wade and LeBron both struggled.

"We understand fully now how tough it is to take down a champion," Spo said.

Game 4 was objectively a huge game. It is trite and painfully obvious, but a 3-1 series is quite different from a 2-2 series. For both teams.

Miami had just felt the full force of Boston firing on all cylinders, while their own Big Three fell well short of what was needed.

Playoff wins and losses all too often get reduced to "this team wanted it more" or "that team played harder" or even the popular "couldn't handle the pressure". Which in a larger sense all might have some truth, as Spo had mentioned after game

3. But ultimately, playoff basketball came down to execution. Offensively, you had to score in the half court, no way around it. That could mean a lot of different things, but more often than not it meant making tougher and tougher shots against good, well-prepared defenses. And the same applied on the other end. Could a team crank up the pressure, take away the other side's best half-court actions, force contested looks, and then close it out with the rebound?

It was said often that the NBA playoffs were a completely different game than the regular season. One reason was that there were ample days off, more practices, and only one opponent to prepare for. Teams weren't playing three different teams in five days, just trying to survive road trips with their heads above water.

Miami had been relatively sloppy defensively in game 3, allowing Boston to run and score in transition. Rubbing salt in the wound was that virtually no Heat player had made any off-script, contested shots to keep the offense afloat.

"We can't continue to go out and be in a ten point deficit," LeBron explained.

The Heat trailed by 8 in the first quarter, but tightened it up to only trail by three at the half, 53-50.

That lead would only be two going into the fourth quarter. It was a tightly contested, anxiety filled period. After a scrum under Miami's basket, a swing around the horn to Allen in the corner opened up an 84-81 Celtics lead with under two and a half minutes to go. Both teams had done an admirable job forcing the other into tough shots and not giving an inch.

Showing heady instincts, Spo deferred to call timeout after Allen's shot. With Celtics fans on their feet and sensing a win within their grasp, LeBron got the ball isolated against Pierce deep in the corner in front of Boston's bench. He tried a couple halfhearted jab steps as Boston's bench inched closer to the playing floor. Former Heat point guard turned Celtics scrub Carlos Arroyo waved for the Celtics to help Pierce. Glen Davis yelled in a wide, deep pose, holding back his bench mates. Shaq, the former LeBron and Wade teammate, pointed at LeBron's heels dangerously close to the sideline.

Number 6 calmly rose up with the shot clock waning and a low contest from Pierce...

"Big time triple!" TNT's Kevin Harlan exclaimed as the ball snapped nothing but net to tie the game.

Another minute ticked by without a score before LeBron, once again isolated against Pierce at the top of the arc, went to work. It looked like the same move he'd used against Carmelo during the depths of the five-game skid: a left-to-right crossover. But Pierce stayed glued, never losing position. LeBron gave the slightest shot fake, just enough to get Pierce in the air, then slipped past for a left-handed layup that hung on the front rim before finally dropping through.

Undeterred, Pierce slithered by James and hit a nifty lefty of his own over Bosh to tie the game once again.

After an unsightly turnover by LeBron, it appeared that maybe the demons of March were resurfacing. But LeBron, an incredible defender in his own right, stuck with Pierce who heaved a long contested two off the backboard as the game went to overtime.

The Heat had stifled Boston in the fourth. The Allen three and the Pierce layup had been five of the Celtics' 13 fourth quarter points.

On the Heat's first possession of overtime, the Miami offensive set devolved into LeBron backing down Pierce on the baseline late in the shot clock. Sensing time was running out, he spun to his right and lofted an impossibly difficult fadeaway over a leaping Pierce that snapped nothing but net.

"What a shot by LeBron James!" Harlan announced.

On the very next Heat possession, Wade snaked a high pick-and-roll with LeBron. Pierce was caught out of position, allowing LeBron to take the pass on the roll deep in the paint, setting up a two-on-one with Bosh against Garnett. LeBron dropped it off to Bosh, who finished through Garnett's contact — no whistle.

Boston still hadn't scored in overtime when Wade went isolation on Delonte West on the left wing with just under two minutes left. He couldn't shake him and, somewhat foolishly, picked up his dribble with four seconds on the shot clock. But he steadied himself and launched a heavily contested deep two.

Splash.

The Celtics briefly awoke from their overtime slumber to muster four points and cut the deficit to 93-90 with a half minute to play in the game.

Sensing the importance of the moment, the Boston faithful were again on their feet, but the synchronized *DE-FENSE* chant was half-hearted, almost a low buzzing chant of fear.

The Celtics switched on a high pick-and-roll, leaving the capable Garnett on LeBron at the top of the key. LeBron missed a clean stepback, the shot bouncing off the front rim. The switch left Ray Allen on Bosh in the paint; Bosh effortlessly boxed him out and tipped in a left-handed shot to push the lead to an insurmountable 95-90.

"That was one of the highlights of my career," Bosh would later say.

Bosh tied a bow on the Heat's first win in Boston in over four years by snagging the final rebound before the horn.

"Our goal was to come out and compete for two games and hopefully get one and we accomplished that goal," Bosh said. "We're one more win away from our short-term goal, and we just have to keep playing together and keep the defensive frame of mind that we did for the last three quarters."

He had followed up one of his worst games of the season with an exquisite 20 point, 12 rebound performance. The Big 3 combined for an absurd 83 points.

"I haven't had much success in this building," James added. "We put a lot of pressure on ourselves to just come out and do whatever it took."

"Might've been the biggest breakthrough win of the season," Tim Reynolds said.

Saying "this will be our toughest challenge" with one game left in a series has become cliché, and maybe isn't even true. It usually just means the leading team doesn't expect the opponent to roll over, which has happened plenty. More often, it's a way to hedge against losing an elimination game and facing a hostile crowd on the road, just like Miami would if they dropped game five.

So, it was no surprise when Spo in his postgame remarks said, "Wednesday night will be our greatest challenge that we've had with this group so far. We'll get their best games on Wednesday. And we have to be better. If we're real about what we want to do, we have to beat the Boston Celtics at their best."

The Celtics sure looked at their best in the first quarter, especially Garnett who tallied 12 points in the frame as Boston took a quick 24-16 lead. The Heat had one of their best quarters of the entire playoffs in the second, living in the paint and cutting the halftime lead to just two. The third quarter was a dead draw, but Boston opened up a 79-72 fourth quarter lead, forcing Spo to call timeout with under 10 minutes to go in the game. The Heat would claw back and when Bosh pump faked Garnett off his feet and finished with a roaring two hand dunk, the game was tied, 87-87.

And Boston would not score again.

In an incredible stretch that felt more thirty seconds, LeBron bailed out Wade with a corner three to take the lead, hit a stepback three over Pierce on the wing to push the lead to six (then stood there, theatrically hyperventilating), stole a pass meant for Pierce for a two-handed dunk, and finally froze Pierce at the top of the key with a hesitation before hitting a right-handed floater to seal the game, 97-87.

"A team that couldn't close is going to close two consecutive games!" proclaimed Kevin Harlan on the TNT broadcast.

Wade and LeBron shared a long embrace on the baseline. The team that ended both of their seasons the year before had been vanquished. The supposedly tougher, more physical team succumbed, not only faltering in overtime of game 4, but in the final three minutes of game 5 to end the series.

The Heat showed no signs of underestimating Boston, recognizing them as a worthy opponent they had to overcome.

"They make you fight for everything," LeBron said in victory. "You can never take the foot off the gas. You can never take a second off against that team. Like I said, I got the utmost respect for that team. They're the reason why all three of us came together, is because of what they did, that blueprint they had in '08 when they all came together. So it's a great team win and get ready for our next opponent."

TNT's Craig Sager, playing into modern-day mythmaking, asked LeBron in the post-game on-court interview, "At one time in your career you had a reputation for not making the big shots, do you think you kind of erased that for good in the last two games?"

As to what point in his career that was supposed to be, it stood ambiguous. Maybe Sager meant earlier in the season? Because he surely didn't mean the previous two seasons when LeBron was second only to Kobe Bryant in shots made in the last two minutes of close games. He also surely couldn't have meant the entirety of LeBron's first seven seasons when he led the league in those same shots, narrowly edging out Bryant. Could he have meant shots closer to the final buzzer, say in the last thirty seconds? Well no that couldn't have been it either, because LeBron led the league in those shots through his first seven seasons. No, no he had to have meant shots in the final five seconds of a playoff game trailing by one. LeBron only trailed Bryant in such shots since coming into the league.

Whatever Sager was referring to, though statistically incorrect, was a widespread narrative. It likely started in the 2007 Eastern Conference Finals during the first fourth quarter, when LeBron rejected an Anderson Varejao screen to attack left-handed against Tayshaun Prince. LeBron seemed to have a good angle on the rim with Rasheed Wallace late helping off Donyell Marshall. He whipped a pass to the wide-open Marshall for a three that could have given the Cavs the lead with six seconds left. Marshall missed, Detroit grabbed the rebound, and won the game.

LeBron got his revenge in game five, scoring 29 of the last 30 Cavs points to take the series. But the myth stuck — despite LeBron hitting a game-winner in his first playoff series and two buzzer beaters in 2009 alone.

It was a ludicrous assertion, invented out of whole cloth.

LeBron smartly sidestepped the sophomoric question: "I never even got into all that."

He had been incredible in the last two games, and even though in the LeBron career pantheon both games would ultimately be exceeded by much grander performances, Boston could do nothing but tip the cap in a defeat they *badly* wanted.

As the years passed, the myths of the Celtics' stature and how they performed in the series became less myths and just flat-out fish tales.

"The pressure, you could see it," Doc Rivers told Ian Thomsen for his book, *The Soul of Basketball.* "The pressure was eating them alive."

"I really believe we would have beat them," he went on. "That was their championship in some ways; that's how they reacted."

"I always think that if I wouldn't have got hurt, we could have at least made it to The Finals," Shaquille O'Neal said to heavy.com a dozen years later. "I would have fucked LeBron and D-Wade up in the playoffs. I promise I would have. That would have been my role. Like, as soon as they come to the hole, touch 'em up."

It was nice the Celtics thought so highly of themselves in defeat, but that wasn't anything new: to this day they still tout that blowing a 3-2 lead in the 2010 NBA Finals and scoring 67 and 79 points in those two games was only because bruising big man Kendrick Perkins was sidelined.

Chapter 7 - Bar Fights with the Bulls

There are statues adorning the facades of many NBA arenas. It has become somewhat of a rite of passage for ownership groups to heroize great players in franchise history in bronze. Varying poses, varying sizes, but likely half of the venues on an NBA schedule have a statue memorializing greatness.

None are as revered or as well-known as the statue outside the United Center in Chicago.

Yes, it's Michael Jordan. And yes, it is Michael Jordan in his world-famous outstretched dunk pose. It is inarguably a beauty. It also lorded over teams that could never duplicate the Bulls' greatness of the 90s.

Steve Kerr liked to share an anecdote of driving to the game with teammate Jud Buechler when Jordan returned to the Bulls late in the 1995 season:

"I said, 'Jud, does Phil (Jackson) start Michael? I mean he hasn't been here for sixty games, sixty-five games.' And Jud looked at me and he said, 'Steve, there's a general rule. When you have your own statue outside the stadium, you don't come off the bench.'"

The 2010-11 version of the Bulls had made it further than any team in the 13 years since Jordan, Scottie Pippen, Dennis Rodman, Kerr, and Jackson split ways after winning the 1998 championship.

Winners of 62 games, touting the newly minted Most Valuable Player Derrick Rose and the rugged defense, Chicago did not have many problems dispatching the Indiana Pacers and Atlanta Hawks in the first two rounds.

The Bulls won all three matchups with the Heat in the regular season, though only by a total of eight points. While their defense seemingly was tailor made to slow down a team like Miami that wanted to play downhill and get to the basket (by "shrinking the floor", etc mentioned earlier), the Heat hadn't had too much trouble, the losses aside. The Heat could seemingly always rely on steals or deflections turning into transition points.

The Bulls manhandled the Heat on the glass in game one, securing 19 offensive rebounds, at one point necessitating Spo in a huddle to beg his team, "We have got to sacrifice and block out! They're runnin' in!"

Humbled in a 103-82 opening game loss, Bosh, who had been virtually the only Miami player to play well, summed it up succinctly, "We have to look at where we fell short for game one and come back with a better approach."

Bosh had been pushed around under the rim, no different than anyone else on the Heat. He had also been the only one to carry his weight offensively against a rotating cast of physical Bulls bigs, with 30 points on 12-for-17 shooting.

Playoffs are full of red herrings. A team has to win four games, no matter how. It's a cliché, but true, when teams say it's just one game or that a blowout counts the same as a one-point win. Still, that makes for boring media. One game always becomes the series-defining moment, especially the opener. No outliers, no adjustments, just instant judgment. Nobody wants to stand under the spotlight and repeat the same tired lines about losing or winning teams. Patience isn't exciting, and the grind doesn't sell.

The machinations can slice both ways. Rabid fan bases are wont to say things like "that won't happen again!" or "complete fluke!"

While the Bulls' mauling of the Heat on the glass was eye-opening, it seemed like a red herring. The Heat was a top five rebounding team in the regular season, as defined by defensive rebound rate, the total percentage of available defensive rebounds a team actually secured. The rate was slightly down in the playoffs, however the Bulls had been one of the best offensive rebounding teams, in the regular season and the playoffs. The Miami breakdowns seemed much more energy and mentality than scheme and roster shortfalls.

But the Heat heard the noise all the same and knew they had to answer the bell in game two.

To set the requisite tone, LeBron and Wade played one on one in full view of their teammates following the practice between games. "Rose tore our ass up in Chicago, and we came in the next day, we was like we need to set the tone, so we was out there killing each other playing 1-on-1," LeBron spilled years later.

"It was more-so to set a precedent for our teammates because we got our ass kicked," Wade said. "Everybody was just watching us. We was going at it. We competitive, we was going at it, but we was setting a tone for this is how it's gotta go. You gotta be able to go at this. We're two of the best players in this game. We going at each other in the Eastern Conference finals right now. We out there killing each other, and this is what ya'll better do tomorrow. Because we got beat on the boards by 20-something and we have to come with it, and we won four in a row."

The one-on-one game may have set the tone before game two, but Spo pushed a button in the game that would re-energize the entire team: it was *UD time.*

As motivating as it may have been to see Haslem rip off his warmups in game two, as Tim Reynolds of the AP said, "No one knew what you'd get from him at all, no one knew if you'd get anything."

In his first minute of meaningful action since November, Haslem immediately scooped an offensive rebound and drew a charge on Derrick Rose. Late in the quarter, he corralled another offensive rebound leading to a LeBron tomahawk in the lane.

Momentum swung wildly when Luol Deng dropped in a halfcourt shot at the first quarter horn. Undeterred, Miami held the Bulls under 20 points in each of the final three quarters, including a staggeringly low 10 points in the final frame. LeBron put on a show much like in the Boston game 5, taking over with the score tied 73-73 and 4:30 left, outscoring the Bulls 9-2 down the stretch to even the series at 1-1.

"That fourth quarter is going to epitomize this entire series," Spo said after his team outscored Chicago 14-10 in the period. "It's an absolute street fight for both teams."

Haslem's presence couldn't be overstated, but Wade and James had played like the true versions of themselves that had been noticeably absent in game one. The game was played in a phone booth, just how Chicago preferred, and they got beat at their own game, shooting a paltry 35% as a team.

Spo revived a regular-season tactic late in the game: LeBron guarding Rose. Wade had mostly handled Rose and did a solid job, but LeBron brought a longer, stronger presence that easily matched Rose physically. Miami's defense was locked in. With two minutes left, Bosh hedged a side pick and roll, letting LeBron recover on Rose at the top of the arc. Rose made an acrobatic pass to Deng on the wing; Wade gambled for a steal and missed. LeBron switched onto Deng in one motion as Bosh came off Taj Gibson in the short corner to help, and Miami forced a strip. The seamless effort was breathtaking.

"The series has just started," James said. "It's 1-1. We're excited that we were able to come here and get a win. But it's just started."

The Heat up to that point were a heady 5-0 at home in the playoffs and expected a rowdy home crowd. (Yes, everyone has heard the jokes about Miami's fickle, late arriving home fans. I presume that anyone still making those hasn't tried to get to the arena which is right downtown and has virtually one single entrance with Biscayne Bay bordering the entire backside of the arena.)

Miami rode an exquisite performance from Bosh in game 3 (34 points on 13-for-19 shooting) and another stiflingly efficient fourth quarter to shut the door on the Bulls, 96-85.

"I feel when I'm at my best, when I have confidence, no one can stop me," said Bosh.

"CB had it going," LeBron said glowingly. "When we have someone going on our team, we continue to go to him."

This was true and also underselling the fact he and Wade had struggled offensively until the fourth quarter when they lived at the stripe.

MVP Derrick Rose was held to a meager two points in that frame during the frustrating loss.

"It's definitely frustrating," Rose said. "Our will wasn't there tonight."

"There is absolutely nothing easy in this series," Spo acknowledged. "It's still all about enduring, sustaining and finding a way to grind it out."

Game 4 was a go for broke game for Chicago, knowing a 3-1 deficit was not impossible to overcome, but not likely either. The Bulls were a prideful group, led by Joakim Noah who was vocal and animated.

The Bulls jumped out to an 11-point lead in the first, but the Heat erased most of it by quarter's end. The game stayed tight through the fourth. With eight seconds left, LeBron was called for a questionable offensive foul backing down Ronnie Brewer. On the next possession, LeBron took on Rose and forced him into a tough fallaway that fell short, sending the game to overtime.

"It's extremely hard," Rose admitted, "when a 6-8 guy can easily defend you."

Despite LeBron's size and physical gifts, men like him weren't supposed to be able to defend an uber quick, shifty guard like Rose. The frustration from Rose was clear. He struggled throughout the series, never hitting 50% from the field and shooting just 5-for-22 (22.7%) from three. It got worse in the fourth quarters, where LeBron and Wade tortured him into an unthinkable 4-for-19, as he struggled just to shake them, let alone score. "We know offensively, at times, we have rough stretches," James said. "But we give ourselves chances to win every game because we defend."

In OT, the team branded as the one that couldn't close only a couple months prior, closed the door on the Bulls behind an active Bosh, Wade, and LeBron who combined to score all 16 of the Heat's overtime points to send the series to the brink, 101-93.

Mike Miller was enormous in the game, shooting 5-for-8 off the bench and recorded an insane +/- of +36 in his 26 minutes on the floor. While such things can't be quantified or even substantiated, it felt in the building like the crowd and his teammates were feeding off the energy his presence, and more importantly, his play generated.

"If you're a fan of the game, this was a great basketball game," surmised Wade after the game.

"It's one game away," James stated.

Miami could smell a quasi-coronation. The Bulls were supposed to be the tougher, more physical team, "organically" built (whatever that means). In short, they were, in theory at least, the anti-Heat in many of the same ways the Celtics were. Grit and grind would become the slogan of the Memphis Grizzlies, but the Bulls embraced the same ethos. Ugly, grind it out, not afraid to get their hands dirty.

"You can't forget those bar fights with the Bulls," Bosh would say a decade later with great respect. "They were huge, they were heavyweight, braaaaaawler."

And yet, Miami was beating them at their own game. The Heat clearly had multiple gears offensively the Bulls couldn't reach, Rose included. But the series was not a track meet. It was a half court contest of execution in a jam-packed space. And the Heat was answering the bell every time.

Despite what Boston claimed, the Heat wasn't going to be intimidated by tough nosed and dogged play. They had been through a maelstrom of criticism and negativity all season. Playing the games was the escape, for two and a half hours, from what everyone else had to say. And the Heat players, despite their best efforts, heard a lot, and of course denied hearing a lot.

"Look, this series is an absolute bloodbath," Spo said, echoing common refrains as after previous games. "It's about as competitive and physical as it can be."

The return to the Madhouse on Madison wouldn't be as intimidating as game one. The crowd was in a furor, but there was a twinge of angst to go along with it. The Heat didn't have a problem in game two, nor in a more tilted setting back in Miami for games three and four. They enjoyed a position that they hadn't had all season: the pressure wasn't on them.

And they played like a team that knew it could fall back on a game six back in Miami. The game was ugly, sloppy, and low-scoring. And when Spo called timeout after a rare Ronnie Brewer three with 3:53 to go, the Heat seemed destined to go back home up 3-2. The 76-64 deficit appeared too much to overcome.

In a blur, it wasn't.

Wade drove past Rose and banked in a tough runner over Kurt Thomas with just over three minutes left. Defended by LeBron again, Rose turned the ball over in the paint, leading to a running floater and a foul. After a Taj Gibson miss on the baseline, LeBron hit a wing three in semi-transition over Rose, cutting the lead to 77-72.

On the next possession, Rose couldn't shake LeBron and instead scored on a tough one-hander in the paint after a spin move, pushing the lead back to seven.

Rose foolishly fouled Wade, a poor three-point shooter, on a three that turned into a four-point play.

On the next possession, Rose briefly freed himself from LeBron after several screens high on the floor. Haslem, savvy as ever, slid off Taj Gibson to force a wild floater that missed. Sensing the momentum shift, LeBron galloped into a wing three in front of the Bulls bench to tie the game.

Two minutes earlier, Chicago fans were booking flights to Miami. Now, the game was tied in what felt like the blink of an eye.

The Heat's relentless trapping defense forced another Rose turnover trying to escape a LeBron-Bosh double team. LeBron calmly dribbled down the clock under ten seconds near half court. With Brewer (who'd drawn a key charge in game 4) defending, LeBron skipped trying to muscle him down low. A couple of stutter steps up top got Brewer leaning just enough, and LeBron let fly a two-pointer from the top of the circle. Bottoms up.

The Madhouse on Madison sat in stunned silence. The East's best team was about to go out like this? Taking shots without even throwing punches back?

Rose had other ideas. Driving to the basket, he drew a crucial foul on LeBron. The frustrated, underperforming MVP now had a chance to make his mark on the series. He calmly knocked down the first free throw. And subsequently spun the second out.

Bosh knocked down two pressure-packed free throws to extend the lead to three points. The Bulls had life and one more chance.

Rose probed up top and passed to Korver on a pindown. Haslem made a smart play, leaving Gibson to close out on Korver until Miller recovered. But Korver made a crucial mistake, picking up his dribble while LeBron hounded Rose near the timeline, and Miller closed in. Rose darted left, then back towards Korver with just under five seconds left. Dribbling into a Gibson screen on the wing, he slipped slightly as Haslem closed out. LeBron, recovering from the screen, delivered the final blow, swatting the MVP's game-tying shot high into the air.

A blur.

No one could believe it, on either side.

"We don't even know what happened," Wade said. "I'm not going to lie to you and say we do. I can't remember all the plays. I just remember the timeout, and Coach just looked at us and said, 'We've done this before. We've been in games where we've gone on a 12-0 or 14-0 run. Just believe.' We came out of that timeout believing if we get stops, we can give ourselves an opportunity. That's all I remember."

"I don't think I've ever experienced that," said Kurt Thomas, the Bulls' bone-crunching big man. "It seemed like they just hit one big shot after another. I thought we had a nice lead there, and it just slipped away. We let a golden opportunity get away."

"It's a tough one," an incredulous Taj Gibson said, shaking his head. "It doesn't really hit you yet that you're on vacation now."

How Miami could play so poorly for 44 minutes and so magnificently for the final four was anyone's guess. They didn't miss a shot in the last four minutes and gave up only three points.

"You can see that we have two, three players that have no fear," Pat Riley said. "Chris steps up there and makes two free throws that he's got to make. LeBron and Dwyane struggling a little bit with their game most of the night, but they made some big, big shots. That's what it's all about."

"You could've heard a pin drop in Chicago, they could not believe what had happened to them," said Eric Reid. "It was one of the most amazing comebacks and road victories in the history of the franchise."

While the Heat downplayed winning the East, focusing on bigger goals, it still felt like a coronation before the coronation, the Finals barely an afterthought. They outmuscled longtime rival Boston in five games, then schooled the Bulls, the new kids on the block, in five more. They closed nearly six of their last seven playoff games with lockdown defense, honed in September at the military base, and clutch shot-making from Bosh, Wade, and LeBron.

"Miami is going ham!" LeBron and Wade remarked after seeing footage of fans in the streets of Miami, awaiting the return of the Eastern Conference champs.

"You gotta give Miami credit," Noah admitted. "They're Hollywood as hell, but they're a very good team."

Chapter 8 - Nadir

Awaiting the Heat were the veteran Dallas Mavericks, a rematch of the 2006 NBA Finals where Dwyane Wade became a superstar and Pat Riley notched the final playoff wins of his illustrious career.

It was hard to imagine Miami wouldn't steamroll Dallas like they did Boston and Chicago. The Mavs had swept the season series 2-0, much like Chicago had over Miami, and Boston held a strong 3-1 edge in the regular season. But this was a different Heat team, now battle-tested and hardened, with a renewed resolve and brimming with confidence. The offense was still clunky at times, but as they'd shown in back-to-back rounds, when it mattered most, they had three of the best closers in the game to get over the finish line.

Dallas enjoyed an impressive run through the West, albeit one aided by a stunning Memphis upset of the top seeded San Antonio Spurs, who had the best record in basketball in 2010-11. That meant that after the Mavs eliminated Portland in six and waxed the two-time defending champion Lakers in a resounding sweep, instead of facing a team they struggled with mightily in the Spurs, they would face the young upstart Oklahoma City Thunder. Dallas disposed of them in five games and the reality faced the league that OKC was on schedule and going to be a handful, but not quite yet.

Veteran-laced, not flashy, but well-coached and cohesive, Dallas presented a unique challenge.

They had bodies to throw at Wade and LeBron, but no overwhelmingly great perimeter defenders. They also had a nice rotation of bigs to throw at Bosh. They were built more on veteran guile than talented fresh legs. But no one would be turning their nose at future Hall of Famer Jason Kidd or former MVP Dirk Nowitzki. Make no mistake, Dallas was tough, too, hardened by years of criticism of their own. From blowing a 2-0 lead in the aforementioned 2006 Finals to the Heat, to winning one playoff series in the following four years. They had shuffled coaches and players regularly (including deciding against paying Steve Nash who, of course, would go on to win two league MVPs in Phoenix) and seemed to have found the proper alchemy at long last.

Game one followed the same familiar script as the Eastern Conference Finals: a tight, back and forth game through three quarters that the non-closers from February and March closed out rather effortlessly. Both defenses were sensational, leading to the Heat's second-worst shooting night of the playoffs, and the Mavs' worst. "This Miami defense is suffocating! The best in the NBA!" Jeff Van Gundy declared on ABC.

LeBron started the process of closing out the game with a long, drifting three in front of Dallas coach Rick Carlisle to beat the third quarter buzzer and push Miami's small advantage to four.

Spo was preaching more ball movement going into the fourth quarter, and quickly out of a trap LeBron found Haslem along the baseline who whipped it to Mike Miller in the opposite corner for a wide open three. Miami, up to that point, wasn't really a ball movement team, and the individual shot making would come to the rescue again, for both teams. Wade hit a mid ranger and a wing three over Jason Kidd. Nowitzki squeezed through the lane for a tough layup, and Shawn Marion drew an and one deep in the post against Miller.

Holding a ten point lead under a minute to go, Wade blew around a high Dallas hedge, turned the corner and found LeBron cutting baseline (aided by a Bosh back screen) for a massive alley oop to close out the game.

"There's the exclamation point!" Mike Breen shouted on the ABC telecast.

"They have two very good closers," Nowitzki said, "two of the best in the game."

One game was just one game but bringing the Heat one game closer to their goal.

"We'll play better. I'm very certain of that," Carlisle said.

And they did. A stalemate opened up in the first half of game two, but Miami busted the game open with a 13-0 run to take an 88-73 lead midway through the fourth.

"Not long enough, not strong enough, Mark," Pat Riley said to Mavs owner Mark Cuban. "We're just too quick and too long."

Wade stuck a corner three in front of the Dallas bench and held the follow through, relishing in what had to feel like an inevitable 2-0 lead.

Much has been made of the Wade follow through and he and LeBron celebrated on their way back to the bench after Carlisle wisely took a timeout. Possibly Dallas played more focused and with more intensity following Wade's three, but was that the reason they would come back and win? Were they fine with losing an NBA Finals game *up until* Wade's exaggerated follow through? Was there not external motivation in game one and that is why Dallas ultimately lost it in the fourth quarter?

Armchair psychology is a preferred method in sports media and barbershops alike for making umbrella conclusions and pronouncements on multi-faceted events and circumstances. Was the Wade follow through causation or correlation? Did Dallas sense the urgency being down by 15 with not much time left in a Finals game and ramp up the execution? Was that possibly coupled with the opposite; that Miami felt, and humanly so, that the game was trending largely to being a Heat win and they let the foot off the gas on both ends?

The fact of the matter was, once again as is the case in winning in the playoffs, one team executed on both ends and one did not.

Dallas, though down double digits and in a precarious situation so late in the game with a "white hot" Heat crowd bursting at the seams, did not play rushed or nervous. Double teams on Nowitzki ended up in open shots for Kidd and Jason Terry. They attacked closeouts relentlessly, a direct byproduct of the constant Miami double teaming. And defensively, they were the beneficiaries of the Heat virtually playing a prevent offense on several possessions: slowly bringing the ball into the frontcourt and not much player movement besides a Chalmers/ LeBron pick and roll. Struggling to get penetration or collapse the defense, the Heat was getting long two pointers late in the shot clock and not connecting.

After Terry cut the lead to four at 90-86, Spo called timeout to stop the bleeding. Miami tried to get Bosh a mismatch in the post, but Dallas' sharp defense shut it down, forcing Bosh to dribble out of bounds. Haslem missed on the next possession, but Bosh bailed them out with an offensive rebound after

LeBron nearly ran the shot clock out, hesitating before firing a desperate three.

The reset after Bosh's timely rebound wasn't much better. Dallas was all up in the Heat jerseys and yet another LeBron heave didn't connect. The ball pinged around before ending up in Terry's hands to lead a 3 on 1 Dallas fast break, tying the game.

"What a comeback by the Mavericks, timeout Miami!" Breen exclaimed. "A 17 to 2 run and this crowd is *stunned*!"

"You cannot play better defense than the Dallas Mavericks just did on that entire possession," added Mark Jackson as the ABC telecast went to commercial.

Coming out of the timeout, the Heat again ran an unimaginative set far away from the hoop, and Wade clanked a contested three.

"Miami's gotten very poor shots down the stretch tonight," Van Gundy demurred.

On the other side, Dallas was getting good looks, playing aggressively, and hitting their shots. Nowitzki nailed an open three on a rudimentary stagger screen action in semi transition and Dallas, down 15 only minutes before, now led by 3.

"This is beautiful basketball," remarked Van Gundy, speaking only of Dallas.

Now out of timeouts, the Heat ran a flawless play that freed Chalmers for a wide-open corner three to tie the game. Could the team branded as non-closers now close game 2 in dramatic fashion?

Nowitzki had other ideas, squirming around Bosh and narrowly beating the helping Haslem for a lefty layup. Sans timeouts, the Heat hurried up the floor and got a good look at a potential game-tying running Wade three. Harmlessly ricocheting off the back rim, Breen announced what everyone watching was thinking: "One of the most incredible comebacks in NBA Finals history!"

Nowitzki scored the last nine points for Dallas, including two go-ahead shots in the final minute. The Mavericks missed just three shots total in the final 7:13, while Miami missed everything except a single Chalmers three that tied the game at 90.

"We just didn't execute down the stretch," Bosh said. "There's no shock. There's disappointment. But the reality is the reality. We might as well get used to it and focus on the next one."

"No question about it, that's about as tough a fourth quarter as you can have," added Spo. "When it started to slide, it just kept on going."

If there was a team that could handle not just the loss but the noise that would surround it for the next three days, it would be fair to think it would be the Heat.

The Heat didn't look like a team shell shocked from a huge loss to start game three. Seemingly committed to attacking the hoop, they opened a 29-22 first quarter lead in game three, aided by a Chalmers heave a couple steps inside halfcourt to beat the first quarter horn.

The game remained tight the next two quarters, with Dallas cutting the deficit to three headed into the final stanza. Perhaps a closer game would equate to a greater sense of urgency from Miami as opposed to game two with the large lead?

Wade hit a three during a broken play to push the lead to 84-78 with 4:32 left. After some empty possessions and a questionable foul on Bosh, Nowitzki dunked to tie it at 84-84.

In a clear case of results over process, Wade isolated Kidd at the top of the key with little ball or player movement, but nailed a long jumper to regain the lead.

Dirk, unfazed, responded with a tough jumper over Haslem.

Miami returned to the static offense, with Wade working hard to escape a trap from Chandler and Kidd. He passed to LeBron late in the shot clock, who tried to draw a foul on a three but came up empty, resulting in a shot clock violation. "He has a right to be upset on that one," Van Gundy said, as the ABC broadcast replayed Marion jumping into LeBron.

Regardless, it was easy to see the same script playing out as game two, only without a large lead as a cushion and with far less time on the clock.

Miami forced a rare turnover and, even rarer, ran a solid play out of the timeout. Instead of the usual Wade-Bosh pick and roll, Spo went with Wade and LeBron, a much tougher look to defend. Dallas trapped Wade on the right, who smartly flipped the ball to LeBron at the free throw line. Marion recovered quickly and joined Chandler to trap LeBron, who had just come off a screen from Haslem. With Haslem and Bosh guarded only by Nowitzki on the left, Haslem set a moving screen, allowing LeBron to reverse pivot and hit Bosh for a clutch baseline jumper to take the lead.

On the next possession, Wade blitzed Marion, forcing a bad Nowitzki turnover as he tried to pivot into a fadeaway against Haslem.

"The double team confused Nowitzki, and he threw it away," summed up Breen.

But the Heat seemed to not be learning any lessons with its stationary late-game offense. When something resembling movement happened, Dallas was flying around, desperate for a stop. Wade drove hard off the left into four white jerseys, kicking out to LeBron on the wing. LeBron probably could have risen up to shoot, but faked instead, getting the closing Terry to slide by him but also allowing Marion to get a small contest as well. The late clock, hurried shot was in and out.

Dallas' last gasp attempt was Nowitzki at the top of the floor one on one versus Haslem, a look they had ridden all playoffs to great success. This time the well defended turnaround wouldn't go down.

"He's a great player, 7 feet, so he's going to shoot over me," Haslem said. "I've got to make it tough on him."

"It was a good offensive play, and a good defensive play," Spo elaborated. "And he happened to miss."

The Heat led 2-1. They all count as one, and this, on the heels of the epic letdown of game two, felt enormous. It also felt like a gut punch for the Mavericks who could never quite mount the kind of run to take the lead and make the Heat play from behind.

But make no mistake, if anyone thought this was going to be a walkover for Miami, they couldn't think that anymore. Dallas had proven on both ends they were no joke.

A narrative was starting to percolate. Gregg Doyel, in the postgame press conference, didn't waste time:

"Three games in a row for you, fourth quarter, not much. That's the moment superstars become superstars. Seems like you're almost shrinking from it, what's going on?"

LeBron's response was lukewarm: "I think you're concentrating on one side of the floor." Then he offered the explanation: "D Wade had it going offensively, so we allowed him to handle the ball, we allowed him to bring us home offensively."

If Doyel's question didn't land, ESPN's recap swung the hammer: LeBron "had four turnovers, including a pair during the fourth quarter — not counting the shot-clock violation — that helped bring Dallas back." The phrasing made the implication obvious: LeBron was coughing the game away when it mattered most.

It sounded brutal. Four turnovers in a quarter? In the Finals? Who was allowing that guy to touch the ball late?

But peel back the box score and the story changed. One turnover was a fast-break traveling call with Miami up two at the 8:37 mark, hardly a massive moment. Another was a double-dribble call the broadcast couldn't even explain after it looked like Marion had blocked a LeBron shot back into his hands late in the clock. That dead-ball turnover came with Miami up 81–76 and 5:11 left. On the next possession, Haslem fouled Nowitzki, giving Dallas two free points, a detail omitted by ESPN.

And they also left out the rest of his quarter: a steal and dunk to open it, four assists (including the game-winner to Bosh), and logging all 12 minutes. From the 5:00 mark to 3:03, he touched the ball only once, the byproduct of Miami running Wade-centric offense with Bosh and Haslem screening. His last touch was the shot-clock violation play, scrambling to make something from nothing after Wade shoveled him the ball late on the wing.

Doyel was technically right about the low scoring. But the way it was framed (first by a reporter in the room, then by ESPN for millions reading) made it sound like LeBron went full meltdown mode. The reality was far less sensational.

In the ABC postgame show, Magic Johnson perpetuated a myth surely invented out of thin air: "In game two, they decide they want to let LeBron close, but Dwyane Wade was rolling. And you should have kept the ball in his hands."

Yes, LeBron had had the ball in his hands later in game two than game three. However, in a twisted way Miami became easier to defend with the ball in LeBron's hands. Utilizing a great scheme by quasi defensive coordinator Dwane Casey, the Mavs cheated off most of the Heat players. Kidd or Terry would sag off the poor three point shooting Wade. Chandler and Nowitzki could step off Haslem to clog the paint. They even lived with open shots for Chalmers and Bosh, knowing the ball was out of LeBron's (or Wade's) hands. With Wade handling the ball, even though LeBron was all too often stationed in the corner watching the action unfold at the top of the arc, a Dallas defender, usually Marion, couldn't sag off because of LeBron's better long range shooting and adept ability to attack defenders scrambling out of position.

Johnson must have forgotten what the possessions looked like immediately after Wade's corner three and elongated follow through in game two. Because the first two were both Wade! An open missed three, then Wade tip-toeing across the free throw line for another open missed three by Chalmers.

Jon Barry tried to steer the postgame conversation on the air to actual basketball, citing Haslem's tremendous defense on

Nowitzki and the Miami defense as a whole, which had carried over from their stifling, swarming ways versus Chicago.

But the damage was done, the seed was planted.

And LeBron did next to nothing to alter the narrative.

A relatively close game through three quarters of game four turned into a nine point Miami lead with 10 minutes to go in the fourth after former college teammates Miller and Haslem hit a three and a mid range jumper on the baseline, respectively. Under any other circumstances, it would have to feel like the Heat could crank the temperature up on defense and salt the game away to an almost insurmountable 3-1 lead. But no one forgot game two, least of all the Mavericks.

In the immediate two minutes after a Carlisle timeout to stop the bleeding, the Mavs cut the lead to just three. This wasn't going to be a cinch for Miami.

The old thorn in the Heat's side reappeared as the offense sputtered, running mainly with Wade initiating at the top and LeBron standing virtually statuesque in the corner or high out on the wing. At one point an exasperated Jeff Van Gundy bemoaned on the broadcast, "Just get the ball to LeBron James against Terry." Instead, Miami ran a disjointed possession with Bosh fumbling the ball as he attacked the goal, leading to a leak out layup to take the lead by Terry.

Wade stumbled and bumbled on the next possession and LeBron, trying to save the ball in front of the Dallas bench, stepped out of bounds. The Mavs crowd cranked up the decibels on the heels of the 14-4 run and sensing a similar script as game two. "What a turnaround for the Mavericks!" Breen roared over the din.

The Heat could never wrest control back, exacerbating turnovers with missed jumpers, the result of a lifeless offense.

Leading 82-80, Dallas got a great look at a corner three by Deshawn Stevenson after swinging the ball around the perimeter. The shot, however, was short and in a scramble, Chalmers came up with the ball on the baseline and pitched to LeBron. Wade had leaked out behind the last Dallas defenders, a clear and flagrant offside had it been soccer, and LeBron fired to Wade in stride at the other end. Kidd fouled to prevent the easy two. Wade split the free throws, giving the Mavs a chance to force Miami to have to conjure some late game magic.

As the Mavs had done seemingly all postseason, they got the ball to Nowitzki at the top of the circle and let him go to work.

Much to the chagrin of Van Gundy, who was bemoaning the fact that Nowitzki didn't milk the clock more, the former MVP swept the ball over Haslem's hands and muscled his way to the rim for a layup. Pandemonium ensued in the American Airlines Center.

But the Heat had at least one more chance to even the score when Wade blew by Chandler for a dunk. Terry knocked down two free throws to extend the lead back to three. Miami couldn't play the cat and mouse game any longer and would have to hit a three.

A well designed clearout action to get LeBron versus Terry in the empty corner never materialized. Instead, a dummy misdirection action freed Wade up, sprinting to Miller who was inbounding. But Wade flubbed the catch as he looked at the defense converging. Lunging to save the ball from a backcourt violation, he tipped the ball to Miller who could only chuck a wild three up over Chandler.

"Airball!" Breen shrieked.

It shouldn't have shocked anyone; Dallas had pulled the same reversal in game 2, but it was still baffling. Miami had more talent, yet Dallas executed cleaner consistently on both ends. Nowitzki and Terry attacked fearlessly and the Mavs' defense sharpened as the game tightened.

And LeBron? Oh boy.

It became infamous as the worst game of his career, not because he was humiliated, but because he was invisible. Even his defense, often his fallback calling card, disintegrated with repeated breakdowns against Terry in the fourth. The stat line had some juice (9 rebounds and 7 assists), but the meager 8 points stuck out like a sore thumb.

Over time, this game has become more myth than reality, the story of LeBron avoiding the ball, ping-ponging it around the perimeter to dodge taking a shot. A related narrative took hold that he disappeared in the fourth or shied from big moments, feeding into questions about his mental makeup.

By his standards, it was a bad game. Did he leave any real imprint? Not much. Critics had been waiting for a stumble, and this was it. Never mind that he spent most possessions parked in the corner, face-guarded. Some wanted him to demand the ball, hijack the archaic offense, or start firing shots the moment it touched his hands.

It might sound like excuse-making for LeBron, but the fourth quarter was always going to be an uphill climb given Miami's offense against the Mavs' shifting schemes. Too often he was parked in the corner, with no action to free him or get him into the paint, and when he was at the top of the key Dallas could double without repercussion. As Nowitzki put it after

Game 4, "Whoever has the ball, the other two can't have the ball."

Whether by design or drift, Wade seemed to have the keys to the offense. And while his numbers looked solid, it felt like the overall attack suffered for it.

"Obviously, when you have players playing well, playing aggressively, like I've been playing and Chris played, you kind of get passive," Wade said the day after game four. "That's what LeBron kind of got. That's kinda how I got in the Chicago series. We want him to take advantage of his opportunities."

In the years since, players and coaches up and down the Miami organization pointed to being overwhelmed and out-coached. David Fizdale would go so far as to say, "We were killing...the process of LeBron just being great and giving him the space to go... We were still trying to play like the old Heat when we just had Dwyane, he was our star and that was it. We weren't ready to deviate from what we have been doing all year long."

In the fourth, LeBron made the right plays, but they were overshadowed by criticism of his passivity. Early on, he wisely pitched out of a double team to Haslem, setting up a Miller corner three. Minutes later, he again passed out of a trap, creating a wide-open baseline jumper for Haslem.

A bit later, LeBron got trapped and traveled when he couldn't find a pass around Stevenson. Out of a timeout, he smoothly swung to Wade for a Bosh pick and roll.

Against Dallas's zone, LeBron made a textbook cut and fed Haslem at the free throw line. Haslem flipped to LeBron cutting to the basket, but a forced pass to an unguarded Bosh fell incomplete, leading to a fast break the other way.

Through it all, LeBron never hid or blamed the coaches. He knew he fell short of his standard.

Game five all eyes would be on him. "Our star player is in single digits, and we lose by three?" Bibby explained the mindset of the team years later. "That's not going to happen again. That's the mindset we had going into game 5."

"We've all been here before. We just have to keep trusting ourselves and trusting each other," Bosh stated between games.

LeBron tweeted out in the wee hours before the game, "Now or never", a cringeworthy message that surely wouldn't be mocked.

As if hedging against the nonstop criticism levied on LeBron, the pregame broadcast tried to provide some context. "LeBron James took the blame, but all of the Big 3 struggled down the stretch in game four. When all were on the court in the fourth, the Heat missed 9 of 12 shots and had four crucial turnovers," Jon Barry shared.

But as quickly as it came, the context went. Hall of Famer Magic Johnson followed up Barry, saying: "He just has to be more aggressive." The low hanging fruit "analysis" was far from reality, even after talking about fourth quarter shot attempts. Would Magic have agreed it is difficult to get shots up in the fourth quarter if a player doesn't have the ball? He would follow it up with the other low hanging fruit favored by TV guys: free throw attempts. And specifically, that less free throw attempts meant a lack of aggression.

Sigh.

LeBron came out much more "aggressive" which may have been code for the Heat finally deciding that having him stand in the corner and watch Wade handle the ball might not have been the best use of a two-time MVP. Running more actions to get him open jumpers was a sight for sore Heat eyes. However, those jumpers weren't falling. LeBron was making his impact felt setting up others, working abnormally hard on the offensive glass, and stopping multiple shots at the rim.

It was incredible to see the Heat run a play after a second quarter timeout that wasn't a series of screens only to end up dribbling the clock down at the end of the shot clock. It was a back screen on the baseline for LeBron who got a clean catch and turned in for a layup.

But the vaunted Heat defense hadn't shown up to game five and gave up a playoff-high 60 points in the first half.

Nonetheless, with 3:38 to go in the game, a Bosh free throw gave the Heat the lead, 100-97. Dallas quickly answered with a Terry three on a defensive breakdown and a Nowitzki dunk, going right past Haslem on the baseline.

Mike Breen, not usually one to get caught up in hyperbole and narratives, got caught up in hyperbole and narratives. "James still scoreless here in the fourth quarter," he said on the broadcast, mid-Heat possession. "He did not have a point in the fourth quarter of game four, 0 for 2 in the fourth quarter tonight."

Thankfully, Mark Jackson interjected quickly, "That's really not fair. He missed a jump shot, but the Mavericks are doing a very good job of double-teaming LeBron James."

Moments later he would miss a good three point look from the top of the arc. To make matters worse, Terry blew by him, capitulating the Miami defense and finding Kidd wide open up top for a huge three.

The grizzled vet would get another chance versus James, this time pulling and drilling a well contested wing three with 33.3 seconds left.

It was a back breaker for the Heat. Once again, their late game offense had been fruitless while Dallas' had been efficient. And this time it wasn't the individual brilliance of Nowitzki.

"We are getting the same looks we knew we would get," Terry said. "After games 1 and 2, you watch it on film, you see it, and then you realize you're going to have the opportunities. I said to myself, I said to my teammates, 'We're not going to continue to miss those open shots that we're getting.'"

LeBron had a triple double, but struggled with his jumper all night. Bosh scored 19 and Wade had 23, leaving the game briefly with a hip pointer.

"Definitely a big win for us," Nowitzki said after the game.

It now really was now or never.

Miami had the home court advantage, which could possibly equate to two more games at home to finish the series. Dallas' trio of point guards combined to hit 10 three pointers, one seemingly more punishing than the next. If it was of any hope, Boston had led 3-2 in the Finals the previous season, only to drop the two road games in Los Angeles and cough up the series. So, it could be done.

"I remember I went back at night when we were shooting," recalled Bosh, attempting, along with LeBron, to clear their minds. "I was watching him shoot. He just seemed like something was on his mind. I said, 'Hey man, look, we got two games at home to win an NBA championship, we good.' And he said, 'Yeah, you right, but everybody wants me to fail.' And I felt the same way... nobody got it like he got it."

Spo finally benched Bibby, who had gotten his lunch eaten by Kidd and JJ Barea nearly the entire series. Chalmers brought more length and quickness at the point of attack and, hopefully, much better shooting.

In another myth-making attempt in the pregame show, LeBron's fourth quarters were highlighted and his overall shooting versus Michael Jordan and Kobe Bryant in their NBA Finals careers. Luckily, Magic Johnson, who had not been exempt of hyperbole himself during the broadcasts, came to a rescue of sorts with some context in his analysis when asked if the criticism of LeBron was warranted: "He deserves some of it because he hasn't performed to LeBron James-type standards. But at the same time, he's not the only one who's not performing well. Erik Spoelstra, the coach, he's going to have to perform better."

Jon Barry, the former mediocre NBA player, of course had to bring it back to the company lines, guffawing about LeBron being passive (yawn), not attacking off pick and rolls (yawn), the same trite "analysis".

Michael Wilbon, who of all the team members on the pregame show was most likely to take an extreme, emotional stance, surprisingly had the most measured thoughts of the situation at large.

"There is a difference between criticism and ridicule and too much of this has crossed the line," he responded to Barry. "There's a rush to judgment out there that's over the top. Five years ago, people had already judged Dirk Nowitzki as a bum, as too soft, that would never be a champion. Now all of a sudden, they have to reverse those judgments... People need to leave some wiggle room for people to evolve, for players to get better, for players to learn, accept coaching better."

LeBron started the game with the same kind of aggressiveness as in game 5, going 4-for-4 early. His jump shot was falling, even if it looked stiff and jerky, almost releasing as he came down from the peak of his jump.

The Heat cut an early 8 point deficit to two by halftime, but a hot third quarter by the Mavs equated to a 9 point lead going into what could be the final frame of the season.

Dallas' bench had nearly doubled up the Heat's through three quarters, outscoring them 37-19.

A quick, early flurry by the Heat got the game to striking distance at 81-77 and a near steal by Wade in the Dallas backcourt got the Miami fans amped up. The sellout crowd, almost all wearing white, rose to their feet. They wouldn't be standing for long as Barea shook House for a stepback three to extend back to a 7 point lead.

Miami could never really mount a run to overcome the deficit and a nervous crowd turned to a despondent one as Dallas coasted to the win and the title.

As the final buzzer sounded, Nowitzki leapt over the bench to weep with joy back in the locker room, overcome with emotion. He had been resplendent all postseason and even in what was his worst game of the Finals, hit a series of jumpers to keep Miami at bay.

"An unlikely playoff run capped off by Dallas upsetting LeBron James, Dwyane Wade, and the favored Miami Heat," Breen said as the magnitude of the moment was setting in. "A stunning ending to one of the more compelling seasons in NBA history. A bitter finish."

The Heat was gracious in defeat, congratulating Dallas players and coaches, some of whom would cement their Hall of Fame careers with the championship. "This is a true team," Carlisle said. "This is an old bunch. We don't run fast or jump high. These guys had each other's backs. We played the right way. We trusted the pass."

Amid the shock was an overwhelming sense of joy for Dallas, a veteran group of players who had been nearly flawless in the Finals. Overmatched in the talent department, they were better coached, better prepared, and were more efficient throughout all six games. Those disparities were more glaring than the talent gap.

Nowitzki's journey probably mirrored what Miami felt all season, and now ultimately in defeat. After falling to the Heat in the 2006 Finals, Nowitzki won MVP the next year and led Dallas to the best regular season record. But they were stunned in the first round by the eighth-seeded Warriors. At a crisis point, Nowitzki disappeared from the spotlight, facing the crucible of criticism as a "soft European" player. Between 2006 and 2011, Dallas won just one playoff series, and the franchise, and Nowitzki himself, was dismissed as weak-minded and finesse.

And now, here he stood: Finals MVP, exorcising the demons of 2006 in the grandest way possible. First by utterly dominating the defending champion Lakers, then by toppling the Heat. His hero's journey was marked by heartbreak, disappointment, and failure until finally, crowning glory. In a twisted way, the mantle of best player never to win a title was being passed from the gallant Nowitzki to the defeated LeBron.

"I'm so happy for him. I'm so happy for Dirk," Carlisle said.

"I really still can't believe it," said Nowitzki. "We worked so hard and so long for it. The team has had an unbelievable ride."

"They were incredible in that series," Spo said nearly a decade later. "I don't think people give that team enough credit."

Chapter 9 - Come to Jesus

The means did not justify the ends for the Heat's season. Beating the Celtics and the surprising Bulls would never ingratiate Miami to the general basketball world. How could it? This was the team coming out to be introduced in a laser and fog show. This was the team whose goals, implicitly or explicitly, were championships and nothing else.

Adding insult to injury, the immediate aftermath of the loss was fuel to the critics' fire. Bosh wilted to the ground in an emotional outpouring in the tunnel to the losing locker room. With ABC cameras rolling, he had to be helped up and escorted to the door. Normally a sign of passion and importance, this would not receive the normal treatment.

"I didn't know the camera was there," says Bosh now. "If I'd have known the camera was there, I could've kept it together for a little longer."

LeBron and Wade, sitting together at a postgame press conference for the last time in 2011, were in understandably somber moods. LeBron was the first to "crack", when he was asked if he was bothered that so many people were relishing in his failure to win the championship.

"Absolutely not," he answered, partially false at best. "At the end of the day all the people that was rooting on me to fail, at the end of the day they got to wake up tomorrow and have the same life that they had before they woke up today. They got the same personal problems that they had today. I'm going to continue to live the way I want to live... they got to get back to the real world at some point."

It clearly was what LeBron had been feeling ever since the criticism had crescendoed nearly a year ago. But the people rooting for LeBron and the Heat to fail only got more ammunition with a comment like that, the one soundbite to bookend the season.

While innocuous and theoretically true, the comment came off as "you're broke, I'm not" and launched the criticism into overdrive heading into the offseason.

"Your back is against the wall and you're going to react, we're all human," Bosh says now.

There was not much sympathy for the plight of LeBron or the Heat.

The basketball media went in for the kill, dissecting LeBron's psyche and picking apart the Heat's Big Three with relentlessness.

Jay Caspian Kang wrote for *Grantland*:

> *LeBron did not shrink up in the moment. He did not miss big shots or free throws. He did not turn the ball over or travel or call a timeout. Instead, he just kind of wasn't there. And what was even weirder than the public's lack of surprise, or LeBron's hostile postgame press conference, or even the defensiveness with which he carried himself throughout the season, was just how the villain in this particular tragedy felt staid, warmed-over.*

The great Henry Abbott wrote in his *TrueHoop* postmortem of the NBA Finals:

The story is of LeBron James' failure. He was as bad as I could imagine he'd ever be. He was atrocious. Atrocious.

Earlier in the playoffs we talked about how he was, I thought then, being brilliant in conserving energy early in games to be fresh for crunch time. Now I realize he was just being lazy.

"The Heat lost. And the universe is celebrating," wrote a high-trafficking blog called Basketbawful.

Drew Magary of Deadspin piled on:

There's nothing wrong with rooting for LeBron James to fail. It says nothing bad about you as a person to wish ill upon someone who is monstrously talented yet at the same time is also a world-class dipshit. LeBron James has never been arrested or caught with naughty drugs or done anything explicitly "immoral," I suppose. But that doesn't matter, because he's still a piece of shit anyway. His reaction in the wake of losing last night was even more predictable than his on-court meltdown. His personal blind spot is as large as Lenny Dykstra's or Charlie Sheen's.

The season, judged by any measure short of the stated goal, was a resounding success. But the goal was a championship trophy, and Dallas was the team holding it. In 2011, it was fair to wonder if the Cowboys were still America's Team or if that title now belonged to the Mavericks.

"I couldn't believe it," said Bosh. "I sat there all night. I didn't go to sleep until about 8 a.m. I just sat outside all night, and I was sitting with my friends and I was like, 'Just stay up with me.'"

It had been an eleven month long, never-ending spectacle. The term traveling circus was fraught and overused, but it really had been one. Sold out arenas in every city, all ready to boo the team that everyone hated. The Heat was the top story, no joke, almost every single day. From *The Decision* to the fallout from *The Decision* to the first game in Boston, to Bumpgate, to winning streaks, to the losing streaks, to the playoff domination, to the untimely Finals debacle. It was almost miraculous that the Heat had overcome all the noise and been able to play basketball at all, let alone at a high level.

"The sheer intensity of the entire season...more daunting than anything you would ever find even in a real competitive conference final or final," said Kevin Arnovitz, who had as good of a vantage point of the entire season as anyone.

The intensity, the negativity, all of it resulted in what everyone admitted was a miserable season.

"It was not fun at all," said Bosh. "I was a different person, it was like a baptism, so to speak."

"It wasn't a joyous year to play basketball," added Wade, "at all."

A work stoppage for the players was on the horizon, which only made the question begged go longer without an answer: how could the Heat possibly pick up the pieces from this?

The roster had to change, one way or another. Not necessarily in the Big 3, though that was frequently floated. As Abbott wrote thoughtfully about what the next steps could be for the Heat:

I'd revisit the offense. I'd revisit the decision to fill the roster with old stiff dudes who wouldn't be able to play on 25 NBA teams, but almost won rings here. Joel was almost unplayable in this series. Bibby was a disastrous signing.

The Heat signed players based on their brand, which is a gigantic problem in the NBA. The supporting cast they assembled would have been great in the late 1990s, but it's 2011!

It would be a huge mistake to break up the big three, though. They are not only all young and good, but also underpaid. You can do a much, much better job on the supporting cast.

What's lost in the entire first season of the Big 3 era was the turnstile that the roster became.

"It just wasn't a very good roster," Ethan Skolnick admitted.

"Carlos Arroyo and Big Z were starting!" Tom Haberstroh says now, fully perplexed.

"The rest of that team was sorry!" said Gilbert Arenas. "It was a bunch of million dollar players that was old as fuck!"

Many would never play in the NBA again; a handful would play literally only dozens of minutes more in the NBA.

Carlos Arroyo had been jettisoned in March, signed with Boston, played 190 total minutes for them (none in the playoffs) and never played in the NBA again.

Mike Bibby, the prized late season replacement for Arroyo, flamed out spectacularly in the Finals, played for the Knicks the following season, shot 31% from three, and never played in the NBA again.

Erik Dampier had been serviceable, if not wholly unspectacular for the Heat. He scored one more NBA basket the following season with Atlanta and never touched the NBA hardwood again.

Eddie House had been a good presence and a good shooter but was a huge defensive liability and the Heat lost trust with his game throughout the season. His final NBA season was 2010-11 with Miami.

Zydrunas Ilgauskas had been an underrated safety blanket for LeBron and was fine in his role, until that role was no longer necessary in the playoffs. He did not play in the NBA again.

Jamaal Magloire was well-respected in the Heat organization, but ultimately, he was not an answer as a rotation player. He would appear in 34 more games in his career, all with Toronto, and retire.

The 36-year-old Jerry Stackhouse would end up having the most productive post-Miami career of all those brought in (and out) in 2010-11. He had been cut to make way for Dampier early in the season to address the big man crunch with Haslem's injury. The proud Stackhouse wouldn't play in the NBA the rest of the season but resurfaced the following season in Atlanta and saw action in the 2013 playoffs with the Brooklyn Nets before retiring.

"I feel like the Heat had like 24 guys on the roster that year, they kept cycling through guys," Windhorst joked.

The Heat's bench scoring was in the bottom five of the league during the season, a combination of the creaky vets and ill-fated injuries to Miller and Haslem. The point guard conundrum seemed to have been solved with Chalmers, while Wade or LeBron could handle those duties in spots.

The roster was one thing. The basketball philosophy was quite another.

The philosophy worked, until it didn't. Old, complicated offensive sets bogged down throughout the playoffs, and Miami leaned on Wade and LeBron to bail them out with elite isolation shot-making. Dallas's zone smothered that, and when Wade got banged up and those shots stopped falling, the Heat was left holding the bag.

By the time anyone realized it, it was too late; Miami was running a vintage Pat Riley/Stan Van Gundy offense built around a ball-dominant guard and a big man, a system that completely undercut what LeBron could and should have brought to the table.

Hall of Fame coach Rick Adelman summed it up best saying, "People assume a good team is easy to coach. But the pressure to maintain the trust of these talented players, and keep the whole thing from disintegrating, is very hard."

That was what Spo found himself tasked with. *Keep the whole thing from disintegrating.*

A dozen years later, Jason Quick of *The Athletic* penned what Spo experienced the night of losing the Finals to the Mavs:

Stunned and hurt, Spoelstra didn't leave the arena after the loss. He was tortured because he felt his coaching played a role in the upset. Despite having James, Wade and Bosh, Miami was stymied by Dallas. On defense, the Mavericks clogged the paint, making it difficult for James and Wade to penetrate. On offense, Dallas neutralized Miami's quickness and athleticism by limiting dribbling and stressing passing to stay one click ahead of rotations.

Spoelstra had no counterattack, and it ate at him.

At daybreak, assistant coach David Fizdale arrived at the arena. He found the coach sitting behind his desk, both stewing and devastated.

"As soon as I opened the door, I could tell it had been one of those nights," Fizdale said. "Probably the longest night of his life. It wasn't his best look."

They had long been friends, dating to 1997 when they worked in the Heat video room, and they talked openly about their hurt and frustration with the series.

"It was crushing for him, and he blamed himself a lot for it," Fizdale said. "So we sat there, two old friends, teary-eyed and hugging it out, feeling as small as you could feel."

Then, amid the sniffles and clearing of throats, Spoelstra snapped into form. He locked eyes with Fizdale.

"This is typical Spo: he looked at me with bloodshot eyes and said, 'Never again! Lay it on me ... how do we fix it?'" Fizdale said.

They brainstormed late into the afternoon. The Heat offense was revamped, scrapping non-scoring bigs from posting on the strong side to open more space for James and Wade to attack. And on defense, they accentuated their trapping schemes by adding more switching coverages, designed to hinder teams like Dallas from beating them with crisp passing. In a matter of hours, they had performed a clean sweep of the Heat playbook.

"It was a pretty important moment in time, where failure actually galvanized us to victory," Fizdale said. "But a big part was Spo saying, 'You know what? I'm flawed. We are flawed. We are not going to let them blame LeBron for this, and we are going to do what is necessary to never feel this way again.'"

Ron Rothstein, who spent 26 years on NBA benches, including six as Spoelstra's assistant, said by the time the Heat staff reconvened the next season, he noticed a different Spoelstra.

"He was bound, driven by that experience," Rothstein said. "I never really talked to him about it, but I saw it in his eyes. We would all be in the office talking, and with him there would be this silence. I know he was hurting; we were all hurting. But to his credit, the things that didn't go well, he was smart enough to own up to it. He learned from his mistakes."

The playbook wasn't the only thing that changed. So too did Spoelstra. He had tried so hard in his first four seasons to sound like a head coach, carry himself like a head coach, that he never got around to being a head

Lee Jenkins wrote in *Sports Illustrated* what Spo was demanding of others in his orbit to avoid the same fate again:

> *Spoelstra installed an organizational "improvement program." He ordered coaches to read books and attend clinics, then write reports about what they learned. One staffer was instructed to mine every Malcolm Gladwell article for relevant thoughts. Spoelstra, who listened to John Maxwell leadership CDs on the drive to work every day, was taking the equivalent of 30,000 jumpers again. He discovered a book by Carol S. Dweck called Mindset and became consumed with the distinction between a growth mind-set and fixed mind-set.*

Spo visited Oregon football coach Chip Kelly who had turned college football on its head with a hyper-fast offense, wanting to snap the ball after each play as quickly as possible, eschewing the old school tenants of time of possession. Spo, realizing the crossover of speed and the pressure it inevitably puts on defenses, mentally and physically, was all in.

He "outlined principles that would allow the Heat to play up-tempo and unclog the lane for dribble penetration. He named it the 'pace and space' offense," wrote Tom Haberstroh.

Riley remained resolute and calm amid the storm of defeat, backed fully by Mickey Arison. Spo would bounce back, he was too competitive not to. But what about the players, the ones who'd made bold claims and ultimately came up short? Those same players who'd endured a nearly yearlong gauntlet of criticism, hatred, and then public disappointment? It wouldn't have been surprising if the Heat had returned broken, defeated both on the court and in spirit. For a time, and even longer with the looming lockout, the consensus was clear: LeBron was mentally fragile, happy to ride shotgun to Wade, and the Heat could never recover as a team.

LeBron went into hiding, saying he was so low he didn't step outside his house for two weeks.

"You definitely didn't want to be around me the first couple weeks after the Finals," he told Dan Le Batard. "I sheltered myself from everybody. It gave me time to sit back and think about ways I can become a better person, ways I can become a better man and a better basketball player. I was devastated. I've had a few low points in my life and that was definitely one of them."

He and Wade went on a pre-planned Bahamas trip. "We started having different conversations about why we lost and how we lost," Wade said. "Everything that I was getting from LeBron in that year, even though he had a great year, and even in that moment, was hesitation. If we gonna reach the level that we're going to reach, and how I can help us, is to take that hesitation out of one the games greatest players... you that dude, go be that dude."

"I said to LeBron, 'You're not a villain—that's not even who you are,'" said Rich Paul.

"I made a pact in the Bahamas that the guy who I was last year wasn't going to be me going into the future," recalled LeBron. "I knew if I was going back to the person I was before, we'd be a better team. It was that simple."

Bosh also got married in the summer, likely planned as an afterparty to the championship the Heat was surely going to win. "I couldn't be down too long," he reflected. "Our wedding, it was a great party, and everybody came and that kind of got us back into a good feeling...huge party, we tore Miami up...the spirit was back a little bit. Best wedding Miami's ever seen."

Slowly but surely, the players returned with new priorities. Spo's philosophy wasn't the only thing evolving. LeBron publicly studied post moves with Hall of Famer Hakeem Olajuwon. Bosh expanded his range. "He came back and added that three-pointer, and it changed our whole team," Wade recalls.

And Wade himself evolved by symbolically taking a step back.

"We said we want to win rings, for us to win rings...you have to be who you are," Wade remembers intimating to LeBron. "I can't stand in the way of that."

"It had to be bigger than me, which is hard to do. I just had to look at myself in the mirror and say this is not why you playing with LeBron James and Chris Bosh."

The roster also, thankfully, evolved. The Heat drafted a feisty point guard, Norris Cole, to be Chalmers' backup. They signed Rony Turiaf, an undersized big man who had championship experience with the Lakers. And the offseason trump card: signing veteran utility man Shane Battier.

Battier was a household name from his days at Duke where he won a national championship and was named college player of the year. He was drafted by Memphis where he was part of a reclamation project for the downtrodden franchise, fresh off relocating across the country from Vancouver. With Battier as a key cog, Memphis went from 23 and 28 wins in his first two seasons to 50 wins and the franchise's first ever playoff appearance in his third. He was traded to Houston in the summer of 2006, becoming a key contributor to the Yao Ming and Tracy McGrady teams.

But Battier's reputation would truly explode in 2009 when he was the feature of a *New York Times Magazine* article by Michael Lewis called "The No-Stats All-Star". Battier was a solid player albeit with unspectacular stats. Lewis, however, wrote that Battier's understanding and implementation of analytical information made him invaluable, in both Houston and Memphis. He shot virtually nothing but three pointers, devoured scouting reports, and coupled those with player specific data to get an edge defending the best players in the NBA on a nightly basis.

Battier was highly sought after, but his teams rarely made deep playoff runs. He'd only advanced past the first round twice, including the 2011 playoffs when his Grizzlies upset the top-seeded Spurs, clearing the path for the Mavericks to dominate the West.

"My criteria for joining the team was I wanted to play for a contender where I had a major role," Battier explained. "I wanted to be a guy that brought a team to a higher level."

That was the goal bringing Battier into the Heat fold; he was a consummate professional and got along with everybody. He also wasn't wearing the battle scars of the 2011 Finals or the whole season in general.

"That first year for them was really about growing pains," he observed. "It was obvious that entire year that they were playing an awkward dance ... those guys were so good that they got away with it until they didn't."

Battier also was drawn to the Heat because of his friendship with Mike Miller, who had been his teammate in Memphis for four seasons during the most success the franchise had ever enjoyed.

"Myyyyy homie," Battier says endearingly. "Mike is one of my closest friends in this league and he's a big reason I chose Miami."

The presence of the Duke-educated Jimmy Buffett parrot head would be a calming influence in many respects. First, he knew his role: play defense and shoot (and make) threes. Second, he wanted to win. And third, he wasn't a creaky veteran who peaked in the 90s.

Banking on improved health for Haslem and Miller, the bench suddenly was looking much stronger (and younger) than it had only months before.

The Heat was determined to not replicate the 2010-11 season: everyone would have to evolve. "That formula wasn't the one that works," Bosh said succinctly.

"The Heat had always had a comically inefficient offense for the talent they had," pointed out Wosny Lambre.

LeBron would no longer be a pawn, relegated to watch the other four players from the corner. He would be a juiced-up queen on the chessboard.

"They said, 'LeBron, you're Karl Malone out there,'" said Tom Haberstroh. "'You need to learn how to be Karl Malone, learn how to post up guys, and, more importantly, learn how to set screens and then roll to the rim.'

"LeBron James has always been the air traffic controller being able to see everything," he continued. "And one of the hard things for LeBron was to come to grips with the fact that when he turns after the screen, he's no longer being able to see the floor."

Putting LeBron at the focal point of multiple actions, while there would inevitably be a learning curve, would be a nightmare for defenses. Guarding him straight up was hard enough, now teams would have to defend him from every possible place on the floor.

"He's a lot more comfortable. He's really settling into being LeBron James," said Wade.

The longest NBA work stoppage in 12 years at long last ended on December 8, 2011. A condensed season of 66 games in just over four months would kick off on Christmas Day, featuring a heavily anticipated rematch:

Miami at Dallas.

Chapter 10 - Frothing at the Mouth

Most of the Heat had kept a relatively low profile during the offseason and most of the lockout. LeBron of course had been working on his game, first with Olajuwon and then at the Los Angeles Drew League where various NBA players stopped through to get competitive basketball in front of standing room only crowds. He also opened the doors of a boutique shop in Miami called UNKNWN, selling "highly coveted goods", including collectible sneakers and designer clothes.

LeBron spoke with ESPN's Rachel Nichols before the season, addressing the prior season's negativity head-on.

When Nichols pointedly asked how he performed in the Finals, he pulled no punches.

"Not great at all, not how I know how to play the game of basketball ... I just know I didn't play well, I didn't have enough game-changing plays like I know I'm capable of."

He seemed contemplative and soft spoken, a man who had been truly been humbled.

"I'm not here to ask for any sympathy or ask for no apology," he said.

Nichols prodded about the yearlong narrative of the Heat, and LeBron specifically, being and embracing themselves as villains.

"You start to hear the villain ... I started to buy into it ... I started to play the game of basketball in a mind state that I never played at before ... being angry, and that's mentally. And that's not how I play the game of basketball."

And in what would be an underrated and forgotten line, but a sign of things to come, he warned, when asked if he was still the villain: "His game can be the villain, but I'm not that guy."

As much as he and the Heat began to downplay the villain role, they surely wanted to be just that on Christmas Day in Dallas. Not only would the new-look Mavericks be getting the rings they earned back in June, but it would also be a long, drawn out, televised ceremony that the Heat would have to patiently wait through.

The Heat to a man never discredited Dallas or made excuses for the Finals failure. In retrospect, they almost unanimously admitted that losing the Finals was the best thing that happened to them for the long-term success of the four years together.

"One of the best things that happened to us media-wise is that we lost in the Finals," Wade explained years later. "It humbled us, it put us at our level, and it allowed us to focus on what was real and why we had got together."

"We learned the pain that Dirk and Jason Terry and Jason Kidd went through," Bosh said. "Nobody cares, get over it and just win."

"If we'd have won in the Finals ... we'd have been jackin'," Wade would say with a giggle.

And the Heat was jackin' on Christmas Day.

"These guys were frothing at the mouth," said Battier. "There was an amazing edge about this team, an edge from losing to Dallas. I was like holy cow these guys are angry, *angry*. The training staff was angry, the coaches were angry, the players were angry in a good way. I'll never forget being in the tunnel and I could feel the heavy breathing and you could feel the edge. The edge was so defined. These guys are some dogs."

Defending champs often start slow, as Dallas did, but Miami was hungry and fast in the blowout. Leading by 35 early, the Heat began their climb back in earnest. LeBron was dominant—37 points, 10 rebounds—punishing in the post and making play after play in transition.

The Heat in general looked re-energized, not beaten down from the previous season and its crushing conclusion. The offense in Dallas looked completely different than it had in June in Miami; neither Wade nor LeBron hardly ever were stationary and not in the action, no more standing like statues in the corner. Both moved freely off-ball—along the baseline, through the paint, across the key. Complex sets gave way to a freer offense, helped by a Mavs team with little to prove and missing defensive anchor Tyson Chandler, who was now a New York Knick.

It might have seemed like a blip or a fluke, but it may as well have been a warning: the Heat was back and the players had not taken the lockout or the embarrassing Finals defeat lightly.

They dusted the Celtics two nights later, 115-107, leading by as many as 20. The rookie Norris Cole scored 20 points and Wade, LeBron, and Bosh combined for 68.

LeBron had 35 the next night in Charlotte, a 96-95 Heat win, and then made 16 two-point field goals on his birthday, December 30, in a win at Minnesota.

"The lockout ... it helped me out a lot because I was able to establish my family in Miami throughout that time that I had off," said LeBron, who seemed more at ease than at any other point since he got to the Heat.

"When his family moved here, I saw more smiles on his face," Juwan Howard added. "He felt at peace."

The hot start would roll to 5-0 and 8-1, the best start in Miami franchise history before a three game slide on the back end of a West Coast road trip, with two of those losses being in overtime back-to-back nights.

Returning home, the Heat blasted the West's one seed from the previous year, San Antonio, 120-98, and pummeled the Lakers and then the Sixers. LeBron also hit his first three pointer of the year versus the Spurs, noteworthy only because he had stated he wanted to maximize his efficiency and eliminating the three would in theory enable him to be more aggressive and punish teams closer to the basket.

The condensed schedule was taxing on everyone in the league; at one point in January the Heat played 6 games in 8 days and went 5-1. The focus, mentally and physically, would have to be paramount for any team to be taken seriously.

Those that were watching closely noticed an interesting trend with the much-ballyhooed pace and space

"With a month of basketball in the books, it seems that he (Spo) might need to tinker with his mantra," wrote the great Tom Haberstroh. "With Wade on the floor, the Heat were running and destroying teams in transition. The 'pace' was there. But in the six games that he has been sidelined with leg injuries, something interesting has happened: the Heat have slammed on the brakes. They have ditched the high-octane offense in exchange for a halfcourt offense built around the floor-spacing of its three-point shooters Mike Miller, James Jones and Shane Battier.

"The numbers tell the story. While LeBron does his part to break the box score, the Heat have transformed its principles on the fly without Wade on the court. With the Heat this season, there have been two separate offenses: one that thrives on pace and one that thrives on floor-spacing."

An Eastern Conference Finals rematch with the Bulls didn't look anything like the bloodbath playoffs matchup had. Yet, it was highlighted by LeBron jumping over John Lucas on a beautifully designed back door alley oop. "James just jumped right over Lucas!" an incredulous Mike Breen exclaimed on the Sunday main event broadcast. The defending MVP Rose would yet again bungle two late game chances, missing at the line then short arming a push shot in the key that would have tied the game.

"Like the playoffs in January," Wade said.

"The way I see it, every time we play the Bulls it's going to be like that," Bosh added. "It's always going to be an atmosphere where nobody wants to lose and that's how the playoffs are."

The win and LeBron leaping over Lucas were not the only storylines of the day: because of a marathon route shutting down much of the accessible roads to American Airlines Arena, LeBron had ridden his bike to the game, captured on Twitter by user @peter1lee.

Apparently, it wasn't an isolated incident; Shandel Richardson of the *South Florida Sun-Sentinel* reported: "At some point this season, he occasionally began riding his bicycle to practice instead of driving. Then it turned into riding to morning shootarounds. And then games. Suddenly, James was spending more time on the bike than driving around in expensive cars."

Miami was rolling along, not just on two wheels. At one juncture they won three straight road games by double digits... in three consecutive nights.

And in a completely unforeseen and insane delirium, the Heat wasn't the top story in the NBA in February 2012. That would be the New York Knicks, and much more specifically their point guard, previously unknown Harvard grad Jeremy Lin.

Chapter 11 - Linsanity

Lin was a basketball version of a farm arm, filling in for a myriad of Knicks injuries that had crept in during the short, frenzied season. But Lin wasn't just getting spot duty. He was starting due to the lack of bodies available. And he was *ballin'.*

He had played 55 total minutes during the season, never scoring more than 9 points. Thrown into starting duty on February 4 versus New Jersey, he played 36 minutes and scored a career-high 25 points in the 99-92 Knicks win. He bested that career high the next night versus Utah with 28 points in the win. Then 23 and 10 assists two nights later in Washington versus the Wizards.

The term was overused and had lost all meaning by 2012, but Lin was a legitimate sensation. His Twitter following exploded not in days or months, but in hours. The Taiwan native was greeted to cheers and flags in Washington, the crowd chanting his name as he walked off the floor in victory.

Lin wasn't a spot up shooter or another kind of one trick pony. He was the starting point guard, running masterful pick and rolls in Knicks coach Mike D'Antoni's spread out, run and gun offense.

In baseball, rookie pitchers often bamboozle veterans early on, but hot starts usually fade once hitters scout their tendencies and adjust by the second matchup.

The same, or at least something similar, could be said for basketball players. But Lin was on tape by now. And it didn't matter.

He absolutely shredded Kobe Bryant and the Lakers for 38 points in the Knicks fourth straight win.

"I think it's a great story," Bryant said. "I think it's a testament to perseverance and hard work. Good example for kids everywhere."

Linsanity, as it was dubbed, had officially hit the nos.

The zenith was north of the border, in Toronto, where Lin, sitting at 25 points, dribbled at the top of the key with the game tied at 87.

One on one isolated versus veteran Jose Calderon, he calmly walked into a three pointer and launched with 2.5 seconds to go.

No doubt about it.

"BANG! Jeremy Lin from downtown and the Knicks take the lead!" boomed legendary voice Mike Breen.

Lin skipped down the floor nodding his head to the hysteria.

"Amazing!" a breathless Breen added.

"I'm thankful that the coach and my teammates trust me with the ball at the end of the game," Lin said. "I like having it at the end of the game. I'm just very thankful."

The Knicks would win their seventh in a row since Lin began playing in earnest, a 100-85 demolition of the Kings at Madison Square Garden.

He had scored 136 points in his first five starts, most by any NBA player since the NBA merged with the ABA. And he almost single-handedly accomplished what no player had been able to do: utterly take all the attention from the Miami Heat.

During the same stretch, the Heat had won seven out of eight games, barely noticed in the NBA at large. For a team that had seemingly been topic one, two, and three in the NBA consciousness since July 2010, it was a welcome respite. And as much as they refused to publicly admit it, they were jealous of the attention Lin was receiving.

They would get their chance to experience Linsanity almost three weeks to the day it began.

Multiple Heat reporters remembered Miami players arguing about who would get to guard Lin. Chalmers was the natural point guard defender, but Wade and LeBron wanted their chance at the young sensation.

They would all get their bite of the fresh meat.

And, really, it shouldn't have come as a surprise; LeBron loved the spotlight, remember? *Attention whore* and all that. He *had* to have the limelight.

Other teams had tried a variation of the Heat's trapping defense versus Lin, but no other team had the athletes on the perimeter that Miami did. And it showed, painfully so for Lin.

"Heat players are pumped up!" announced Marv Albert before the game even tipped off.

Two minutes into the game, Chalmers, defending Lin full court, poked the ball away in the backcourt for an uncontested two hand dunk.

"He's been all over Lin!" exclaimed Albert.

That would continue all game as Miami, decked out in all black jerseys, resembled the kraken consuming a helpless ship. In pick-and-rolls, with Bosh often coming up to trap, the Heat's quicker guards repeatedly stripped, poked, and yanked the ball away. Lin finished with eight turnovers in total to match his eight points on 1-for-11 shooting as the Heat finished strong to win going away, 102-88.

When TNT sideline reporter Craig Sager intimated to Dwyane Wade in a question that the Heat was tired of hearing and answering questions about Lin, Wade downplayed it again, instead offering up praise.

"He deserves all the credit he has been given," he said. "Our point guards did a great job tonight. He's a good player but we put a lot of pressure on him, and it was successful."

Lin after the game looked like a guy that had had his eyes opened.

"I can't remember another game where it was hard to just take dribbles," he said sheepishly.

"I don't know if anybody's tuned in to watch us lately, but that's what we do," Wade declared.

A game such as this one would serve as a growth moment for Lin, who hadn't seen the type of speed and pressure and had no off-speed pitch to give the Knicks any kind of relief.

"All game long, Jeremy Lin was in panic mode," wrote *Bleacher Report*'s Michael Haley. "By the third quarter, Lin looked like he just didn't want to be there."

The game served as a reminder: the Heat was still hungry and still deserving of the marquee status that had been thrust on them in the summer of 2010.

They had won nine straight double-digit games and were starting a short Western road trip after the All-Star Game, where Wade, Bosh, and LeBron would all be playing.

On the heels of a blowout win in Portland sans Bosh, the Heat rolled into one of the most disliked outposts on the NBA schedule: Salt Lake City to face the Jazz.

Bosh once again would be out, and the Heat was staring down the barrel of an 18-point deficit late in the third quarter.

And then *LeBron* happened.

LeBron controlled the ball almost every possession, driving for two paint shots before drawing a rare quadruple team near the foul line, which set up Joel Anthony for a baseline dunk. Early in the fourth, he split a pick and roll and hit a midrange jumper to cut the lead to seven. On the next possession, Miami ran a clearout pick and roll with LeBron and Anthony, and he stepped back for an elbow jumper. A minute later, he nailed a jumper out of a post touch in front of the Jazz bench. Sprinting down after a Norris Cole miss, he again drew four defenders and kicked out to a cutting Wade for a baseline dunk. He followed that with another jumper to cut the lead to two with five minutes left, then after grabbing a rebound, used a stagger screen on the wing to drain a long two that tied the game.

LeBron got blocked by Josh Howard on one jumper, but immediately chased him down for a block on the other end, causing confusion that led to a Haslem dunk.

Wade blatantly fouled on a three pointer and Miami trailed by two with 1:15 left. LeBron, unfazed, casually dribbled near the timeline. Catching Howard trying to cheat over an Anthony screen, LeBron went the other way knocking in an open three to take the lead. Running the same set up one with 30 ticks left, Utah defended the high screen well. Slow-footed center Al Jefferson forced LeBron out wide to the wing. Undeterred, LeBron uncorked a twisting, contorted long two pointer with his foot on the line, hitting nothing but net and giving the Heat a three-point lead. Running to the Heat bench as Jazz coach Ty Corbin called timeout, he scowled at the stunned Jazz crowd.

"Please! Unbelievable!" an incredulous Craig Bolerjack shouted on the Jazz broadcast. "Not from this world!"

"The most unbelievable shot I have seen this year," added Matt Harpring.

"He is *not* from this planet!" Bolerjack, still at a loss, exclaimed.

Trying to break down the shot, Harpring in sheer disbelief narrated the replay: "This is video game status right here. He's hot, he's off balance, one leg. I am not sure how he even got that off."

Utah scored quickly, and Wade split a pair of free throws before another bone headed foul, trying to sky in for a highlight reel block on Devin Harris, who got a soft bounce and converted the three-point play.

What had only moments before looked like a sure Miami win on the back of a masterful final frame from LeBron, was now a one-point deficit with 4.5 seconds left.

Running a quick pick and roll, the Jazz iced the action with forward Paul Millsap stationed at the elbow, squared up on LeBron with Howard trailing on LeBron's hip. He flipped a pocket pass to the opposite elbow to an open Haslem for the game winner.

Clank.

"He passed it again," mumbled Harping as the Jazz faithful roared. "LeBron James passed...the ball...again," he re-emphasized.

"I'm stunned he gave it to Haslem," Bolerjack said, possibly having been handed a fresh sheet of narratives to unload before the broadcast ended.

What Harpring and to a lesser extent Bolerjack were referring to was dubious. Much like Craig Sager had done after the LeBron master class to eliminate Boston in the previous season's playoffs, they seemed to be force feeding a narrative that simply didn't exist, never mind completely disregarding what they had witnessed the entire fourth quarter. The Heat scored 27 in the final frame, 17 by LeBron. Also unmentioned was Wade committing a foul on a three, missing a key free throw, and then fouling yet again unnecessarily with the Heat clinging to a two-point lead.

"I just try to make the right plays and do what it takes to win basketball games," James said. "At the end of the day, games are not lost on one shot at the end or me not taking a shot. But I know the chatter will begin."

And begin it would. But it was a bad faith talking point; it had been going all the way back to Sager ten months ago. The idea that LeBron didn't or wouldn't take big shots had never been the case. And the one hand clap of an argument seemed nullified with the simple notion that if LeBron and the Heat had punted on the game when they were down 18 and packed it in knowing the game in Los Angeles two days later versus Bryant and the Lakers was more worthy of their attention, less criticism would have come his way than if he scored 17 in the fourth to get Miami the lead, made the right basketball play on the final possession to try to nullify his running mate's stupidity, and lost.

The Heat hadn't been in enough close games to warrant any kind of reaction to a game lost in the final moments. Let alone a wild declaration of "LeBron James passed the ball again!"

The fascination surrounding the hysteria of LeBron James and manufactured talking points was asinine. To exacerbate the theater of the absurd, a common theme had been percolating and then full on reached a boiling point in the last two seasons: *Michael Jordan would never have passed in that situation.*

It sounded great, magical even. The stuff of myths. Because that is just what it was.

That talking point could have worked maybe soon after Jordan's second retirement, maybe even flown after his third retirement and in LeBron's first couple seasons. But this thing called the internet existed, and it was easy to find massive moments where Jordan (*gasp!*) passed the ball, and the evil twin: the *missed* potential game winner.

Anyone who had followed the NBA for more than a decade should have remembered Jordan passing the ball to Steve Kerr in Game 6 of the 1997 NBA Finals for a game winning jumper to clinch the series. Some should have been able to remember Jordan giving the ball up near the timeline in Game 6 of the 1993 NBA Finals that resulted in a John Paxson three pointer to also clinch that series. In one series alone, the 1998 Eastern Conference Finals, the penultimate series in which Jordan would ever play, he had a missed game winner and a turnover in the final seconds of back-to-back *Eastern Conference Finals* games.

But the thing was, passing the ball to an open teammate never was (and never will be) the wrong play, let alone an indictment on mental makeup or some way of diminishing a player. Jordan never was criticized for those plays in mammoth moments, or any other moments for that matter. Why LeBron was made no sense. Not from a statistical perspective, not from a logical perspective. It seemed like a lazy, yet popular and oft repeated way to criticize a player who was one of, if not the best player in the league. Who, by the way, had just had a mind-bending fourth quarter. LeBron's fourth quarter in Salt Lake City featured the most made field goals in a fourth quarter for the entire season. But apparently the pass at the end to an open teammate was a final judgment on the mythological *clutch gene* ("'Killer instinct' is code for 'taking a contested jumper to win a game,'" Tyler Puryear astutely pointed out).

The goalposts always seemed to be moving when it came to LeBron, and this topic was no exception. Was clutch defined as only a game winning shot? Or did it mean fourth quarter play? Or fourth quarter play with a game winning shot? Or just making shots late in games? Or was it *taking* the final shot, as seemed to be the current nadir. Was it only the playoffs? Did all shots and other actions from one's teammates in a fourth quarter not count? It only appeared that the one criterion that LeBron didn't achieve in a given fourth quarter, clutch moment, whatever, would be the one used in that instance.

The same poor logic and bad faith would be used in the future on LeBron's career in general. As to the genesis, it really is unknown. Most likely on a low-hanging fruit morning reaction show that became pervasive and only came to a boil after the Finals. Because remember, aside from game winners (well actually game winning *buzzer beaters*) LeBron had been thoroughly dominant in the lead up to the Finals.

Wade's poor play continued in Los Angeles two nights later with a five turnover, six foul game in a loss to the Lakers.

Miami wouldn't hit the final stretch of the season as dominant as how they'd begun; that would have been a tall order, with the condensed schedule and the endless coverage still buzzing around. Every game wasn't a final declaration on the Big

3 as it had been the season prior; an increasing sense of apathy until the playoffs became apparent.

But the Heat, keenly aware of its social standing and ability to lead any news program or front page, made a deafening, silent statement on March 23.

Posted to LeBron's Twitter account, the entire team was photographed with hoodies on, heads down, the hoods pulled over each player's eyes in solidarity; Trayvon Martin, a teenager, was killed in Sanford, Florida, as he was returning to a gated community, carrying candy and iced tea. A neighborhood crime-watch volunteer, George Zimmerman, said he acted in self-defense and hadn't been arrested. #WeWantJustice was the accompanying hashtag.

The tragedy stoked emotions in the Heat and across the country; many of the players had children, many had children similar in age as Martin, and many had children who wanted to dress as Martin had been when he was killed.

"This situation hit home for me because last Christmas, all my oldest son wanted as a gift was hoodies," Wade said. "So, when I heard about this a week ago, I thought of my sons. I'm speaking up because I feel it's necessary that we get past the stereotype of young, black men and especially with our youth."

"I couldn't imagine if my son went to a store just to get some Skittles and a pop or iced tea and they didn't come home," Haslem added. "We've been following the story, individually, very closely. It's just unfortunate. We just feel like something needed to be done about it. It's only right. It's only fair... I think it's at least a start in the right direction."

Sports had long been a landscape to *not* share views on societal problems or "politics". Michael Jordan infamously had either been quoted or said to the effect that he wouldn't take a stand on an issue because "Republicans buy sneakers, too." Speaking out was viewed as bad business, bad for *the brand*, regardless of right or wrong. A team as polarizing as the Heat standing up for something so black and white, pardon the pun, caught attention.

"Is it James' responsibility to throw his weight behind the hot-button issues of the day?" asked Roy Burton of *Bleacher Report* "No. And none of us would have faulted him if he had remained neutral in this situation. But in the case of Trayvon Martin, James decided to take a stand. And without uttering a single word, he spoke volumes."

"The Heat took a stand on Friday for something bigger than basketball," wrote the great Michael Wallace for ESPN. "LeBron James, Dwyane Wade and their teammates on Friday left no doubt about where they stand. Together... perception must change. And the Heat did their part to both speak out and stand out with their actions."

The Heat would drop a back-to-back against Orlando and the one seeded Bulls in the middle of March, met with general shrugs as most assumed a Chicago vs. Miami rubber match in the Eastern Conference Finals was a shoe-in.

Even a late season pair of back-to-back losses to Boston and Chicago weren't greeted the same as they would have been only a year earlier. LeBron was so efficient and dominant on both ends that it became increasingly difficult to ignore. In those two losses he scored 36 and 30 points, respectively. The three pointer had slowly crept back into his game, but he was definitely not dependent on it, living in the paint as much as he could, both with designed postups, duck-ins, and head down line drives to the basket.

Another strange phenomenon had enveloped LeBron, obviously due to his disappointing Finals performance, but odd, nonetheless.

The same player who was third in the 2010-11 MVP voting, had been a one-man wrecking crew in eliminating the defending Eastern Conference champions and then the secret weapon to send the actual MVP and his team home, was universally disrespected as a top player in the league.

It didn't help, of course, that the lockout had delayed talking about basketball games and had to conjure content in peddling hypotheticals and manufactured lists (sounds familiar?). One of the main culprits for the theater of the absurd was the program that didn't even try to shy away from the hot take system: *First Take.*

It pains me to even write about the First Take jackals, but truthfully so much of what they put forth on their show shaped national narratives, true or false.

Even though the NBA was in a holding pattern, there was only so much football an all-encompassing sports show could draw upon. So, naturally, a pivot to the NBA and (gasp!) the manufactured lists emerged. Only weeks before the season began on Christmas Day, Skip Bayless and Stephen A. Smith unapologetically made their top 5 players lists on ESPN. Bayless, a notorious critic of LeBron, instinctively didn't have him in his very important top 5 list, favoring Wade, Kevin Durant, Kobe Bryant, Dirk Nowitzki, and Carmelo Anthony. Smith, interjecting often to voice his disagreement, then unveiled his equally important top 5 of Wade, Bryant, Dwight Howard, Nowitzki, and Durant.

The senselessness would only deepen: Anthony touted for his "clutch gene" but lack of "jewelry", Bryant lauded not by what he did on the court the season prior, but rather what he had done in all the years prior (make it make sense) as well as "always be closing". Howard was renowned by Smith for "doing too much on both ends of the floor". How people watching could believe the nonsense let alone take it at face value was anyone's guess, especially on the heels of this doozy: "Kareem wasn't Kareem until Magic came along", a reference to Howard needing better point guards to be more effective offensively.

Smith fashioned himself as a historian of the game, having grown up in The Bronx and covered the early career of Allen Iverson in Philadelphia. Be it as it may, a comment like that should have torched all his credibility, even on a low hanging fruit debate show. Not only had Kareem Abdul-Jabbar set the New York City high school scoring record and won three city championships, he also was a three-time college player of the year, winning the national championship each season, won Rookie of the Year, an NBA championship in his second season, and five Most Valuable Player awards all before Magic Johnson was drafted by the Los Angeles Lakers. The blatant disregard for a top NBA career ever should have done irreparable damage. Instead, it wasn't even a footnote, a telltale sign of what the show was peddling daily.

The phenomenon was illogical then and would be going forward, highlighted by Nick Wright fantastically years later: how was it that players eliminated before or by another player could or would be "ranked" higher than the one that eliminated the former or advanced further? In this specific case LeBron, and to a lesser degree Wade.

How was Wade ranked higher than LeBron in these very important top 5 lists? Had he not also lost to Dallas and Nowitzki, who was ranked lower than Wade but higher than LeBron. Hadn't LeBron advanced further than (excluding Wade and Nowitzki) the others on both lists? How could LeBron be punished in the public eye (mainly regurgitated from the show) for winning three playoff rounds, dominant in all three, but ultimately losing the final round, which only one other team could boast of winning?

No sense could be made of it, but it would snowball into its evil twin which would become even more preposterous: that losing in the Finals was worse than losing *before* the Finals. This "take" spread like a virus and no one pushing that idiocy ever had any reasoning.

And to be fair, the entire idea of counting records that players had in Finals appearances never was a topic before 2011, likely another low hanging fruit to latch onto. People could easily recite Michael Jordan's 6-0 Finals record, but no one outside staunch basketball junkies could list off Larry Bird's record, or Magic Johnson's, or even Kareem Abdul-Jabbar, who wasn't Kareem until Magic showed up, let us remember.

It wasn't a debate as much as it was a complete fallacy, destroyed with the easiest of questions: So, LeBron's 2010-11 season wouldn't have been a failure if he and the Heat had lost to, say, Boston in round 2? It would have been better for his legacy not to have had the fourth quarter avalanche in game 5, better for his legacy to not have the dominant shut down stretches in games 2 and 5 in Chicago, both scoring and shutting down the league MVP?

So absolutely ludicrous it was, that smart basketball journalists even began mocking it. The common thinking (well, the non-batty thinking) being that when LeBron dragged a severely limited Cavs team to the Finals in 2007 and lost to a superior, veteran-laden, Hall of Fame bunch in the San Antonio Spurs, it would have been better for his *legacy* (whatever that even means) to lose earlier in the playoffs? The byproduct being either not having his bananas 48-point game in Detroit in the Eastern Conference Finals to wrest control of the series and ultimately advance to the Finals, or have that game but still lose that series?

I hope as you read this, your eyes are rolling or your head is spinning at the asininity. But the story of the Miami Heat and ultimately LeBron James, couldn't be adequately told without touching on the actual talking points that prevailed, both on the heels of the Finals and during the lockout and during the actual season, even as LeBron was playing some of the best basketball he would ever play.

In a late season game in New Jersey, he scored the Heat's final 17 points of the fourth quarter (clutch or no clutch?) to lead them to a 101-98 victory.

A late season meeting with the Bulls in Miami turned ugly and unnecessarily physical, and the Bulls mustered only 11 points in the fourth quarter, harkening back to the Eastern Conference Finals, in the 83-72 Miami win, without Bosh.

"It was a physical, competitive game against two teams that defend," Spo said. "That tends to lead to a little bit more passion. And nobody was really backing down."

Chapter 12 - We Got 'Em

Chicago had brought back virtually the same team that had lost to the Heat in five games back in May, only really adding veteran Richard Hamilton, hoping to find some kind of relief in late game situations for the all-too-often bogged down offense. The problem with Hamilton was that he was definitely on the back nine of his career and while he could score and shoot well from the midrange, much of that had to be manufactured with Hamilton dipping and darting around myriad screen actions to which Miami routinely just switched.

The Bulls' playoff flameout the year had been met with general shrugs because even though they were the top seed that had been an incredible overachievement completely out of left field. Miami was supposed to be the big bad bullies and they had ultimately succeeded in conquering the East, Chicago notwithstanding. Though not nearly as dominant in the lockout-shortened season, the Bulls proved that they were no fluke. Rose was still a pain to defend, the defense was still the crippling crux of the team, and they never took nights off.

That's what made the events of April 28 so jarring.

The Bulls secured the top seed and were slated against the team the Heat had easily disposed of in the first round in 2011, Philadelphia. The Sixers were mired in NBA no man's land, a low seed that was feisty but not going to make waves and would shortly be headed for an all-time NBA tank job.

Trailing by 12 late in the fourth quarter in the first game versus Chicago, the Sixers received a Machavelian gift from the basketball gods as the Bulls were still playing all their starters.

Rose, driving through the lane and jump-stopping hard, crumbled to the ground in pain. He immediately grabbed at his knee.

"Uh oh, uh oh Rose came down bad!" Kevin Harlan announced on TNT.

It was a torn ACL, taking Rose out for the remainder of the playoffs and leaving Chicago's playmaking options severely limited.

In reality, the injury all but eliminated one contender from the championship picture on the first day of the championship chase. The Heat couldn't worry about what was going on in other series, even though to a man, they knew the Bulls were a tough team, but they did not fear them or think they wouldn't have been able to beat them again in a series, with or without Rose.

Instead, hours later, LeBron put on another insanely efficient game, 10-for-14 from the floor and 11-for-14 from the free throw line for 32 points in a 32-point stomping of the New York Knicks, 100-67.

"I'm a different player this year, a different person this year compared to last year," LeBron said. "I've waited to get back to the postseason, prepared myself all season, throughout the offseason to get back to this point."

"I think the Miami Heat right now are feeling great about their performance," Amare Stoudemire said after the Heat's second largest postseason win. "Which they should."

Game 2 was closer, a 104-94 Heat win, where Battier and Miller hit more threes combined than the entire Knicks team.

A frustrated Stoudemire punched a fire extinguisher in defeat, reporters noticing a trail of blood in the Knicks locker room. A mini story, for the second time not revolving around the Heat but rather the Knicks, had sprouted.

"I am so mad at myself right now," Stoudemire tweeted after the game. "I want to apologize to the fans and my team, not proud of my actions, headed home for a new start."

Stoudemire had played well, going 6-for-9 from the field, it was just glaringly obvious Miami was the better team, top to bottom, and had been all season. They stifled the Knicks in game 3 with a suffocating second half and highlighted by Chalmers' 5 three pointers.

The Knicks eked out game 4, a fourth quarter duel by Anthony and LeBron spoiled by a disjointed Wade iso possession against Stoudemire that resulted in a missed three at the buzzer (clutch gene?).

But Miami eliminated the Knicks, 106-94, behind 67 points from the Big 3 and 5 three pointers from Battier and Miller. The series win was nice, albeit expected.

"We will savor this win tonight," LeBron said. "And then we get to work tomorrow and get ready for Indiana."

LeBron, and the organization, would also savor him being named the 2011-12 Kia NBA MVP. He had, after all, been resplendent in coming back from the dumps of the 2011 Finals collapse; he shot a career best from the floor and the three point line (53 and 36 percent, respectively) tied his career best mark in rebounds per game, all while finishing third in points per game and thirteenth in assists per game in the league.

"We're just so proud that we can observe and watch and experience the level that you play at and where you can take yourself and this team," Pat Riley told LeBron at the ceremony.

LeBron truly seemed humble in such a big moment, honoring his mother, wife, and sons and then inviting the rest of his Heat teammates onto the stage with him. "If those guys don't sacrifice what they sacrifice, I wouldn't be up here," he said.

In closing his remarks, he acknowledged that while the award was humbling and put him in rare company as a three-time winner in four years, "this is not the award I want ultimately, I want that championship. And that's all that matters to me."

Few, if any, pundits thought Indiana would present any kind of issue for the Heat. Of course, that was before Bosh suffered an abdominal injury in the first half of the Heat's game one win.

Bosh was a lightning rod for criticism, despite the fact he was a consummate professional and had been incredibly good for the Heat. He had shown up post-lockout noticeably stronger and more comfortable in his role on both ends of the floor. His offensive role, more so than any other player on the Heat, was fluid; one night he could get 20+ shots, as he did in a February game in Cleveland, on another he could get as few as eight, as he did four nights before that in a shellacking versus the Bucks. While he had been a face up demon in the post during his time in Toronto, the days of Bosh isolation post-ups were few and far between in Miami; he operated much more from the perimeter in pick and roll and catch and shoot situations, the beneficiary of defenses endlessly bending to Wade and LeBron.

Indiana had jumped out to an early lead on the Heat, and the play in which Bosh was injured was finishing a nice pump and go for a dunk over Pacers big man Roy Hibbert. The play looked rather routine. Bosh stayed in the game to knock down the free throw before exiting with over a minute to go in the first half and Miami trailing.

"It's unfortunate Chris went down," Wade said. "But we told him, 'Be healthy. We got 'em.'"

The Heat tightened the screws in the second half as they had so often in their previous five playoff series, this time overcoming zero made three pointers but buoyed by 61 points from LeBron and Wade to win a closer than expected game 1, 95-86.

"It came down to execution in the fourth quarter and you've got to give credit to Miami's defense," Pacers coach Frank Vogel said in defeat.

Though victorious, Miami had hit more turbulence in a stretch that now spanned nearly 24 months of rough air. But this kind was different; the Heat hadn't suffered time-consuming injuries to their Big 3, and outside of the freak Haslem and Miller injuries the season before, had generally been a healthy outfit. Aside from the health aspect, Spo was staring down the barrel at an issue that likely had not even been considered up to that point: that while the Heat had big men on the roster (Haslem, Dexter Pitman, Rony Turiaf, and Juwan Howard) none had a skill set even remotely resembling that of Bosh.

"There was definitely an oh shit moment when Chris went down," Battier admitted years later about the untimely injury, going on to say that Bosh "gave us an element you couldn't replace."

How would the Heat adjust with only two thirds of the Big 3 available for an unforeseen amount of time?

The answer was: not swimmingly.

In game two, both teams shot well under 40% from the field and combined for four three pointers made, and the Heat got no more than five points from any player outside Wade and LeBron. The duo both missed chances to tie or take the lead in the final minute, and the Pacers celebrated an uglier-than-it-sounds 78-75 win, wresting homecourt from the stunned Heat in the process.

"Chris was missed, no doubt about it," Wade said. "But that's not the reason we lost this ballgame."

While true, it was hard to ignore the seven points his replacements produced.

"Welcome to the playoffs, for us," the pragmatic Spo said. "That's how we're viewing it. This series has started. They won on our home court. Now we have to collect ourselves, gather ourselves and get ready for game 3. That's all that matters right now."

It didn't seem like the Heat had collected or gathered themselves as they stared down a 2-1 deficit after getting bludgeoned in Indianapolis, 94-75.

Dexter Pitman had been given the starting assignment at center, trying to match physicality with Hibbert and the rugged David West. That lasted three minutes before Spo punted entirely on the idea ("Dexter Pittman experiment failed," Shane Battier still laughs).

Wade was atrocious, lacking any lift on his shot and screaming at Spo during a heated timeout. LeBron, while scoring 22 points, wasn't impactful either. The Heat made four three pointers, bringing their total to five for the series through three games.

One of the best offenses during the regular season, albeit with Bosh, hadn't broken 75 points in back-to-back playoff games and now trailed a middling team 2-1. The entire Big 3 existence may have never looked as grim; Bosh wasn't going to be returning anytime soon, the Heat seemed incapable of matching the strength and physicality of the Indiana frontcourt, and Wade was leading the group of struggling Miami players.

"They got their asses handed to them... it was an epic disaster," remembered Tom Haberstroh. "I remember Spo looking at me after that game and being like, *we got 'em*."

"When you lose a game like that, all you try to do is move on to the next one," LeBron said.

It looked like more of the same as Miami trailed 9-0 four minutes into game four. "Miami needs *something* to ignite them," moaned ABC announcer Mike Tirico. A LeBron cutting dunk finally got the Heat on the board with 7:41 to go in the quarter. It was doubtful even after the thunderous dunk that the Pacers faithful packing the house would have thought anything other than a win and a commanding 3-1 series lead was going to occur. But LeBron and Wade weren't having it.

In a performance that is often forgotten in the lore of the Big 3, but just as important as any, Wade and LeBron took turns hitting the Pacers with body blows. The latter looked creaky out of the gate, but soon settled in, his shots no longer hitting only the front of the rim.

Utilizing a game plan that would have been welcome in the Finals, Miami early and often got LeBron in the triple threat on one side of the floor, with all four players in close proximity on the complete other side of the floor. This forced Hibbert to either commit to a full on double and leave a man wide open on the weak side or give token respect and use his length to try to deter LeBron as soon as he made a move. Neither worked.

LeBron hit an array of fadeaways over Hibbert in the first half, Wade started getting shots in tight to go down, and then

Spo started to unleash the anvil smash the league would come to fear. Stationing Battier out way above the three-point line with Wade occupying one corner and Anthony in the opposite short corner, Chalmers was running pick and rolls with LeBron acting as the screener. Because of the vast amount of space created by Spo playing only one big man in Anthony and having Battier so far from the hoop, LeBron was halfway down the lane on his roll before a white shirt could even sniff a contest.

Right before the half, LeBron and Wade feigned an empty corner pick and roll, Wade cutting baseline with no resistance at the rim for a two-handed dunk.

If the Pacers thought they had a grip on what the Heat was doing, it didn't seem like it in the second half. LeBron and Wade scored every which way: slashing, cutting, creating space for jumpers, putbacks. "You're a marathon runner!" Spo yelled at LeBron. "You're not supposed to get tired!"

No other Heat player scored a field goal in the second half until Haslem, bloodied from an elbow to the eye, hit four mid range jumpers to ice the game.

It was an incredible performance, not only by LeBron but by Wade as well, rebounding from his horrific game three.

LeBron, in his best playoff game as a member of the Heat, tallied 40 points, an astounding 18 rebounds, 9 assists, 2 steals and 2 blocks. Wade pitched in 30 points, 9 rebounds, and 6 assists himself. In essence, the two stars had nearly outscored the entire team's output from either of the previous two games in an efficient floor game (54% from the field combined) all while registering the same rebound totals as the entire bruising Pacers starting lineup.

The totality of their games was on full display in easily the largest moment of the season and maybe of the entire era to that point. "We all knew what the stakes were," Battier said later. "If we lose to Indiana, they're blowing up that team and we all have new homes."

The ease with which they dismantled a team at home with a frenzied crowd, riding the wave of the blowout game three, was remarkable. After settling in (coinciding with LeBron's dunk to finally get the Heat on the scoreboard), Miami never looked rushed or rattled, dictating the action with equal parts force and finesse.

"Me and Bron had it going," said Wade rhetorically. "We played off of each other very well. We both were aggressive at the same time. That's beautiful basketball for the Miami Heat when we play that way."

"LeBron had that look," Battier said. "And when he has that look and Dwyane has that look, you want to run through a wall. We knew when DWade and LeBron were playing at their highest level it was a scary, scary thing."

The Heat returned home not only with new life, but a new plan of attack. Starting Battier and Turiaf as the de facto frontcourt, Miami capitulated the Indiana defense again, romping to a 115-83 home win. LeBron and Wade only combined for 58 points on another impressive shooting night (61% combined). Battier, getting good looks while being guarded by prototypical power forward David West, knocked down 4 of 5 threes.

A series that looked gloomy at best two days before was now a 3-2 Miami lead. What had seemed like such a struggle in the first three games now looked dangerously easy. Spo sensed it.

"This is our challenge right now, to leave it behind us," he wisely said. "A lot of good things tonight, but we have to focus on the next one."

Wade showed his focus in game six. In the performance of a maestro, he kept Miami afloat early early with a series of crafty stepbacks, floaters, and hard-nosed drives to the rim, befuddling Hibbert at every turn. He started posting up in the second quarter, making quick, decisive floaters and bank shots. Time and again with solid young defender Paul George matched against him, he knocked down contested jumpers out of the post, many right in front of the cheering Miami bench.

When LeBron also got going in the second half, surely all the Pacers and their fans wanted was to be put out of their misery. But instead, they would have to witness shot after shot from LeBron and Wade, a true tour de force of two players unlocked at the highest level. Hibbert couldn't do anything right, constantly on his heels as LeBron and Wade came lumbering at him, usually off a high screen. He tried to offer resistance, lunging forward to try to meet the all-stars, only to see high arcing floaters fly right by his outstretched arms.

Wade finished with a game-high 41, LeBron added 28 (as they combined for another out-of-this-world 60% combined from the floor) and Miami somewhat easily steamed into the Eastern Conference Finals for the second straight season.

"In the regular season, we've had some good games," Wade contemplated. "But I don't know if we've ever had three in a row like that in the playoffs."

"Ever since Game 3, they've played at such a high level," Vogel said, somewhat in disbelief. "I don't know if anybody can beat them.

"Chris Bosh is an awesome basketball player, but when he goes down, that just means more touches for LeBron and Wade," he added. "That's not exactly an advantage."

It generally felt like Miami had stumbled into a formula without Bosh that they could ride hard until he returned, whenever that would be.

And it appeared that way as the Heat trounced the Celtics in game one of the Eastern Conference Finals, 93-79. Boston was as helpless against LeBron and Wade as Indiana had been, surrendering 54 points on 35 shots to the duo.

Despite a spirited effort from Rajon Rondo, the Heat also prevailed in game two, in overtime. It had to be all but a wrap; the Heat would be in the Finals again.

Except for one small detail: the Celtics were one of, if not the, proudest team in the league and they certainly would not be going down silently. "We'll be ready for Friday," proclaimed Celtics coach Doc Rivers.

LeBron came out with a sensational first quarter of game three, with 16 points on a variety of jumpers and cutting layups. But by the time James Jones knocked down two free throws in the second quarter, the Heat already trailed 37-30 and would only muster 14 points in the second quarter. Trailing by as many as 24, the Heat mounted a small comeback to make the final deficit a respectable-looking 101-91.

"You're trying to fight back the whole time," said LeBron. "We made a run, but it was too much."

The Heat didn't help themselves, missing ten free throws and committing 22 turnovers.

Sweeps are incredibly difficult to come by in the NBA and this was no exception.

Miami found themselves behind the 8 ball almost immediately in game 4, trailing by 11 after the first quarter. But methodically, the Heat chipped away, clamping down defensively in the second half, allowing a paltry 12 and 16 points in the third and fourth quarters, respectively.

Boston's second half offense resembled the 2011 Miami version: clunky, stagnant, and lots of tough shots late in the shot clock after the initial, complex action went nowhere.

A wrap-up foul in transition by Rondo on Wade seemed to light the spark for the Heat: they played much more downhill, with Wade, LeBron and Chalmers taking turns getting in the paint and finishing or getting fouled.

A LeBron layup with 8:54 to go had somehow tied the game. Neither team would lead by more than three the rest of the way. LeBron answered a Garnett push shot with a huge three on a defensive miscommunication to tie the game at 89. He would then draw an offensive foul on Garnett, tangling with him on the baseline right in front of veteran referee Bill Kennedy.

"The Heat will have a chance to win it on the final possession!" exclaimed Mike Breen on the ESPN broadcast.

The final possession by the Heat left much to be desired. LeBron got the ball with six seconds left, tried to drive right, only to be met by three Celtics near the free throw line. He made an attempt at a jump pass back across the floor to Haslem near the short corner, but the pass was deflected, allowing Boston to recover just in time and contest an off balance jumper from Haslem that was woefully short.

"Overtime here in game four!" Breen announced as the Boston crowd went berserk.

The play was slightly disjointed, but more than anything, tremendously defended by the wily Celtics. That play would have much less impact on the overtime than two plays in the middle of the fourth quarter: a LeBron charge where Pierce seemed to be shuffling underneath him and a horrendous double foul call 20 seconds later by the aforementioned Kennedy while Garnett and LeBron were battling for position in the post, resulting in his fifth foul.

With the Heat down one inside two minutes to go in the overtime, LeBron ducked in on a transition possession by Miami, slightly getting tangled once again, this time with Mikael Peitrus. Both stumbled and fell to the floor, the pass attempt flying out of bounds. But whistle-happy official Joey Crawford underneath the basket enthusiastically punched the air, signaling offensive foul and the end to LeBron's night.

LeBron sat on the floor, stunned. Known for rarely fouling, he'd just fouled out for the first time as a Heat player; several of those calls looked iffy at best.

Miami would have to try to win without their MVP. Not getting the ball off a Boston miss didn't help, giving the Celtics an extra possession. Luckily for Miami, they came up empty. However, Battier missed a wide open below the break three on the ensuing possession.

A Rondo free throw put the lead at 93-91 for the Celtics. Now there was no LeBron to use on the final Heat possession. Common knowledge suggested it had to be a Wade shot coming.

"The three beats you, you've got to make them take a two," said Jeff Van Gundy. "You're behind by two, so you're attacking right away."

Spo drew up a good elevator action for Chalmers on the right wing, which the Celtics sniffed out, turning into Battier coming to set a late screen at the top of the arc for Wade.

Wade got Marquise Daniels switched onto him, probably not an advantageous matchup for the Heat due to Daniels length and athleticism in contrast to Rondo. But Wade crossed over and picked up his dribble just to the right side of the arc, pump faking quickly. Daniels flew by as Wade set his feet to the right and let go an uncontested three for the win.

"NO GOOD!" Breen said on the broadcast as Wade grimaced.

"It was a good look. It was on line but didn't want to go in," Wade said. "Got the shot off I wanted and that is all you can ask for."

"I think we executed offensively, came up with some lucky plays and we got stops at the end," summed up Rondo.

"At the end you have a chance to win after 50-plus minutes and losing the MVP. Hey, you'll take that," Spo said.

There didn't seem to be any sense of desperation or disappointment emanating from the Heat side; they had lost a game they clawed back into and missed two chances to win, once in the last seconds of the fourth quarter and once on the final possession of overtime. The margin for error was razor thin, the difference between a 3-1 lead with a chance to close out in Miami and a 2-2 series guaranteeing another visit to the raucous TD Garden in Boston.

"Not stressed the series is tied 2-2," James said. "It's great basketball, great competition. We wanted to get one up here and we didn't."

Brian Windhorst was reporting that Bosh would be available for game five, over three weeks since suffering the injury versus Indiana in what now seemed a lifetime ago.

While it had appeared that Miami could thrive without Bosh, it was becoming more and more apparent how absolutely crucial he was, not only as a mismatch nightmare offensively, but what his defensive versatility brought. LeBron and Wade could shoulder a big load, on both ends, but even together could not replicate what Bosh brought, try as they might. LeBron both drawing and committing fouls on Garnett was a direct result of that: Miami was trying to steal minutes with LeBron, a Swiss army knife of the highest degree, playing as a de facto big man. Boston concluded, as evidenced by the defense at the end of game four, they were fine letting the ancillary Heat pieces beat them, mostly because they didn't believe they could, or would.

All told, a return to Miami for game five felt like an automatic Heat win that would lead to a chance to close it all out in Boston in game six. After all, the Heat in the two postseasons with the Big 3 had lost a paltry three home playoff games, two being in the Finals. Even a hampered Bosh figured to be a key piece missing in a "big" rotation of Anthony, Haslem, Battier, and LeBron.

The Heat storming out to a 24-16 first quarter lead was the least bit surprising. Neither should have been the Celtics 24-18 second quarter win, leading to a neck and neck 42-40 halftime score. But then, following the script of the last game in Miami, the Celtics put a stranglehold on the third quarter, taking a 65-60 lead into the fourth.

LeBron and Wade once again were terrific in the fourth and the Heat drew within one, 87-86, on a Haslem free throw with just over a minute to go.

And then yet another myth was ripe to be made.

Pierce, getting LeBron to defend him in isolation, dribbled the clock down on the left wing in front of the Miami bench. Taking the smallest of hesitation dribbles, forcing LeBron into a false step, Pierce rose up for a giant three.

Nothing but net.

This shot, while massive and a potential series swinging shot, has since been made out to be Pierce exerting his manhood on LeBron, a no regard for human life type of kill shot. It was a great shot, albeit one to take a four point lead with 53 seconds left.

He would also foul Dwyane Wade that would cut the lead to only two, and after two Ray Allen free throws to restore the four point edge, LeBron drove right around Rondo to cut it back to a one score affair. Ultimately, too little too late for the Heat in a shocking home loss.

The Miami offense had been humming in the fourth quarter, the problem was they couldn't get a stop to either wrest back the lead or hold one in the middle of the fourth quarter.

It was a stunning defeat by all measures.

"Every time we got them down, they made runs," LeBron said. "They made us stagnant offensively, got stops and got back in the game."

"We played hard," the ever astute Battier said. "We just didn't play intelligent."

"Just shows you how quickly a series can change, you feel like you're in control, we felt like we were playing better basketball and it's 2-1," Spo said years later of the series swing. "They absolutely took our hearts out in game 5. We did not practice the next day. I had a team meeting and we just talked about our why's and why we put this team together and we were going to have to face the team that we knew we were going to have to go through."

Bosh's return was anticlimactic and overall uninspiring, playing 14 relatively quiet minutes. He too sensed the edge of the cliff the Heat was back up on, now down 3-2.

"It's going to be an extremely difficult time," Bosh said. "But that's what the playoffs are about. In order to get to where we want to go, we're going to have to face huge challenges. And I think we're in the biggest challenge of our lives right now, of our professional careers. We just have to overcome it. It's going to be very, very difficult. But that's how it's supposed to be."

Chapter 13 - The Final Boss

The Heat wasn't alone in sensing the nuclear bomb ready to detonate on their team; the media was in a frothy frenzy.

"What is there to suggest that Miami's going to come through and win a game on the road?" asked Michael Wilbon.

"I don't know if they got it inside themselves to go out and play a great game," pontificated Magic Johnson.

"This is bad, this is very, very bad," spat Stephen A. Smith on SportsCenter. "It's one thing to go *out*. It's another thing entirely to go out the way they look like they're going to go out. I'm not pickin' them to win Thursday night."

Smith wasn't done, talking about endorsements getting in the way of LeBron and Wade's focus, ignoring apparently the MVP season LeBron had rebounded with following the dismal Finals, and what they had done together to lasso the Indiana series.

Will Leitch of *New York Magazine* wrote before the game, "There are many NBA fans whose primary rooting interest this season — and last season and next season — is to make sure the Miami Heat don't win the title. They're one game away from getting their wish."

Adrian Wojnarowski, ever giddy at the prospect of the Heat, and specifically LeBron, failing, opined: "All along, they believed this would be easy, that the NBA would lay down for them. Two years ago, they believed this resembled Team USA, that most of the league would crumble like Angola to them.

"One more loss, and Armageddon awaits for this franchise and its stars. One more loss, and the wall could come tumbling down on LeBron James, these Heat and a world that may see a modern basketball superpower dismantled before everyone's eyes."

"It's over, we already know it's over," Bosh remembers thinking. "We understood in that locker room what it meant. You know what happens if we lose and there's nothing else to say."

"Blueprint I'm convinced was on the line there," Dan Le Batard opined.

"[A loss] would have been hysteria," the even-keeled Zach Lowe said.

"It was a tense time," Battier added. "Everyone knew the ramifications. Everyone knew what the game meant."

"There was pressure," Spo acknowledged.

The outsiders were convinced that Miami, a team that had won a virtual must-win sans Bosh in Indiana, was a mentally fragile team, bullied by the Celtics, a team that wore their emotions on their sleeves and weren't immune to their fair share of hubris along the way.

Maybe the Heat *was* fragile. And maybe the entire experiment of Wade, Bosh, and LeBron really was on trial going into game six. It would have been a hard argument to make against it, maybe only that a shortened season and a Bosh injury wasn't the proper way to evaluate the entire run to that point. But a loss to a clearly inferior team, one that had benefited from only the fifth ever one seed being upset in the first round, wouldn't be excused by the public or the basketball media at large.

The Heat had defended home court in the first two games, but this time there was no heroic playoff surge like Nowitzki's.

Bowing out after leading the series for two years, bowing out halfway home felt like an irreversible failure.

It wouldn't have been surprising, maybe even expected, for the Heat to enter game six dazed and overwhelmed by the immense pressure, both inside and out.

Bosh and Battier felt the excitement from the Boston faithful to dance on the already dug grave of the Big 3.

"There's a lot of bodies in Boston, man," Bosh said later, laughing. "A lot of ghosts; they finished off a lot of guys."

"We get into Boston, and you could just feel Boston fans were ready to bury the Big 3," Battier remembers now. "They were almost giddy."

But what may have been undersold was that in a sense Miami was playing with house money; to so many, they were already eliminated after game five, a mental team that couldn't take punches and ran when the going got tough, as incorrect as it may have been.

With sulfur in the air and bombs ready to explode around them, the Heat appeared, at the least, not tight with pressure or nerves.

"We were actually pretty loose," Battier recalls.

"There was a calmness, a quiet confidence," Spo said.

"I've never been more confident going into a game that I should've been unconfident about," Mike Miller remembers.

Loose or not, the man everyone was watching, whether they loved him or hated him, wasn't going down without a herculean effort.

Up to that point, LeBron had faced more scrutiny, criticism, and outright hate than almost any athlete. It would've been understandable if he'd cracked, not just after game five, but even earlier, given how underwhelming the Finals had been. Instead, he reinvented his game and mindset to win MVP. That made for a great story, but it all meant nothing without a game six win, and ultimately, a series win followed by an NBA title.

"Legacies are at stake," Magic Johnson pronounced before the game.

"Is this the end of the Big 3?" asked Jon Barry "This could be it."

"I don't think the Heat have a chance," predicted former NBA standstill shooter-turned-analyst Tim Legler.

Jeff Van Gundy summed it up nearly perfectly: "Look, the bandwagon of the Miami Heat is empty. You know who's going to get the blame already. Now you don't have to worry about that anymore. Just play ball and enjoy the process."

"Before the game we sensed this power from LeBron," Battier said. "It became very apparent LeBron was a different man that day."

"Killer, we're going to be fine," LeBron told Miller as the Heat walked on the floor.

The LeBron in Boston resembled the LeBron from the 2011 Finals as much as a hamburger resembles a Caesar salad. Dictating the action mostly from the mid-post, he wrecked every defender Boston threw at him. Jab step jumpers on Pierce, turnarounds on Rondo, step throughs on Ray Allen. He got free in the open floor for a thundering dunk with Pierce left dusted behind, as well as a freewheeling and-one on overmatched Greg Stiemsa.

"By the first media timeout it was like *ho-ly cow*, this is the dude right here," Battier said beaming. "You knew six minutes into the game, he's not losing tonight."

LeBron didn't stop, getting Pierce and Stiemsa flat footed in a pick and roll and drilling a wing three. Then ducking in versus Pietrus for an up and under short jumper.

"He right now is in a special zone in the first half," said Breen on the broadcast.

"It just became grim by midway through the second quarter," Boston super fan Bill Simmons lamented.

The MVP polished off a 30-point first half with a flying putback dunk and another mid-post jumper over Pierce.

"Really a historic first half for LeBron James," Van Gundy announced rhetorically.

His 12-for-14 first half performance from the floor was so breathtaking that Breen had to correct himself when he said in the second quarter that it was a quiet 24 points, at that point, noting instead that his otherworldly efficiency had quieted the rowdy Boston crowd.

"We were not prepared for the way he shot the ball that night," admitted Doc Rivers years later.

The second half wasn't nearly as spectacular, but it didn't have to be as the Heat dominated and LeBron checked out with 45 points and 15 rebounds with 3:11 to go and a 22-point lead in hand.

As shocking as Boston's win in game five was, this was even more unprecedented. The Celtics and their fans were loud and confident, expecting a coronation, but instead they were dismantled by a calm, surgical, thorough domination from LeBron.

"One of the most bad ass performances I've seen across sport," Le Batard says to this day.

Battier still is in awe of the performance: "It's very few times I've been around people that are not gonna let you lose," he says. "That day, he was not going to let us lose. He singlehandedly, not only won the game, but ripped the soul out of Boston. Ripped the soul! I ain't never seen that before.

"Pretty sweet win."

Given the circumstances and the untold pressure on himself and the team, it had to be the grandest performance of LeBron's career. On the road in a virtual win or team is blown up scenario, he not only showed up, he showed out. "In an environment like this, you want to have a big game," he said, understatedly. "I wanted to be there for my teammates, no matter what was going on throughout the course of the game.

"This was a gut check for us."

When he told Rachel Nichols before the season that he was going to let his game do all the talking, there was no one, not even LeBron himself, that could have foreseen his game do *this* kind of talking.

"He was absolutely fearless tonight," Spo said in the postgame.

"He played amazing. He was locked in from the beginning of the game like I've never seen him before," Wade added.

"He inflicted some pain here in Boston," signed off Breen.

"Larry Bird was like, 'My favorite is when we win on the road. I love how quiet it gets. I love going into the tunnel and everyone shuts up,'" remembered Bill Simmons.

"There was nothing better than going into a packed house and making the fans leave early and that's what we enjoyed doing," laughed Battier.

"The single greatest LeBron game," proclaimed Wosny Lambre. "He literally turned into a freakin' alien… he ripped their heart out."

"I thought it was sensational, spectacular, and any other superlative," Stephen A. Smith said on SportsCenter following the utter domination. "He was a one man show… he did whatever he wanted to do to whomever Doc Rivers put in front of him as his sacrificial lamb. He was completely dominant, and he did it with ease; he barely broke a sweat. It was almost scary to watch."

"I hope now you guys can stop talking about LeBron and he doesn't play in big games," Celtics coach Doc Rivers said. "He was pretty good tonight. So, we can put that to bed and go play Game 7."

A subdued LeBron most of the season, hopped happily to the team bus with NBA TV cameras on him. Smiling, he said into the cameras, "This what it's all about, man. Game seven, let's get ready, Miami. We're coming home!"

Some in the media decided that the proper reaction to an all-time performance was to perform some gold medal mental gymnastics. Skip Bayless, with a straight face, said in his opening remarks the next morning that because of the game five loss "the pressure fell". He also said that after LeBron missed his first shot of the game, he had said to himself, "Okay, I give up. I'm not going to try hard anymore."

It wasn't entirely certain whether Bayless had watched the game, because surely someone who had would not have come to that zany conclusion. More likely though, almost a guarantee, was there was no possible narrative to be crafted out of the absolute virtuoso showing from LeBron. Because everyone who watched that game saw the same thing: a steely, emotionless, focused to the tilt LeBron exerting all his possible dominance.

At the very least, co-host Stephen A. Smith, who had vocally denounced the Heat and their chances of winning the game, fired back at the smug Bayless: "What we saw last night was one of the greatest, if not the greatest postseason performance we have ever seen," he said, annoyance tinged all over his voice which, for one of the rare times, didn't seem to be an act. "This is some unreal stuff that we saw here last night, but yet you sit here and say, 'oh, he didn't get going until Dwyane Wade gave him a shot.' Let me get this straight, it's a game six on the line, he takes a shot in the first two minutes of the game, and because he Lebricked it in the first two minutes of a game six of an Eastern Conference Finals game, you're going to sit here with a straight face and say he said, 'oh I give up'?! Do you have any idea how nonsensical that statement is?"

Bill Simmons, an unabashed Boston homer, fantastically wrote the next day:

> *You can't imagine what this was like to witness in person. I know Michael Jordan had similarly astonishing games, and others, too, but not with stakes like that. This wasn't just an elimination game. This was LeBron James's entire career being put on trial ... and it only took an hour for him to tell the jury, "Go home. I'm one of the best players ever. Stop picking me apart. Stop talking about the things I can't do. Stop holding me to standards that have never been applied to any other NBA player. Stop blaming me for an admittedly dumb decision I never should have made. Stop saying*

I'm weak. Stop saying that I don't want to win. Stop. Just … stop."

As a Celtics fan, I was devastated. As a basketball fan, I appreciated the performance for what it was. One of the greatest players ever was playing one of his greatest games ever. He swallowed up every other relevant story line.

But the Heat still had a another game to play, and maybe a secret weapon hiding in plain sight.

"I was at shootaround that morning; everything I was shootin' was going in," Bosh remembered. "We were at lunch, and I just said, 'Man, I just feel I'm really going to have a big game tonight. I'm not missin' tonight.'"

The Heat was stuck in the mud in the first half of the home game seven, trailing by 11 with under four minutes to go in the half and down by seven at the halftime horn.

While leading, it didn't feel like Boston was in control of the game, more like Miami had simply not kicked the door in yet. And kick it in they would.

Bosh, the secret weapon, hit a baseline jumper to tie the game near the end of the third quarter, an omen for what he prophesied earlier that day.

Less than a minute into the final frame, Chalmers, coming off a high screen from LeBron, found Bosh in the corner. Bosh, who made ten three pointers all season, knocked in a surprising three to give Miami a one point lead. LeBron dunked in transition to give the Heat the lead again, and following a Boston turnover, found Bosh in the same corner for the same result as before. Miami led by four, 86-82.

It would be all the momentum they would need to steam out the deciding win, 101-88, and head back to the NBA Finals. They had vanquished the team they had united together to beat, *again*. And they had done it flipping the script on its head: forcing Boston to defend smaller, quicker lineups with their plodding, aging vets. Putting Bosh behind the three point line stretched Boston into unfamiliar territory and they paid dearly.

"The most efficient shot in basketball is the corner three, that's not a secret," Bosh now says apoplectically. "You never know when that weapon is needed."

"We didn't mind him taking them, we didn't know he was going to make them and then he made them over and over again," Rivers said.

"He was big time — every shot, every defensive play, every rebound — we missed him," LeBron said admiringly of Bosh. "We're just happy to have him back at the right time. If it wasn't for him and the rest of the guys who stepped up, we wouldn't have won this game."

The Big 3 scored all 28 Heat points in the deciding fourth quarter and once again in a must-win playoff game showed they were the force everyone feared back in July 2010 when they announced their intentions.

"We decided to come together and play together for a reason," Wade said.

The reason, of course, was to win championships. Not two, not three, not four, if you took LeBron at face value. The first championship still hadn't been won. Though a young, dynamic Oklahoma City Thunder team awaited with home court advantage, this Heat team was starkly different from its 2011 predecessor. It wasn't just mental strength—something not obvious after the Game 5 loss—but an evolution forced by their Finals defeat. LeBron returned as dangerous and efficient as ever. Bosh expanded his range and deepened his role on both ends. Wade accepted a secondary role. Chalmers improved, and Battier brought veteran professionalism.

At the core of it all was Spo. Instead of repeating the 2010-11 playbook learned from Riley and Van Gundy, he reinvented his approach—unleashing chaos in transition with Wade and LeBron while freeing them in the halfcourt. The aggressive defense, though taxing and vulnerable against some teams, played to the strengths of Wade, Bosh, and LeBron: a perfect blend of top-end speed, instincts, and collective IQ.

Spo hadn't been afraid to try different things, results notwithstanding. The Dexter Pittman game three experiment in Indiana lasted three whole minutes. Because of his willingness to experiment on the fly, whether from necessity or curiosity, he and the Heat stumbled into what would become the calling card of the Big 3 era: *smallball.*

"I give Spo and Fiz just a ton of credit for really being creative," said Battier. "It would have been really easy to go back to what they did the year before and say you know what DWade, LeBron just carry us. We're going to give you guys a bunch of isos just clear out and try to lead us to a championship. They really reimagined who we were on the fly."

And while LeBron was the Swiss army knife, Bosh was the catalyst, able to defend bigger players while simultaneously raising hell against the same slower, stodgier bigs. Battier being a capable three-point shooter coupled with his ability to also defend bigger than he was unlocked the scariest version of the Heat, the version Oklahoma City would feel full force as they doubled down on their antiquated philosophy.

Chapter 14 - We're Not Coming Back Here

Despite Miami's return to the Finals, Vegas favored the Thunder, and most pundits, whether wary after the Heat's collapse the year before or eager to defy the Big 3 narrative, picked Oklahoma City.

But the Heat's game plan would draw from what had been the undoing for the Thunder's previous opponent, the San Antonio Spurs: sixth man James Harden and his dynamic playmaking leading the second unit and then late in games as the main offensive initiator.

"He was the key to the series for us," Bosh explained. "We had to stop him. He was the guy making the plays."

"We were really, really dialed in," added Battier.

Even though the Heat dropped game one in the zoo that was Chesapeake Energy Arena in Oklahoma City, the team was unfazed, confident even.

The difference in the game had virtually been a late game avalanche by the Thunder, buoyed by a crowd that had aided in sending so many teams to the chopping block.

LeBron still was drawing headlines, this time for off-the court reasons: he ditched social media (his self-proclaimed "zero dark thirty" to focus during the playoffs) and replaced his phone with books, often seen reading in the locker room before games.

"For me, it's relaxing honestly," James had said before Game 1. "You spend so much preparation for the games, sometimes you just need to get away from it for a little bit. The reading has helped me get away from the game a little bit, and I'm able to zero in once I'm done and get ready for the games."

He was currently reading Jay-Z's book *Decoded* after ripping through the Hunger Games trilogy, the autobiography of Jerry West, *The Pact,* and *The Tipping Point.*

Players had read books before games long before LeBron, but everything he did drew immediate infatuation and takes, even an act so simple as reading.

In game two, the Heat withstood the Thunder late game avalanche after leading big early (18-2) and they were on full, terrifying display. LeBron and Wade combined for 56 points, Bosh in his first game back in the starting lineup had a strong 16 points and 15 rebounds. "It's been so long since we've had them all together," Battier said. "They played like the All-Stars that they are and that's the effort that we need."

Battier nailed five threes, defended by a combination of plodding center Kendrick Perkins and rangy but reluctant forward Serge Ibaka.

Spo's discovery was working and working in a big way.

"I said that when we won game two, we're not coming back here," Bosh remembers now.

Miami had the chance to play the remainder of the series all at home, given that they won every game. "Once you lose home court, especially as a young team, it's really demoralizing," explained Battier.

In a twist of fate, the Heat was now in the position Dallas had been only one year prior: the road team that stole a game and would have three bites at the apple at home to knock off the favorites.

"We had that taste, we knew what it meant," said Bosh.

LeBron apparently knew what it meant, completely in control again in game three, this time hitting a corner three pointer late in the third to give the Heat a two point lead (one of four total field goals the team hit in the frame) and then finishing two tough downhill drives with under four minutes to go.

But Wade didn't want the game to be over and hold a 2-1 lead just yet. Nursing a five-point lead, he was stripped at the time line by Thabo Sefolosha, who made a layup and was fouled by Wade. To add insult to injury, Wade bricked on the next time down the floor, Westbrook answered with a midrange pull-up and Spo had to call timeout with a sudden one-point lead and only a minute and a half to go. What had felt like a win going away suddenly felt like a game from the 2011 Finals.

Bosh and LeBron hit three free throws and Wade stole a foolish Oklahoma City inbounds pass to ice the game and atone for his furious attempt at self-sabotage.

"Last year I don't know if we was experienced enough as a unit to deal with what came at us," Wade said. "I just feel like we understand the situations more and we can deal with it better."

That seemed completely accurate: Miami looked and felt like the veteran team that had been through the playoff rollercoaster of battles, Oklahoma City like the young, green upstarts they still were.

And at the end of the day, as good as Durant was (second in MVP voting and an absolute terror to defend), one team simply had LeBron and the other did not.

"He was great. He's been great for us all playoffs," Haslem said of LeBron. "I don't know if he looks up at the clock or score sheet, but he knows when we need him to make big plays and come through for us, and he comes through."

Whatever LeBron saw in himself in the 2011 Finals, coaching and philosophy and opponent be damned, he must have said *to hell with this, I will go down with no bullets left in this chamber*. Surely the philosophical shifts freed him up, but he also hadn't played so aggressively, so downhill at any other moment in his Heat career. And Oklahoma City was feeling the pressure; trying to defend LeBron with a multitude of defenders from Durant to Harden to Sefolosha and stationing long, feared shot blocking big man Serge Ibaka near the rim. None of it mattered.

And suddenly, Miami sat in the exact same position as the year before: a 2-1 lead in the Finals with the momentum. What LeBron had accomplished and rebounded from notwithstanding, it was fair to ask how LeBron would respond *this time*. While nowhere near as dominant or in control of his game or himself in the previous Finals, LeBron had not been a wandering man in those first three games and all signs pointed to a series win... until they didn't. Was there really something to be said for LeBron freezing up with the ultimate goal so close?

Game four was an inauspicious start for the Heat, getting jumped 33-19 in the opening quarter with Westbrook scoring ten of those and shooting almost every time possible.

Miami quickly righted the ship in the second quarter, drawing to 49-46 at the halftime break. LeBron scored the last eight points of the third for the Heat and suddenly one quarter was all that separated Miami from an all-but-over 3-1 series lead.

And then *the cramps*.

With the game tied 90-90 a tick under halfway to go in the fourth, LeBron drove to the middle, falling to the floor at the dotted line. The Thunder tore down the court looking to capitalize on a 5-on-4 opportunity until Wade swatted an off-balance Derek Fisher layup. LeBron, laboring at the other end, cherry-picked a layup of his own but was jogging gingerly. The Heat lucked out not having to foul while LeBron was clearly compromised, benefitting from Westbrook's thirst for shots as Bosh collected the rebound, the Heat called timeout, and LeBron exited the game, clearly locked up from cramping.

LeBron had a history of cramps, dating as far back as his fourth year in the league and resurfacing in other tight, humid, summer playoff games, like in the 2009 Eastern Conference Finals versus Orlando.

Almost immediately, the Thunder took the lead back with LeBron off the floor. It was fair to wonder *is it happening again?* LeBron was writhing on the ground in front of the Miami bench after having been escorted off the floor by Juwan Howard and head trainer Jay Sabol.

"Ah, shit!" he shrieked on the bench.

"Late in Game 4, when LeBron started limping and finally toppled to the floor, everyone in the arena had the same reaction," wrote Bill Simmons. "Wait, LeBron can get hurt? LeBron feels pain? It was like seeing Michael Myers keel over. When he was carried off, the crowd audibly gasped in disbelief. They're carrying him off? They're carrying LeBron off? I assumed that he belatedly realized he'd blown out his knee because, you know, he's a fucking cyborg. As it turned out, he only had cramps. Even that seemed kind of amazing. LeBron James gets cramps? LeBron James needs to drink water?"

Not so fast. LeBron only missed just over a minute of action, even though he hardly looked magically healed. "I just told myself, 'If you can get in and make one or two plays,'" he said.

Following a Westbrook turnover, Bosh tied the game back up with a tough, stumbling layup. Another Westbrook miss and the clock ticked inside three minutes. And LeBron had the ball, isolated at the top of the arc with the game tied and a chance to do what he flagrantly had *failed* to do one year earlier in game four: make a game-changing play on the biggest stage.

And he did just that, sizing up Sefolosha and hitting a pull-up three to beat the shot clock. He hobbled back down the court as the whiteout crowd went ballistic.

Wade added a layup, driving right past the low-effort defense of Westbrook. A Westbrook layup over three Miami defenders would be as close as the Thunder would get, succumbing 104-98 as LeBron watched the final minute from the bench.

The Heat had overcome likely the best game of Westbrook's career (despite all the shots whenever from wherever) 43 points, 7 rebounds, 5 assists as well as Durant's 28 points. But, as was the game plan, they had smothered Harden to the tune of eight points, four turnover, and five fouls in 37 minutes. And they had overcome *the cramps*.

"He was hurting," Wade said of LeBron.

"That three was just sheer will and competitiveness, to contribute in some way," Spo said of the isolation three on Sefolosha, which turned out to be the last shot Miami needed to keep the lead the rest of the way.

"I was just trying to make a play," LeBron said. "If I was out on the floor, I wanted to try to make a play with the limited mobility I had at that time, and I was happy I was able to come through."

While LeBron may have been the headline, the story was the absolute team effort to keep the Thunder at bay in what may have as well been a must-win.

Bosh had 13 points and 9 rebounds, Norris Cole came in to bridge the first and second quarters as the Heat was chipping away at the deficit and had eight huge points in eight minutes.

And then there was Mario Chalmers, who had been guarded by Durant to start the game.

"I took that as a little sign of disrespect," Chalmers said.

He was a highly confident player who truly thought he was the best player on any court he stopped on. And in game four, he could not be overlooked, scoring 25 points on 9-for-15 shooting and making the Thunder pay time and time again for focusing on Wade and LeBron.

"Mario Chalmers *magnificent* tonight," Breen said on the wind down of the broadcast as Chalmers embraced Gloria James entering the tunnel to the locker room. "What a fourth quarter."

A long camera down the hallway caught Wade, several yards behind Chalmers in the tunnel, shouting after his teammate: "Hey, Mario *motherfucking* Chalmers! Mario *motherfucker*!"

The Heat had won game two only five days earlier, and now would have a chance to shut the whole thing down in one calendar week. The daunting challenge would not be lost on the Thunder, however, a team that could go on their avalanche-like runs at any moment, meaning no lead was ever, ever safe.

But Miami, for maybe the first time in the Big 3 era, had to feel somewhat comfortable. They had withstood the Westbrook barrage, the Durant conundrum, and had suffocated sixth man of the year Harden.

Simmons, for *Grantland*, wrote, "Last night, the mood of Oklahoma City's contingent ranged somewhere between 'sullen' and 'crestfallen.' Their boys didn't just blow the championship; they wasted the best game Russell Westbrook ever played."

Oklahoma City was doing itself no favors, matching the Miami small ball with stubborn minutes of slow, plodding big man Kendrick Perkins.

And, once again, one team had *that dude,* and the other team did not.

"LeBron was playing like a rich man's version of the fifth-best basketball player of all time," Simmons wrote, referencing the similarity in LeBron's performance to that of Larry Bird. "I don't care how much you hated 'The Decision' — if you can't appreciate what LeBron James is doing right now, you need to start following another sport. It's one of the greatest night-to-night athletic feats we have ever witnessed."

A frothing, whiteout Miami crowd would get unchained almost as early as possible as LeBron got loose thirty seconds into the game for a one handed slam, bringing them all to their feet.

And in what would become an ominous sign of things to come for Oklahoma City, Battier knocked down his second look at a three pointer from a probing Chalmers, and Wade scored on a tremendous one-handed alley oop layup in transition.

Bosh got in on the action, figuratively licking his lips with the slow-footed Perkins defending him, getting to the rim at ease. Cole and little-used Mike Miller hit three threes in the final three minutes of the first quarter. Oklahoma City seemed content on not defending anyone but LeBron and Wade, and the "little 12" were making them pay early and often.

A LeBron runaway layup after a Chalmers steal elicited "An avalanche from Miami!" from ABC play-by-play man Mike Breen.

The Thunder, however, did not wave the white flag, whittling the lead to ten at the break. Despite being up 3-1, at home, and with all sorts of players hitting all sorts of shots, Miami had to know a ten point lead could be evaporated by the Thunder in a blink.

In fact, within a minute and a half the Thunder were right back in the game, trailing 61-56, before Chalmers snuck behind the sleepwalking Oklahoma City defense for a wide open corner three.

A pair of Battier threes, a Chalmers runner, and a LeBron slash over Ibaka, coupled with some stifling defense all led to a Bosh corner three to extend what now felt was an insurmountable lead, 85-63.

"Everything going down for Miami!" Breen exclaimed.

That only continued as Miller nailed a wing three on yet another botched Thunder defensive possession against a rudimentary action.

Bosh patiently waited at the front of the rim as the Thunder had two defenders in the vicinity of LeBron (neither really defending) and slammed home a two-handed dunk. A 25-point lead felt as safe as any; wrestling the game away with the kind of momentum the Heat was feeling from their amped-up home crowd would have been an all-time legendary feat. It wasn't going to happen.

Spo emptied the bench with three minutes to go, a ceremonial hand off from LeBron to Fab Five legend and NBA journeyman Juwan Howard. Before checking out for the final time of the season, LeBron embraced Bosh, burying his head into his shoulder. He hugged James Jones on the bench as Wade lifted two hands to the adoring Miami crowd.

He then found Miller, the one for whom the Big 3 had all taken less money to sign, and who had rewarded them for their faith with an awe-inspiring 7-for-8 three point shooting night, and the two hugged, rocking back and forth.

Spirited "DE-FENSE! DE-FENSE!" chants followed the substitutions, quieted only by Thunder guard Royal Ivey drilling a three pointer right in front of the celebrating Heat bench.

Pat Riley, typically stoic and emotionless, flashed a small smile and clapped as Battier exited the game moments later, the prized free agent signing rewarding the faith by hitting timely threes all playoffs.

"There's a moment of disbelief," he would later say about realizing he and the Heat were NBA champions at last. "Ho-ly cow, that's what it takes to win an NBA championship."

Wade hugged his young sons as they jumped the front row to take in the final seconds with their two-time champion dad.

Breen and Van Gundy applauded, rightfully so, everyone they could on the Heat, from Riley to Howard to Spo.

Then Van Gundy, an NBA lifer who sadly could never get over the hump to win a title as coach, summed up his feelings: "I love to see the joy on players' faces, the unbridled joy it's a remarkable thing. They have all the fame and the money, and yet the accomplishment of being the best at what you do in any one year brings incredible joy." The ABC crew knocked it out of the park, cutting to a slow-motion replay of the Heat bench, led by LeBron, jumping and waving their arms as Van Gundy hit on the incredible joy.

"What a difference a year makes," Breen added, "2011 had such a bitter ending, making this celebration all that much sweeter."

"We couldn't cry, we couldn't laugh," said Randy Mims. "The biggest deep breath…"

LeBron and Spo, at last, embraced as champions, having conquered the heavy criticism aimed at both.

As the Heat dribbled the clock out on the championship, LeBron met Durant at half court, surely an embrace of empathy, LeBron having experienced the same defeat only a year prior.

"LeBron James captures that elusive title he so desperately coveted!" Breen announced. Seemingly sensing his moment to passive aggressively address the asinine criticism and hatred levied on LeBron in the past two years, he continued, "Well, this finally put an end to all the criticism (in today's world perhaps not) but even anyone that's ever rooted against him, if you love the game of basketball, you've got to *respect* and admire what LeBron James brings to the court every time he steps on the floor. A remarkable talent at both ends of the floor, and one of the most unselfish stars the league has ever seen."

Outside of the local broadcast teams and reporters, perhaps no one had more perspective and more license to comment on LeBron. He had announced every Finals game LeBron had played in, all seven games of the Eastern Conference Finals, and about half the playoff games in previous rounds both years since LeBron joined the Heat. Breen was anything but a sensationalist, a historian who, like Van Gundy, loved the NBA and the incredible athletes for whose games he called.

Of course there would still be detractors, those who didn't like *The Decision* or the decision to play in Miami or still couldn't get over LeBron's attempts to fend off the detractors during 2011. But make no mistake, he had been resplendent in 2012, not only during the season as MVP, but maybe even better in the elevated stakes of the playoffs. His averages of 30.3 points, 9.7 rebounds, 5.6 assists and 1.9 steals per game all while shooting a robust 50% from the floor had never been equaled in NBA history. Facing a quasi must-win in Indiana he had responded with the 40 point, 18 rebound, 9 assist masterpiece. Facing a literal must-win a few weeks later in Boston, he again answered the bell with the 45 point, 15 rebound, 5 assist drubbing of the Celtics. Following the game one loss in Oklahoma City, he delivered again in a resounding 32 point, 8 rebound, 5 assist night. And, as one final *I'm him* moment to the winding, lockout shortened season, he polished off a triple double, incredibly his only one of the playoff run.

However the measurement of *doing it the right way* is made, LeBron emphatically checked those boxes. When he said to Rachel Nichols before the season that he would let his game do all the talking, he wasn't lying. He had been much more subdued, much more somber in 2012, all while unleashing unholy hell on the league.

"I know how bad he wanted this championship, but to see the way he played, the way he went and *got* it, I was so proud of him," said Wade.

"LeBron's brilliance lifted everyone else along with him," penned Simmons. "Everything Miami did offensively went through LeBron."

"He has long been the NBA's most polished player," wrote Zach Lowe of LeBron, "and in this series, he corrected the only blemish on his record by dominating the only playoff round he had yet to command. He grew into some unholy combination of point forward and power forward, grabbing rebounds, dishing assists all over the floor, guarding every position and contributing Hall of Fame-level production even when his jumper wouldn't fall.

"James can now take his place without argument among the very greatest players of all time."

"Your decision to come to Miami was not made without difficult choices, nor ramifications for the way those played; in light of everything you've been through in the last two years, what is this moment like for you?" Doris Burke asked in the pre-championship presentation din.

"It means everything," LeBron demurred. "I made a difficult decision to leave Cleveland, but I understood what my future was about, and I understood that coming to Miami and being a part of this organization and being able to put together this team, I knew we had a bright future. This is a dream come true for me... this is definitely the way that it pays off."

"There's some stark contrast to the guy we saw in last year's Finals, what put you in a place to get back to being LeBron James?" Burke followed up.

"Losing in the Finals last year put me back in place," LeBron humbly said. "At the end of the day, I just looked at myself in the mirror and said, 'You've got to be better, both on and off the floor.'"

That comment from LeBron stood as the essence of the long, winding champion's journey he had taken. The 2011 Finals in some capacity or another would follow him the rest of his career, becoming more and more confounding and less and less impactful to his "legacy". But make no mistake, as the man himself said, without that letdown, there would have not been the LeBron he became. Which parts of him, that is unknown. But there would have been no need for him to alter his game or his approach, no real need for Spo to alter his static, archaic offense, or for Wade to defer of his own volition. There wouldn't have been much reason for Riley or Andy Elisburg to sharpen the roster had they won in 2011, either.

"Complacency is the enemy of progress" is an oft-used quote prophesying of the dangers of sitting on one's laurels. The progress necessary to unlock, as Battier said and the rest of the NBA painfully came to find out, LeBron as the queen on the chessboard likely wouldn't have occurred sans the embarrassment and devastation of 2011.

A mental shift was the way it was easily explained, which may have been at least partly accurate. But the version of LeBron that from opening tip on Christmas Day until exiting with three minutes left in game five of the Finals completely barnstormed the league couldn't be explained away that easily. He had come back more efficient, more comfortable in the post, a more willing screener in the pick and roll, and embraced defending all five positions.

It couldn't be understated that Savannah and his sons being with him in Miami now on a permanent basis had assisted in the shift. "I'm thankful for the fact that I have a family - fiancée and two kids," he told the press. "No one had gone through that journey, so I had to learn on my own. All the ups and downs, everything that came with it, I basically had to figure it out on my own."

"LeBron's title means we can at very least embrace him as a basketball player, which really, was always his most accessible quality," wrote *GQ*'s Bethlehem Shoals. "The hype and mythology surrounding him took on a life of his own. We've gotten back to that first game, to that smiling kid who made us gasp every time up the court."

Shoals wasn't the only media member who explicitly had grown tired of the LeBron handwringing at every turn, nonstop, for the previous two years ("We've all just about maxed out on LeBron hysteria, at least those of us interested in James and not a shell we can affix our rancor to").

The great Kevin Arnovitz, the man tasked with heading the incredible *Heat Index* team, wrote:

> *I'd been quietly pulling for the Miami Heat to win the title since April—and not because I find LeBron James to be sympathetic or because I like the Heat's brand of basketball or even because I have a lingering attachment to the Heat after covering them in Miami during the 2010-11 season.*
>
> *I simply wanted it all to be about basketball again, because the public exercise of trying to probe James' inner life had grown tiresome. The ease with which epithets like choke artist, fraud and much worse have been*

Arnovitz was one of the most measured writers in the game, and the fact his annoyance with the coverage of LeBron oozed out spoke volumes.

The ever-eloquent Arnovitz concluded the fantastic piece (titled "LeBron James and the End of All That"): "All that talk is over. The next time James falls short—and he almost certainly will at some point—we'll measure that failure in the context of the game, not in the language of hysteria."

As much as the championship, and the season by and large, was going to be about LeBron, it also was about a *team* that withstood the hurricane of negativity and criticism and as individuals pushed forward and through to the ultimate end.

Wade overcame balky knees to play his three best games of the playoffs in the back half of the Indiana series, absolutely unable to be guarded, slithering and conniving his way to the basket.

Bosh, who other than LeBron faced the most scrutiny on the team for his chameleon role, unlocked what Spo wanted to do stylistically playing small ball. His 19 points in game seven versus Boston were crucial and he stretched Oklahoma City's defense to the limit, literally, with his ability to space the floor.

Chalmers, though not held in as high regard publicly as he held himself, never shied from the moment and always answered the bell. He defended relentlessly, usually against players much more qualified than he, and when the ball came to him to make big shots, he had delivered.

Battier, the prized free agent of the summer of 2011, banged against bigger men all season and then made their lives hell on the other end, continuing his rep as one of the best "three and d" players in the league. He shot nearly 58% from three in the Finals, eclipsing DeShawn Stevenson's NBA record from the previous Finals.

Mike Miller, oft-injured and in and out of the lineup, never demurred and more than justified his signing with the seven three pointers in game seven, a Finals record for a non-starter, clearly limited with his back injury. "I don't know how this guy was playing," Spo said. "I literally only planned on playing him three or four minutes tonight, then he started knocking down threes, so we left him in there."

"I was so happy he had the performance he had," Battier reminisced, smiling widely.

Haslem, the OG, fairly or unfairly was often tagged only as the physical guy, the enforcer. But what was often missed on those types of labels was that he provided the Heat exactly what they needed, when they needed it. In game four against Indiana, bloodied and battered, he took the baton from the exquisite LeBron and Wade performances and closed the door on the Pacers. He had 12 points and a staggering 17 rebounds in game four in Boston. And he was now a two-time NBA Champion, Miami's proud son.

And then of course, undeterred and finally smiling, was Spo. Championship hat backwards and grinning for seemingly the first time since LeBron and Bosh arrived in 2010, it was easy to forget he was only 41 years old. He'd weathered the storm, with

Riley and Arison's undying loyalty of course, and emerged an NBA champion, grizzled and dirty, but a champion no less. "We love you, Miami!" he shouted on the stage. "Thank you for your patience! We remember last year! We wanted to make up for it."

"It's about to go down!" Wade and LeBron both yelled as they entered the hallway to the locker room, prepped with dozens of bottles of champagne for the freshly minted champions. As they entered, there was Riley, already attempting to uncork a bottle and douse the Finals MVP and his mate. "That champagne moment," said Wade, "that's one of the best moments of winning a championship."

The locker room celebration was nothing new in terms of championship celebrations. Bosh poured champagne on himself, everyone vied to douse Riley, still in his Armani suit.

The feeling was one of jubilation, and undoubtedly of relief. The championship expectations had been placed on the heads of the Heat, and particularly the Big 3, from the moment of formation, only heightened with the ill-fated pep rally and openly embracing the championship talk. Whether or not that was a reality inside the locker room would ultimately be irrelevant. Many teams annually have championship aspirations or expectations, implicitly or explicitly. Only one team will hold the trophy in June. That is the reality. And even though LeBron's words and the overall tone of the Heat from the summer of 2010 were slightly misconstrued with regards to championships being easy simply based on the talent of a team, 2012 proved, as if the concept needed proving, that championships are in fact extremely difficult.

That's why this title, with the exception of the usual bad actors, garnered so much respect: it was anything *but* easy. From the lockout-shortened regular season to the Bosh injury, to the earnest comeback down 3-2 to Boston. There were no real times to take a deep breath and relax, and when it seemed like there was, reality came calling with more opposition, more hills to climb.

And they collectively had ascended them all. And the way with which they disposed of the Thunder made it very hard to not assume more success in the near future.

"It's been well documented that we've been through quite a bit but that's part of the fire that we had to go through together and it makes this moment that much more gratifying," said Spo.

"It was validation that losing in year one and winning in year two was all part of it. It makes the story even better," Maverick Carter added, smiling fondly.

"When you've never won a championship before, you don't actually know what it takes," said Battier, who had won championships at Duke but soon found the NBA challenge the most daunting of his career. "And you fight like hell and you sacrifice and you work and you hope. You hope that the effort you've put forth is good enough to win a championship. When you cut down those nets, when you win the championship and pop the champagne, you say, 'Holy crap that's what it took? It took everything.'"

LeBron was as good as he had ever been, which is to say an all-time talent nearly completely unlocked and now completely unburdened.

On the winning sideline as the final seconds ticked down in Super Bowl XXIX, quarterback Steve Young had facetiously, but maybe half-seriously, acknowledged a monkey on his back. He had been ever in the shadow of four-time champion Joe

Montana since being anointed his replacement in a contentious changing of the guard in the mid 1990s. LeBron, now wiser to the workings of the media and also softer spoken and thoughtful, surely would never admit the same. But there was no denying there had been a weight of expectations he had felt, both to live up to the mantle placed on him as a high schooler and also the expectation to win a championship and therefore take his rightful place among the all-time greats.

A championship didn't make a great player, but the list of the truly great Hall of Famers who hadn't won titles was very recitable and had become even more so with the endless handwringing discussions of LeBron's greatness. Greats like Barkley, Malone, Stockton, Reggie Miller, Patrick Ewing rolled off the tongue. It was a foolish exercise, truly. Playing at the highest of levels for so many years wasn't only accepted if a championship ring accompanied it. Greatness was greatness, the fact the discourse ever got to the point of ignoring that for *jewelry* was a tiresome, low hanging fruit for media and fans, one gobbled up and regurgitated at an ever-alarming rate.

That is why so many, like Arnovitz, were so outwardly grateful the Heat won. The general narrative could now, hopefully, return to basketball and not a day-by-day accounting of completely invented legacy scoreboards.

Grant Hughes of *Bleacher Report* wrote about LeBron and the shifting perception we should have of him:

> *There's no getting around the fact that James is everything we should want in a superstar.*

*He's confident, supremely talented, a good citizen and a
mature adult. We can pretend that he needs to have a
sharper edge, but the truth is that we should be praising
him for retaining his humanity in the ultra-competitive
NBA world.*

*James' "nice guy" image is good for his own sanity, great
for the league and even better as a reminder to fans that
it's good to keep things in perspective.*

The Heat proved many wrong, and congruently proved many right. But championships quickly fade into the rearview mirror; the NBA is definitely a *what have you done for me lately* league. And so, the question to ask, naturally, what was the Heat encore going to be? On the one hand, it was hard to envision the Heat, now free and unburdened and having found the nearly unstoppable formula, not ripping off more deep playoff runs and more championships. On the other hand, the young, hungry behemoth in Oklahoma City now found themselves in a similar situation as the 2012 Heat: reeling from defeat and determined to return victorious.

It was quite normal for championship teams to return with varying degrees of lethargy; winning a title unearths a certain complacency, usually, borne of the exhaustion in conquering the mountaintop and the spoils that come with it.

Bill Simmons wrote, "LeBron peaked in a similar way during those last two and a half playoff rounds, and really, you couldn't blame him if he coasted from here — his hunger satiated, his point proven, the monkey pulled off his back and subsequently stomped to death."

There would be little time for complacency for one LeBron James as he was soon headed to London to attempt to secure a second Olympic gold medal. Wade and Bosh withdrew due to their injuries. When Team USA emerged victorious, with LeBron still every bit of the worldwide mismatch he had been in the NBA, he capped off one of the best seasons of *basketball* ever: an MVP in a shortened season, not to mention all the media hoopla, a Finals MVP, a first-team All-Defense nod, and now an Olympic gold medal.

From Simmons: "During the Summer Olympics in London, observers were pleasantly surprised by a subtle shift in LeBron's personality: less clowning, more leading, more measuring himself against the other guys. Four years ago, he may have spent an hour shooting half-court shots. In 2012, he kept throwing himself into shooting contests with Durant and Kobe, determined to prove he could hold his own. Anytime one of the USA practices became heated and turned into something of a dick-measuring contest, something that tends to happen when you gather the best players in the world on the same floor, LeBron left little doubt who mattered most. By all accounts, he was clearly the best player on the team. And it wasn't close."

LeBron spoke to the great Associated Press beat writer, Tim Reynolds, of his mindset heading into the new season: "I'm nitpicking now, obviously, at my own game. I want that. I want to be uncomfortable. I want to continue to push the envelope and get to a point where I feel like I'm trying to master everything. Now, I can't be the greatest at everything. There's better rebounders than me. There's better passers than me. There's better scorers than me. But I want to be able to maximize my potential in everything I do."

Miami organizationally had made difficult adjustments between the 2011 Finals and the 2012 season trying to maximize the potential of the stars they had, but what adjustments were there to make following a title?

It should have been obvious that a Pat Riley-led franchise would not stand still. Well-known for his phrase from his self-help book *The Winner Within* that following accomplishments "the disease of more" creeps in, he surely would not fall victim to his own forewarning.

And the Heat, as they did in the summer of 2011 by snagging a pro's pro in Battier, picked off two more in free agency: Rashard Lewis and, in a stunning move, Celtics future Hall of Famer Ray Allen.

The fact Allen took less money with Miami spoke volumes.

"As we said a couple of years ago when we started to rebuild the team, I think it's important year in and year out that you continue to try to add quality talent and players with experience, who want to make a commitment to winning," Riley said. "I just mentioned LeBron and Chris and Dwyane, and they take it from there."

The Heat would *not* be running it back, not exactly at least.

"Spoelstra and the Heat staff deserve a lot of credit for figuring out the right style of play and filling out the roster," blogged Haralabos Voulgaris. "Initially I wanted to see a lot of LeBron playing PG, but he's much, much more well suited to playing the 4 and that's precisely what the Heat did last year during their playoff run.

"Fortunately for Miami there aren't too many bigs in the league that can really punish Miami for playing small and as long as Miami is willing to surround LBJ with a bunch of 3-point shooters they'll be absolutely devastating."

And, in another rare occurrence, the Heat took a backseat to another team.

Chapter 15 - Neutral

In a painfully drawn-out summer of negotiations, the Lakers finally pulled the trigger in August, landing Eastern Conference star Dwight Howard from Orlando and aging former MVP Steve Nash from Phoenix.

All eyes suddenly turned to the Lakers, fresh off two disappointing playoff runs, and how they had retooled on the fly to try to catch the Heat. Kobe Bryant's text to LeBron in 2010 seemed self-assured and confident ("Go ahead and get another MVP, if you want. And find the city you want to live in. But we're going to win the championship. Don't worry about it."); the reality was the Heat had won more Eastern Conference Finals series than the Lakers had won total series since the text.

It was near unanimity that the Lakers had hit a home run with the Howard trade, even though he, like Wade and Bosh, had also passed on the Olympics because of injuries, a back surgery that he still had not fully recovered from. Trade grades poured in giving the Lakers glowing marks. The *Sports Illustrated* NBA season preview cover featured Dwight Howard and Steve Nash flexing/growling behind the headline *NOW THIS IS GOING TO BE FUN.*

If there was complacency for the Heat before, there wouldn't be now.

The season previews were nearly as unanimous as the trade grades and reactions of Howard's arrival: it was going to be Miami versus Los Angeles in the Finals, how could it not be? Many of those doing the prognosticating should have, but apparently didn't, learn from the Heat in 2011; the championship is not won in the offseason.

But if there was any concern for the Heat in 2012-13, it wasn't voiced after receiving their rings on opening night and trouncing the Celtics, 120-107. The Big 3 combined for a whopping 74 points and the new additions Ray Allen and Rashard Lewis combined for 29 points off the bench.

The dominant story of the night was several Celtics players ignoring Allen in a faux tough guy exhibit of loyalty against their betrayer (eye rolls). "I was just trying to focus as much as I could. I am such an intense person," Garnett said without saying anything. "It was a blank. Obviously, he's on the other side. It's time to play the game, man."

The Heat roared out of the gates with a 12-3 record through December 1st after allowing 30 points in the second half of a 102-89 win over Brooklyn. It all seemed too easy. LeBron was right back at his MVP levels and the Allen addition was remarkably smooth. Through the first month of the season, he was shooting a robust 51% on three pointers, many wide open as the defense had to pick their poison regularly.

What seemed like a meaningless mid-December game versus Golden State turned into a thriller, as young Warriors guard Klay Thompson knocked down five threes, and second year forward Draymond Green got free from Battier and Allen for a game-winning layup.

"I think I showed too early," Battier said. "It was my responsibility. I got anxious. They made a nice play and burned for us our overanxious play out there, my overanxious play."

It was a hint of things to come for Golden State.

"He played hard, it was great competition out there between me and him," James said, unbeknownst to him that a relationship would develop between he and the fiery second round pick from Michigan State. "I've also respected him especially in college, a big-time player and no one really gave him a shot, but you can tell he knows how to play the game."

"If what happened the other day against Golden State, allowing an absurd, easy basket with less than a second left to lose at home, had happened at any point in the previous two seasons, we would have traded Dwyane Wade, fired Erik Spoelstra and wondered whether LeBron was clutch as America howled at South Florida's misery," opined Dan Le Batard. "But now, spoiled and satiated, not unlike our team, we shrug our shoulders and try to TiVo fast-forward through the next 60 games. Perspective isn't what you usually find at the best parties."

There were the inevitable blips and losses, but the difference from previous seasons was how those were now covered. Gone were the sky is falling proclamations after each and every loss, questioning legacies, front office moves, and who knows what else. It was a long season and the champs had earned the benefit of the doubt.

Riding a four-game winning streak into a Christmas Day Finals rematch with Oklahoma City, the Heat once again withstood a furious Thunder festive upset attempt, behind a mind-blowing 88 points from the starting five, led by LeBron 29 points, 9 assists, and 8 rebounds.

"I'm tired as hell right now," James said after the emotional, close game.

Wade, as he had done in the Finals back in June, seemingly tried to lose the game in the waning seconds, this time turning the ball over attempting to go behind the back in the lane, leading to a Durant dunk and cutting the Heat lead to one.

As much as the Heat was flying high in the early part of the season, so too was the Thunder, sitting at a 20-6 record going into the game and not having suffered back-to-back losses all season. There was no letdown from the Finals disappointment, as they sat in first in the West.

"Both teams really played up to the billing," Wade said. "An excellent basketball game."

The Heat would then embark on a four-game road trip featuring three of the worst teams in the East: Charlotte, Detroit, and Orlando. In a slightly eye-opening week, the Heat took only two out of four on the road trip, and overtime was necessary to shake the lowly Magic by two.

As much as the regular season could be monotonous and rote, there was still a huge matchup awaiting: the pre-Finals matchup with the Lakers, of course. At Golden State the night before the road game, LeBron became the youngest player in NBA history with 20,000 points and 5,000 assists as the Heat made quick work of the Warriors, avenging the close home loss from December, 92-75.

"It means everything," LeBron said of the record-setting night. "It means a lot. First of all, like I continue to say, it means I've been able to be healthy. To be out on the floor and do what I love to do, I love the game of basketball and I try to give everything to the game. And hopefully it continues to give back to me."

Riley and Spo gave LeBron the game ball in the locker room, the history lost on neither of them.

All the starters would have fresh legs the next night in LA, after sitting out the fourth quarter against the undermanned Warriors, who were missing their leading scorer, Stephen Curry.

The game had likely looked like a can't-miss for TNT when the schedule came out; the two title favorites on a Thursday night, no competing NFL games and only another NBA game preceding it on TNT. In reality, it was a tour de force and a mismatch in intensity from the outset.

The Heat's first eight points came off four straight live-ball Lakers turnovers: Haslem stole one that turned into a Chalmers-to-LeBron alley-oop; Bosh followed with a steal leading to a LeBron tomahawk; Wade added one of his own for a flying dunk; and finally, LeBron picked off an inbounds pass and fed Wade for a backdoor two-handed slam.

The Lakers didn't roll over, but the fire with which they played seemed completely manufactured. They trailed virtually the entire game, but cut the lead to 86-83 before LeBron calmly sank a deep, long two with 4:19 left. Undeterred, L.A. tied it at 90, but they wouldn't score again. LeBron took full control, the clutch gene on full display. First, he found Ray Allen curling off a pindown for a free-throw-line fadeaway. Then he drove left on Metta World Peace (the artist formerly known as Ron Artest) and drained a short, fading jumper to stretch the lead to 96–90.

"Championship trust," Steve Kerr called it on the broadcast. LeBron and Wade combined for 66 points, and along with Bosh tallied eleven steals between them.

"We closed out the trip the right way, and we want to build from it," LeBron said.

"That's a championship team," Lakers coach Mike D'Antoni marveled. "They turned on all the juices, so it's a good measuring stick. That's what they do."

"We never really got into a great flow offensively until late in the fourth quarter," Spo remarked, undoubtedly happy about the end of the road trip, but would never openly admit to such satisfaction.

Even though it was just one game — as Kerr and D'Antoni noted, a matchup between a champion and a supposed contender — the Lakers looked no closer to Miami's level than they had the year before, even after adding Dwight Howard, Steve Nash, and all the hype that followed. The adjustment period for new stars, a new coach, and Kobe Bryant's uncompromising standards hadn't been factored in when people crowned the Lakers as the West's sure thing. Two years earlier, another team had already laid out a roadmap for how bumpy that process could be.

In a rare scheduling blip, the Heat would have six days off before their next game, and in the meantime would sign a colorful new presence, to say the least. Literally.

Harkening back to the first season of the Big 3, the Heat decided to sign veteran journeyman Chris "Birdman" Andersen to bolster their thin big man rotation which to that point consisted of Haslem, Bosh, and a pinch of Joel Anthony.

Andersen was most well-known for his colorful neck to toe tattoos and his high-flying acrobatics, most notably in the Slam Dunk Contest. He had a massive wingspan and even at age 34 still had some bounce in his legs and figured to be a welcome rim-running big man that could alter shots and give the rest of the big man rotation a powder.

Not missing a beat, LeBron and Wade again combined for 66 points in a 123-116 overtime win against Toronto. The Birdman did not play, only three days after being signed, still getting in playing shape; the last game he had played was five minutes back in March of 2012.

Chapter 16 - Streaking

The Heat went an innocuous 2-2 in their next four games before a sleepy matinee in Toronto versus the Raptors on Super Bowl Sunday. It was the last leg of a four game, seven-day road trip before heading home for a five game homestand. Toronto just wasn't very good, but had some talent. It was a terribly kept secret that the Toronto early afternoon game was a trap game, heavily favoring the home team since it was virtually the only game on an opponent's schedule during that early time frame.

Toronto buckled under the Miami second half defense, which allowed only 35 points, and the

Heat ran away with a convincing 100-85 win, the Big 3 scoring 81 of the Heat's points.

"They're the champs," Toronto guard Demar DeRozan said in defeat. "We couldn't stop them. We couldn't slow them down when they got it going."

Bosh was still booed every time he touched the ball by the scorned Toronto fans. "I was hearing a lot from the fans," he said. "I thank them for continuing to stay on me and call me names and stuff because that helped my focus a lot. I was like 'I need to get in this to shut them up.'"

"It's good to get this one to close out this road trip so we can enjoy this evening and enjoy the second game," Spo said, referring to the Super Bowl to be played later that night.

The win, and the game itself, normally wouldn't have been noteworthy, not in an 82-game season and definitely not against a team bound for the lottery on a sleepy Sunday morning.

But, as the team congregated at the Real Sports Bar and Grill adjacent to the Air Canada Centre to watch the Super Bowl before a late flight back to Miami for a Monday evening game with Charlotte, the seeds were planted in earnest for what would become one of the defining stretches of the Big 3 era.

As the team clambered onto the bus after the Ravens finished off a last-minute goal line stand to win football's ultimate prize, Shane Battier, a man of many words but not a man of excess, stood up and delivered a liquified speech, or more accurately, said a few impassioned words.

"Enjoy what we've accomplished but like anything in the past, it's in the past," Battier said, summing up his speech. "Enjoy the moment and seize the moment. Just do your best this very minute. That's all we can control. That's all we can do."

"He speaks, I won't say like a politician, but like an absolute leader," Spo said. "It was great. I love it when that happens and Shane takes the mike."

"There's something about Toronto," Battier said. "It's inspirational. I feel it here. It's one of my favorite NBA cities."

The speech may have been stirring, but there was little chance anyone within the sound of Battier's voice could have expected what the team would go on to do.

After handling the Raptors, the Heat stood alone in first in the East (which secured Spo as the head coach for the East in the upcoming All-Star Game) and a respectable fourth-best record in the NBA, a noble title defense when so many teams can fall flat trying to replicate the urgency from the first title chase. The Heat hadn't underachieved, but they also hadn't been world beaters. The San Antonio Spurs stood a head above the rest of the league at a gaudy 38-11, though few thought of them as true contenders in the West after what Oklahoma City had done against them the previous spring.

Returning to Miami, the Big 3 picked up right where they left off, combining for 74 points in holding off the Hornets. They finished off the five-game homestand undefeated, touching up the Blazers, 117-104 behind a heady 32 points and 11 rebounds from Bosh. The Big 3 combined for 86 points.

A six-game winning streak was nice, but hardly noteworthy other than knocking off three Western Conference playoff teams in succession: Houston, the Clippers, and the Lakers. The Heat had already pulled off two six gamers earlier in the season.

On the heels of the homestand was a four-game road swing, starting at Oklahoma City. The Heat jumped the Thunder in the first quarter, 32-17, and never looked back in a comfortable 110-100 win to sweep the season series and win their sixth in a row overall against the Western Conference behemoths.

"That was the game, that first quarter," said Kevin Durant, who had 40 points in the loss, 15 from the free throw line. The frustration emanating from the Thunder was palpable. Wade had struggled, scoring only 13 points on 13 shots, but LeBron and Bosh had 59 and 24 rebounds together in a game that was truly never close.

"Thought we imposed our will, playing our style of basketball," said Wade. "But have their number? No, we're not feeling that way. We've just won two games against them. That's it."

LeBron's record-setting streak of six straight games scoring over 30 points on better than 60% shooting from the floor came to a screeching halt as he scored 39 on an underwhelming 58.3% from the field.

The only thing stopping the Heat's momentum was the NBA All-Star Game in Houston, which was well-represented by the Miami organization between Spo coaching and the Big 3 starting in the annual no defense invitational.

The Heat used an insane 40-point fourth quarter, 24 from Battier and Allen, to dispose of Atlanta six days after the last win in Oklahoma City. They dump trucked the plucky Bulls, 86-67 behind 27 forced turnovers and stifling half-court defense that allowed a paltry 26 points in the second and fourth quarters.

"We're putting together some good basketball right now," LeBron said. "We're defending. We're creating turnovers. We're winning the turnover game offensively. We're the best shooting team in the league...so if we don't turn the ball over, we get good shots at the rim, we could also have a good chance to win."

LeBron continued his brilliant basketball with a triple double and Allen added four threes off the bench in a blowout of Philadelphia, followed by recovering from a 22-point blown first half lead to hold off the dismal Cleveland Cavaliers, 109-105 to reach an 11-game winning streak.

In a wild, defense optional home game versus Sacramento, it took 79 combined points from Wade and LeBron to outlast another cellar dweller, but the streak reached 12 games.

"No matter what their record is, they made plays just like us. They gave everything they had and more," James said.

"They've got a couple of guys that can turn the notch up pretty quickly," Kings coach Keith Smart said. "LeBron and Dwyane played an incredible game. It took a Superman-type game from both of those guys."

LeBron not only had 40 points but a staggering 16 assists and Wade made 19 field goals. "Video game numbers," Spo said of the effort.

Rob Mahoney, a great writer in his own right who understood and contextualized the game with the very best of them, wrote of LeBron's insane February, which was punctuated by the performance against the Kings:

> *LeBron James has been so fantastic this season that his supernatural play has gone from headline story to steady undercurrent. For many, there's simply no revelation to be found in a transcendent player doing transcendent things. LeBron is expected to be great, and the fact that he lives up to—and exceeds—even the wildest expectations doesn't resonate in the same way that his failures to do so might.*

A nice two-day break between home games gave the Heat to produce more memories, this time of the off-court variety. In the early months of 2013, a viral trend had sprouted on social media and snowballed to absurd proportions. A dance trend to the catchy beat of the song "Harlem Shake" by American DJ and producer Baauer was running rampant where groups of people would dance the shake to the beat with quick, up-close cuts of individuals with the rest of the group dancing in the background.

"When you're kicking ass on the court, you can pretty much do whatever you want off of it," wrote Michael E. Miller of the *Miami New Times*. "The Chicago Bears had the 'Super Bowl

Shuffle' back in 1986. Now the Miami Heat have made their claim to this year's meme, the Harlem Shake."

The video, shot in the Miami locker room, featured all the players dressed up in costumes that were mostly neither here nor there: Chris Bosh in a bathrobe, cowboy hat and sunglasses with a giant gold boombox. Dwyane Wade in a giant stuffed bear head. Mario Chalmers dressed as Super Mario. Ray Allen in a Phantom of the Opera-style white mask. The dance moves were attempts at best, but the video belied what the Heat had become: a tight-knit group that, from the ashes of 2011, cared very little about public perception and happened to be really good at basketball.

"As close as we are in that video, that's how close we are on the floor, and our play shows it," LeBron told the media.

"They really enjoy each other," noted Jason Jackson of the local Miami Heat broadcast.

The video was the lead topic on the hot take shows, of course, and was viewed millions of times. Copycats would emerge from many other sports teams, but none quite caught on like the Heat's. The trend peaked in search hits about a week later.

When it was time to return to the court, the Heat overcame one of LeBron's worst games of the season to outlast the feisty Grizzlies, who were on an eight-game winning streak of their own, 98-91, as the Heat winning streak swelled to 13 games.

"I thought this was one of our better wins of the season," Spo said. "It was tough. We had to work for everything. We had to find a different way to win, deal with frustration...and then make some plays down the stretch."

Double-digit win streaks aren't uncommon in the NBA. Good teams will usually string wins together with a mix of strong play, a favorable schedule, some rhythm, and a little luck. So the Heat reaching 13 straight wasn't shocking. And with four games against weaker opponents ahead, 17 certainly wasn't out of the question.

The Heat swept those four games, though they needed a LeBron game-winner against the lowly Magic after blowing a 15-point halftime lead, to reach 17 straight, a mark hit only five times before, including earlier that season by the Clippers.

"It's about getting W's and trying to find a way not to get L's," Wade said.

The Heat had to find a way to not get an L in Philadelphia for win number 20 in a row, blowing yet another double-digit halftime lead, but Wade kept active on the offensive glass under 30 seconds left in the game to get the Miami lead to three and ultimately ice the game.

"Twenty is special," Wade said. "Win twenty games in a row, it's awesome. You can't get around it. We're going to try to go for the next one."

Only three other teams in NBA history had reached the coveted 20 game win streak, most recently the 2007-08 Houston Rockets featuring none other than Shane Battier.

Tom Haberstroh, writing for ESPN, noted the absurd level of play required for such a streak, specifically in the clutch.

Wednesday's win over Philadelphia underscores a hallmark of the Heat's remarkable run and their 2012-13 season as a whole:

He would go on to cite the reason for the Heat being almost unbeatable in the clutch, which was hiding in plain sight.

How much longer could the streak last? The Heat had already cheated death against weaker teams, but also steamrolled contenders like Chicago, Indiana, Oklahoma City, and both Los

Angeles squads. One game, though, stood out on the calendar: a Monday night in Boston against a proud Celtics team still bitter over the Ray Allen defection and their blown 3–2 lead the previous summer.

"It's not unreasonable to suggest Miami could be going for its 30th straight win on the road against San Antonio on March 31," Zach Lowe penned. "Regardless, they've clearly established themselves as the favorites to win the title."

The Heat would not allow themselves to publicly look ahead, appreciating the streak but focusing solely on the next opponent. To even get to the Boston game unscathed they would have to win two more on the road against two teams still fighting for the playoffs: Milwaukee and Toronto, where the streak began over a month ago.

As many predicted, the Heat had no trouble against either of them, winning both by double digits.

"After a brief flicker of competitiveness, the Heat buried the Raptors in Toronto yesterday under a pile of smartly created open 3s — mostly by Ray Allen, who hit four in a span of about 4:30 in the fourth quarter as Miami pulled away," wrote Zach Lowe for *Grantland*.

"There's no time to relax," Bosh said succinctly after the 22nd win in a row.

On an ABC broadcast of a different game, but on the day the Heat streak touched 22 in a row, Jeff Van Gundy offered this question to his broadcast mates, Mark Jackson and Mike Breen: which is more impressive, winning 33 games in a row or winning a title?

Van Gundy, ever a contrarian, sided with the win streak, prompting Jackson to joke that he should be drug tested.

It was great conversation fodder for around the water cooler, but what did the numbers say, asked Haberstroh in ESPN.

"The Heat have about a 1-in-3 chance at winning the 2012-13 title, or 2-in-5, according to bettors," he wrote. "But the odds of a team with Miami's record winning 23 straight are microscopic by comparison. About 0.4 percent, or about 80 times as unlikely."

The public at large is not good with probabilities or game theory; the numbers to a mathematician would make perfect sense, the answer to Van Gundy's question a cinch. Haberstroh minced no words for the casuals:

> *A championship is greatness, too, but usually in the "last man standing" sense. Championship teams can have off nights. Heck, they can afford to have an off week. But win streaks don't allow for that margin of error. Take, for instance, the 2007-08 Celtics who "won it all" despite losing 10 of their 26 postseason games. And as a reward, they received a ring, a banner, a parade and a place in history.*

> *There will be no such ring for the Heat, even if they do something that has happened one other time in NBA history and fail to win the title. To some, the lack of commemorative hardware makes Van Gundy's claim a load of nonsense. Ultimately, the Heat will be widely judged by what happens in June, not in March, because that's how we've been conditioned in this championship-or-bust culture.*

But streaks have an immortality element, too. Before being reminded of this streak, did you even remember offhand who won the 1971-72 title? Probably not. (The Lakers did.) This happens across sports, too. Which resonates more, Joe DiMaggio's 56-game hitting streak in 1941, or the 1941 World Series? The streaks leave a greater impression because championships happen every year.

The hunt for 23 would be slightly muted, with two of the proudest Celtics out, Garnett and Rondo. But thinking Boston would roll over and become the 23rd straight opponent to die at the Heat's hand was foolish. After all, only five years before, Boston had ended the second-longest winning streak in NBA history by the aforementioned Rockets; they had experience in this ending winning streaks thing.

"I'm looking at the Boston Celtics to be the team that will put an end to that streak," Stephen A. Smith declared, never wanting to miss a chance to bloviate.

It began to look dire in the first quarter when the Celtics, behind a career night from Jeff Green, finished the quarter on a 17-0 run to lead by 12. No one on the Heat could cool off Green, a subpar shooter, who was hitting jumpers and making contested layups at will.

"There's no excuses for them playing that much harder than us," Spo offered between quarters.

Boston had all the momentum, stretching the lead to as much as 17 early in the second quarter.

"Down 17, it's easy to say, 'You know what, it's not our night,'" Wade said.

That was before LeBron wrested momentum, and possibly some manhood, from the confident Celtics.

Boston guard Jason Terry, double teamed deep in the backcourt, lost the ball to Wade near the timeline. Without looking, he flipped an underhand pass to Chalmers who found Cole streaking from the top of the key. If Cole was streaking, LeBron was flat out flying. Cole scooped the ball high in the middle of the paint, Terry turning to defend. LeBron caught the ball out of the air in literal full flight at the restricted circle, Terry's attempt at defending too late. LeBron threw him back out of the air as he finished a nasty one-handed alley-oop. The Miami bench leapt up, assistant coach David Fizdale darting to try to avoid the explosion, held back by Juwan Howard and Ray Allen.

"WHOA!" exclaimed ESPN announcer Mike Tirico, never one to succumb to hyperbole or over-exuberance.

"It looked like he jumped out of the mezzanine," remarked color commentator Hubie Brown, watching the replay. "That's sending it down with some power."

The fact the dunk was on known nemesis Jason Terry was not lost on LeBron. "Yeah, I saw him down there," LeBron said smugly after the game.

"The dunk heard 'round the world," Jorge Sedano called it.

Boston re-calibrated, and led by 13 with just over 8 minutes left in the game. Would the streak die on the vine at 22? The Celtics fans had packed the building not to see the streak reach a holy 23, but to see the knife go through the heart at the hands of their beloved C's, sans Garnett and Rondo.

LeBron, Wade, and Bosh were having none of it. LeBron answered a Jordan Crawford three with one of his own from the top of the arc to beat the shot clock, Wade stole the ball near the Heat baseline and flipped to LeBron for an effortless two-handed dunk, and Bosh got a layup on a beautifully designed back screen action to make it 96-90.

LeBron would have two more buckets and assist on three others before Doc Rivers called timeout, the 13-point lead now evaporated and the Celtics in fact now trailing, 101-100.

But LeBron would gamble on the ensuing Boston possession, leaving Chalmers to try to cover the entire baseline and get out to contest an Avery Bradley corner three that gave the Celtics back the lead.

Unfazed, and after an oddly long review process to show the ball going out of bounds off Jeff Green's foot, LeBron gathered his own miss and laid it in to tie the game back up.

When LeBron got the ball isolated against Jeff Green just off to the left side of the key with only 20 seconds left, he not only had a chance to add to his sensational second quarter dunk on Terry, but keep the streak alive, on his broad shoulders.

LeBron baited Green with a pair of hesitation steps as he shuffled left, getting Green off balance just enough to uncork a deep two from the left angle.

"James steps into a jumper... *and rattles it in*!" said Mike Tirico on the ESPN broadcast.

The game was not over yet, 10.5 seconds left and Boston called a timeout to inbound the ball on their end of the floor in front of the Heat bench.

An unlikely hero emerged, overshadowed by LeBron's fourth-quarter brilliance: Shane Battier. Tasked with defending the red-hot Jeff Green, who was sitting on a career-high 43 points, Battier was Miami's last line of defense. Boston spaced the floor, planting two shooters on the strong side while running Pierce and Terry in weak-side action to occupy LeBron and Wade.

Green attacked downhill to his right. Battier, ever the sly defender, barely touched him but timed it perfectly, swiping the ball as Green went up for a layup. When Green tried to steady it with both hands, Battier got on top again, knocking it out of bounds and burning precious seconds.

Pierce later missed a three, and Battier added more gamesmanship, bouncing the ball off Pierce's back to drain the clock, a trick rarely seen outside of high school gyms.

Twenty-three wins in a row, a new threshold in the annals of the storied history of the NBA, firmly in second place for the most wins in a row.

"It's a special opportunity that we have with this group, and you don't want to take it for granted," Spo said in normal muted fashion after the win. "You want to treat every day as a special opportunity to be with this group, to share these moments together, but more importantly to take a step closer to going after our goal and every day that we improve puts us in a better position in a quest where nothing is guaranteed for anybody."

"The Heat players wanted that streak to continue," said Ethan Skolnick, "and I think that was evident in Boston."

If the streak felt threatened in Boston, it looked dead in the water two nights later in Cleveland.

Trailing 55-34 at the half, and by as many as 27 in the third quarter, all signs pointed to this innocuous Wednesday night in Cleveland being the whimpering end to an enthralling month and a half streak. LeBron, still being booed every time he touched the ball, was still getting into the paint relentlessly. And the unsung hero of the Boston game arrived in a flurry in the third quarter. Battier hit three threes, and a soft miss on another caromed to Bosh, cutting a once-ridiculous deficit to just ten.

LeBron blocked Alonzo Gee just inside the free throw line and found Ray Allen streaking down the wing for an open three with 15.5 seconds to go and the lead down to a very manageable eight points.

With Wade and Bosh on the bench to start the fourth, Spo rolled with a lineup tailor-made for LeBron to succeed: three shooters (Chalmers, Battier, and Allen) and one big man, Andersen, and let LeBron force double teams and pitch to shooters stationed around the arc or a mammoth crashing target in Andersen.

LeBron quickly drew free throws for Andersen, then hit a three from nearly the same spot where Allen had closed the quarter. Moments later, a pull-up three with 10:30 left somehow tied the game, and suddenly the boos had all but vanished. In just over nine minutes of game time, a 27-point lead had evaporated so quickly and cleanly it hardly seemed real. Even gruff Heat head of security David Holcombe was clapping as the Heat jogged to the bench during a Cavs timeout.

The timeout barely slowed Miami. LeBron drilled another pull-up three, found Allen at the top for one of his own, then jumped a passing lane for a steal and hit Chalmers for a layup. On a floppy action, Allen freed himself in the corner for yet another three. The lead was down to seven, and what had seemed over minutes earlier now looked destined to roll on—the streak still alive at 24.

"That guy right there doesn't want to lose in this building," Wade said of LeBron who finished with a brilliant 25 points,

12 rebounds (a career-high seven on the offensive glass) and 10 assists.

"One of the best comebacks I've ever been a part of," LeBron demurred. "I knew there was a lot of time, so we never panicked. We were down 27 with 18 minutes left. That's a lifetime in basketball."

Cavaliers players had sensed a comeback was brewing, even when the score was so lopsidedly in their favor.

"We knew it was coming," Cavs big man Tristan Thompson said. "They were the NBA champions last season. They're not going to lay down. Champions don't lay down even when they're down by 27. We knew they were going to make a push. Guys went out and made plays, so you have to give them credit."

"That Cleveland game was awesome because it was one of the only games where we didn't have it," said Battier.

The win also completed "The Reunion Tour", a self-proclaimed moniker because Miami had visited Wade's home in Milwaukee, Chris Bosh's former team in Toronto and Ray Allen's in Boston before LeBron's return to Cleveland, this time complete with a fan storming the court to tell LeBron personally to come back to Northeast Ohio.

"He said he missed me and come back, please," an unfazed LeBron said. "It happened once before in (Madison Square) Garden, so I wasn't worried. There are metal detectors here, so we were OK. I embraced it."

The Heat blew out three lottery teams in a row as the streak reached an unthinkable 27 games.

They were *the* story of the NBA, and how could they not be? When the Rockets won 22 straight only five years earlier, the run drew attention, but nothing like the glare on Miami.

Houston was an everyman group, with Tracy McGrady sidelined for much of the streak and Yao Ming also hurt. They were scrappy, professional, and easy to admire, but even afterward, no one saw them as real contenders. The Heat was different. They looked like the nightmare critics had warned about back in the summer of 2010: a true super team, now fully equipped with the right complementary pieces, operating at its peak.

By the time the streak reached its height, it was clear—this wasn't a fluke. It was dominance unfolding in real time

"All the justified focus on the individual numbers obscures a larger, better story: These Heat look almost nothing like the 2010-11 version that melted away against Dallas in the Finals," wrote the great Zach Lowe for *Grantland*, "and they don't even look much like the team that took the floor for the bulk of their championship campaign last season."

With LeBron playing at the highest level of his career, it was mind numbing to think he had been put in the corner to watch Wade run iso and high pick and roll actions in an actual NBA Finals. What once was a stagnant morass, replete with a series of stodgy off-ball action and late-clock dribbling, was now anything but.

"It's gone away from just pounding the ball," Dirk Nowitzki was quoted. "It's all about spreading the floor with so much shooting. I guess we were lucky to have caught them in the Finals that first year."

"Miami is a pass-happy team that whips the ball around the floor, shifts bodies all over the place in carefully coordinated motion sets, gobbles up the most efficient shots available, and generally destroys opposing defenses in a way that is both visually pleasing and nothing like how they played in the past," Lowe continued. "League observers used to talk about Orlando's four-out/one-in system, with four shooters surrounding Dwight Howard in the post or on the pick-and-roll. Miami and Erik Spoelstra have one-upped that by often playing a five-out system, with all five guys moving around the 3-point arc as the Heat run through a series of rehearsed actions while hunting for gaps in the defense."

Next up, the old friend Chicago Bulls in the Madhouse on Madison would get their chance at the high-octane offensive machine.

"We played them on Thursday, nobody played Tuesday," Bosh remembers. "Tibs was going to be ready; sat everybody and then had 'em fresh and had a game plan for us."

Out of the gate, the Heat found themselves trailing, down ten at the quarter break and nine at the half. But they had been down all streak, the Bulls were shorthanded, and the Heat had the Big 3.

A 22-14 third quarter got the Heat within a single point going into the fourth and this, too, felt like an inevitable win on the march to history. Except the Bulls, like the Celtics, a prideful and hungry team, had other plans.

LeBron sat the first three minutes of the final quarter and watched his teammates only muster a single point on a Wade free throw. With 6:40 to go, Kirk Hinrich hit a running jumper in transition to balloon the Bulls' lead to seven. The Heat had erased far worse deficits during the streak, so on paper this shouldn't have been much. But Chicago dragged them into its style of slow, grinding, methodical basketball, and the shots just weren't falling, no matter how clean the process looked.

LeBron broke through with a strong finish on a Bosh entry pass, slipping free of Deng's fronting defense. Deng came right back, drilling a three over Wade. Moments later, Wade answered with an and-one, jawing with LeBron on his way to the bench for a timeout. But it felt like one step forward, two steps back: Wade and LeBron both collapsed under the rim on the next possession, leaving Butler wide open in the corner for another three that pushed the lead back to eight.

The Heat's offense looked rushed and out of rhythm, capped by Wade clanking a wild running bank shot. On the other end, LeBron bailed them out with a chase-down block on Hinrich, swatting away what should've been an easy layup.

He appeared perturbed when the referees ruled a common foul when Gibson took a swing around the collarbone area on his drive with just over four minutes left. In retaliation, he put his shoulder into a Boozer screen after he split the free throws. "I like it!" exclaimed Jeff Van Gundy on the broadcast.

The refs assessed LeBron with a flagrant one foul, a curious decision only moments after declining to do so on Gibson.

"There's this overreaction they're taught to call," Van Gundy said disgustedly of the call.

LeBron allowed Hinrich to drive by him, only to pin the ball on the glass with two hands for a sensational block and give Miami slight hope. When Bosh completed a three-point play in semi-transition, it felt like the Heat was going to do it again, snatching victory from the jaws of defeat. Bosh rejected Hinrich again, starting a Heat fast break and the momentum felt firmly Miami's. That is until Chalmers clanked a walk up three and Battier got whistled for a relatively weak loose ball foul on the rebound.

The Heat got away with Boozer only making one free throw, but when Hinrich wrestled the ball from Bosh (clearly fouling him) off an offensive rebound and found Gibson for a baseline jumper on the other end, the streak was seriously slipping away in real time.

Although the Heat got two quick scores in the paint (a LeBron dunk and a Ray Allen layup), the kiss of death appeared to be Boozer squeezing an offensive rebound between Battier and Bosh and scoring directly off the miss with under a minute to go.

"I didn't have a good game. Yeah, we lost, let's get out of here," muttered Bosh.

Miami had made it nearly two calendar months without a loss, it had to be jarring to walk off losers.

"Wednesday night's game was the greatest NBA regular-season game ever played," wrote Bill Simmons. "Repeat: Wednesday night's game was the greatest NBA regular-season game ever played."

"It's one of the best that this league has ever seen," James said of the streak. "We recognized that and rightfully so."

"We haven't had a chance to really have a moment to know what we just did," he added. "We had a moment, just very fortunate, very humbling and blessed to be part of this team and be part of a streak like that."

What was the reaction supposed to be? Muted in defeat or celebratory in appreciation for the 27 games that had come before?

"We understand, probably more so later on in our careers, the significance of that. And then that was it," Spo said. "I had everybody come in, put a hand on each other and we took that moment to acknowledge it, to acknowledge each other, that experience, but it was never about the streak."

"A five second moment of reflection," Wade called it.

There was a sense of relief that the streak was over and that the team's sights could now be set on the ultimate goal. "Everybody was happy about it but LeBron," said Ethan Skolnick.

The streak and its largesse couldn't be understated; the Heat hadn't lost for one third of an NBA season, consecutively. Simmons was particularly impressed with the professionalism of the roster:

> *You know the biggest reason the Heat won 27 games? You know, other than the part where the greatest player in 20 years suits up for them? Ray Allen, Udonis Haslem, Shane Battier, Mike Miller, Rashard Lewis, Juwan Howard, even LeBron and Wade and Bosh ... these guys are all professionals in the truest sense. When you're grinding out win after win after win for almost two solid months — with the media spotlight shining brighter and brighter, with every opponent playing you like it's a playoff game, with the stakes swelling just a little more every game — the professional routine becomes more crucial than anything. You need adults. You need guys who can stay focused, keep grinding out those workdays and say things like, "It's 3:30 a.m., we have a game tomorrow, you need to go home." The 2013 Heat have an overload of adults. Don't think it was an accident.*

Seventeen of the wins had been by double digits. Twelve had been against teams that would make the 2013 playoffs. Thirteen had been on the road. LeBron had shot under 50% from the floor in four of the 27 games and had shot over 60% in ten of them. The Heat had scored 141 points, held a team to 67 points, and won five by five points or less. They had easily wrapped up the top seed in the East and could, if they so chose, coast out the rest of the regular season.

Chapter 17 - Verticality

LeBron had 36 points two nights later as the Heat whomped the New Orleans Pelicans, and then on a Sunday nationally televised matchup with the West-leading Spurs, Bosh nailed a game winning three for the Heat's 29th win of their last 30 games, this one without the presumptive MVP LeBron or Wade.

LeBron and Wade would sit out a loss to the Knicks, and then, tying a bow on the incredible regular season, the Heat won their final eight games, including rematches with the Bulls, Celtics, and Cavaliers.

The streak ending hadn't submarined the end of the season or the collective will; the Heat had lost two games since Groundhog Day. That number would remain two as they blasted the helpless Bucks in a sweep in the first round of the playoffs, winning the final game without Wade, out due to knee soreness.

"He gave me the nod saying he wasn't going to go, so I knew I had to pick it up a little more and try to bring us home, bring this win home for us," LeBron said after he tallied 30 points, 8 rebounds, 7 assists, and 3 steals in the win.

"It's big," Wade said of the time off. "Obviously, we're one of the oldest teams in the league, maybe the oldest team in terms of rotation players. Guys have some bumps and bruises coming out of this series, so it's going to be great to get some rest. But also, we have to take this time to continue to stay sharp, to continue to stay in shape as well."

"They had the whole package," Bucks coach Jim Boylan said. "When you can afford to sit a guy like Dwyane Wade and perform at the level they performed at, that's a championship-caliber team."

The sweep afforded the Heat a full week off awaiting their next opponent, ultimately the undermanned Chicago Bulls, the very Bulls who had ended the winning streak.

But before the series began, there was housekeeping to be done in Miami: LeBron being christened as the 2012-13 Kia NBA MVP yet again.

As good as he had been in 2011-12, and, of course, buoyed by the 27-game winning streak, LeBron had been transcendently better in 2012-13. He eclipsed his career highs shooting from the floor, the three point line, and rebounds per game, while also being the most feared perimeter defender in the league, capable of hijacking a game as easily against a point guard as a center. He finished the regular season with nine straight games shooting over 56% from the field and for the season had 17 games shooting 65% or better, more than in his first two seasons in Miami combined.

"Almost 50 years around the NBA I've had an opportunity to observe great players," Pat Riley said at the ceremony. "In my humble opinion, the man we are looking at right here is the best of all of them."

Miami was too veteran and too professional to be thinking of revenge for a regular season loss, more likely rolling their eyes at the prospect of having to play the Bulls style: physical, mucky, no rhythm.

And that is exactly how game one played out, of course aided by the rust of a week with no games. A bumpy first three quarters was a footnote to the 35-point fourth quarter exhibit the Bulls put on, an answer at the ready for every Heat run.

"There's no excuses," said Spo. "We're not making any excuses for time off or anything else."

"There was no win to celebrate," wrote Bosh years later. "The Bulls had beaten us, at home no less. And I needed to take my mind off it, with the help of McNuggets, fries, and a brain-freeze inducing McFlurry. Oreo. Always. Order. Oreo.

"I also knew Spo was going to make us feel that loss the next day. After the game, he hadn't said much more than, 'Practice tomorrow.' That meant we were in for what he called The Hunger Games—practices worthy of the name, where he'd push us as hard as we could go. We started the day with a film session, which was brutal."

What looked like another dog fight in game 2, Heat leading only 42-38 with under four minutes left in the first half, couldn't have gone much more south much faster for the Bulls, yielding a 62-20 run from that point on and getting gashed, 115-78.

The Bulls, outclassed on the floor, racked up six technical fouls and two ejections, the most by any team in a playoff game since Boston had that many against Indiana in 2005.

"I don't know how many techs we got... I would call that not keeping your cool, not being very Zen," Bulls center Joakim Noah said.

"We got sidetracked and you can't do that," Bulls coach Tom Thibodeau said. "We allowed frustration to carry over to the next play. You come in here, you're not going to get calls. That's reality."

The side show took away from the Heat absolutely dominating, obviously, across the board. The team shot 60%

from the floor, 50% from three and outrebounded the team thought to be more physical and tough, 41-28.

But the series only being 1-1 regardless of the score was not lost to the Heat.

"No matter if you win by 20, 30, or one point, it's a 1-1 series," LeBron said. "They came in and did their job. They got one on our floor and took home court. So, we've got to try to go to Chicago and get it back."

"We're still in the hole," Spo said, referring to having losing homecourt advantage after the game one loss.

But the Heat once again was the more mentally tough team that also executed better, winning game three, 104-94, and blowing the Bulls off their home floor in game four, 88-65. Tightening the screws in the fourth quarter of the home game five, the Heat allowed a paltry 14 points, hearkening back to the first Big 3 season, and advanced to their third straight Eastern Conference Finals.

"We gave it everything we had," LeBron said. "I have no energy left."

"They're a great team. A great team," Thibodeau said in defeat. "They're not going to beat themselves. You have to beat them."

"It only gets more difficult and more challenging," Spo said as the Heat awaited either the Knicks or Pacers as their next opponent. "That's what competitors want."

Indiana would ultimately come through the series victorious, setting up a rematch of the 2012 playoffs when they led 2-1 and the Heat, without Bosh, had to lean on introspection and insane individual efforts from Wade and LeBron.

And, as Spo had warned, it would get more difficult and challenging almost immediately.

Indiana, much in the same vein as Chicago, was a slow, methodical, defensive team that wanted to grind the opposition into dust on both ends. What the Bulls lacked in playmakers outside the injured Rose, the Pacers had in spades with young, rangy wing Paul George, wily sixth man Lance Stephenson, and bruising forward David West.

The Pacers were slightly archaic offensively at best, and wholly unimaginative at worst. But defensively, armed with strong, long, committed defenders, they were a completely different matchup than most teams. Stationed in the paint with everything funneled to him was 7-foot 2-inch Roy Hibbert. Other teams had tall, long centers. Other teams had similar philosophies of ensuring everything in the paint ended up at a static shot blocker. But Indiana, behind fiery coach Frank Vogel, had so strongly petitioned the league to call contact with Hibbert a certain way that an arbitrage opportunity presented itself for the Pacers.

In the NBA rulebook, an obscure wording ruled the day in almost every Pacers game:

A player is entitled to a vertical position even to the extent of holding his arms above his shoulders, as in post play or when double-teaming in pressing tactics.

This word salad became quickly known in NBA vernacular as "verticality", meaning simply if a defender was straight up, even if he jumped and made contact, no foul was to be called.

While the verticality rule applied to everyone, the way it seemed to be enforced almost exclusively for Hibbert drove other players crazy, none more than LeBron. Earlier in the season, he had vented about it, saying, "He takes a lot of teams out of what they are accustomed to doing, because he is so great at the rim, protecting the rim, and they allow him to use his verticality rule more than anyone in our league."

Officials were tasked with making bang bang calls, adjudicating "straight upness" and who initiated contact. Because of the emphasis, those calls were overwhelmingly going Hibbert's way.

"As long as he's allowed to bend the rules protecting the rim, the Pacers are in the catbird seat," wrote the great Mike Prada for *SB Nation*. "The best chance of beating the Pacers is to get Hibbert off the floor, and the only way to do that is to challenge him at the basket. Rarely has the interpretation of a single NBA rule determined so much of the league's hierarchy."

Hibbert and his verticality notwithstanding, the Heat tore off 60 points in the paint and looked like they had held off the pesky Pacers in game one, until Ray Allen missed a crucial free throw and Paul George hit a deep miracle three to send the game to overtime.

In overtime and the game tied at 99 apiece, Vogel made an interesting decision to take Hibbert out of the game as the Heat trotted out the Big 3, Allen, and Battier. LeBron, unsurprisingly, got Pacers point guard George Hill on a switch and drove right by him for an uncontested layup to take the lead with 11 seconds left. The game appeared over after a scrum at midcourt with six seconds left, but the ball somehow made its way to George who dribbled into a potential game winning three-point attempt. With Wade contesting the air space, George flailed as the shot touched nothing but the baseline. The ensuing whistle could barely be heard over the roar of the Miami crowd, thinking

George had airballed the game away. Instead, the flail would be rewarded with three free throws, the second miracle in under five minutes of game time for Indiana.

"It's tough to tell," Steve Kerr said confusedly on TNT.

Wade was incensed, the call at worst was incidental contact; George kicked his back leg out, exaggerating any contact if there was.

Unbothered, he knocked down all three free throws to give the Pacers a stunning 102-101 lead.

Vogel once again yanked Hibbert, leaving no rim protection as the Heat set up a final out-of-bounds play to win it.

Spo, by now a grizzled vet on the whiteboard, drew up a nice action to combat the Pacers' off-ball switching; Allen flashed across, ducking under what was set up to look like a Bosh screen. Bosh instead took off to set a pindown for Cole screaming up from the strongside short corner. All the off-ball action freed up the entire middle of the floor, as LeBron flashed to the top of the arc. Paul George was trailing, but slightly overcommitted, allowing LeBron to get him on his hip as he caught and dipped toward the rim like a locomotive. With no Hibbert in the paint, and all other Pacers players strewn out defending on the perimeter, LeBron was met with no one to contest at the hoop, laying it in gently with the left hand as the buzzer sounded.

Wade, standing on the bench, leapt in the air in celebration before the ball had even dropped through. The stoic Spo, watching intently, leaned with anticipation then clapped his hands emphatically together once, a primal celebration in his world.

"Great play drawn up by Erik Spoelstra," Kerr mused as TNT showed multiple angles of the game winner.

"Two teams fought hard," LeBron said. "We were able to make one more play."

That one play would be second guessed and dissected, everyone to a man wondering why Vogel elected to keep Hibbert off the floor. Most focused on the final play of the game, but he was also off the floor for LeBron's layup to initially take the lead at 101-99 late in overtime.

"I would say we would probably have him in next time," Vogel admitted.

The Heat, even throughout the winning streak, had found ways to win in the clutch, as Haberstroh had so elegantly noted. This didn't seem like anything more than par for the course in a tough postseason game.

"Welcome to the Eastern Conference Finals," Spo said with reverence. "Back and forth the whole way."

After the Heat's offense stalled late in game two — turning an 88–84 lead into a 97–93 loss — the concern grew. For all their regular season firepower, this was now the seventh straight playoff game where the offense bogged down, rescued only by flashes of brilliance from the Big 3.

Bosh and Haslem ensured that the Heat offense wasn't going to be stagnant early in game three, taking turns hitting jumper after jumper. LeBron didn't even score until more than halfway through the first period as Bosh knocked down four jumpers (two threes) and Haslem drilled three jumpers of his own and a short shot. Hibbert, the paint giant, was continually having to go out of his comfort zone, literally and figuratively, to half-heartedly contest the shooting exhibition.

When it was LeBron time, it was something the Pacers definitely weren't ready for: an absolute tour de force from the post.

"The Heat offense suddenly remembered what their most effective play is," YouTuber Nick Hauselman said bemused.

"It was something we wanted to get to just to help settle us and get into a more aggressive attack," Spo explained. "We wanted to be a little more aggressive, a little more committed to getting into the paint and seeing what would happen. LeBron was very committed and focused not to settle."

LeBron abused whoever the Pacers threw at him, patiently picking apart indecisive help defense for a series of short, left-handed shots and assists to baseline cutters behind the befuddled Pacers defense.

"He was in the post doing a lot of work, and I think we have to do a better job of helping Paul out," Hibbert said. "LeBron can't get five or six dribbles to get a post move... We have to make adjustments. He's obviously a low-post threat but we have to make adjustments."

Bosh, Wade, and LeBron combined for (only) 55 points on incredible efficiency: 22 for 41 combined, with just two turnovers. The Birdman Chris Andersen added 9 points and 9 rebounds off the bench, himself going 4 for 4 from the field (congruently, he had not missed a field goal since game four of the Chicago series).

The Heat so thoroughly disposing of the Pacers on the road seemed like the ship had been righted; had they discovered the formula to knock Indiana out of their game plan? It wasn't an outlier performance from three (only six made threes) and

Hibbert had shot an ungodly 15 free throws, five more than the Big 3 combined.

Indiana responded powerfully in game four, answering the efficient effort of the Heat from game three with their own: shooting 50% from the floor as a team, and out-rebounding the Heat 49-30. Wade and Bosh combined to shoot 6 for 21 from the floor and LeBron, in almost the exact same scenario as game four in Boston the year prior, fouled out of the game. The final foul, under a minute to go in a 96-92 game, was quite an exhibit from referee Derrick Stafford, whistling LeBron for a foul on a routine screen where Lance Stephenson stepped on his foot.

"It was a couple of fouls that I didn't feel like were fouls, personal fouls on me, but that's how the game goes sometimes," James said.

The Heat had stormed back from an 81-72 deficit to take an 86-83 lead in the fourth on an abnormal three-point play where Wade was fouled foolishly by West, mustered a layup onto the glass which was then goaltended by George.

But Miami only mustered six points over virtually the final six minutes of the game. And, like the 2012 Eastern Conference Finals, now faced a 2-2 series.

And with Indiana clinging to a 46-40 lead in the third quarter of game five, history very well could have seemed like it was repeating itself. But the same LeBron that appeared in Boston for game six a year earlier appeared in Miami for the third quarter, scoring or assisting on 25 of 30 Heat points and turning a six-point deficit into a thirteen-point lead heading to the fourth quarter.

"That's LeBron showing his greatness and making it look easy," Spo said incredulously. "What we talked about was doing whatever it takes and competing for each other without leaving anything out there. His engine in that third quarter was incredible. He was tireless, he was making plays on both ends of the court, rebounding, covering so much ground defensively and then making virtually every play for us offensively. It's really remarkable."

LeBron's dominance was aided by one of Haslem's best games of the season. Defended by Hibbert, Haslem was stationed in the short corner on most possessions, but never directly in the paint or near the basket, forcing Hibbert further away from defending the hoop. Necessitating that Hibbert both defend him and the paint got the slow footed big man all sorts of turned around, at one point stepping into the key to preemptively shut off a LeBron drive only to get blown by on the baseline for a Haslem dunk.

The Heat, mindful of their 2011 Finals mistakes, moved LeBron everywhere: running side pick-and-rolls, spotting him off the ball, and even posting him at the elbow in traditional horns sets. When Indiana couldn't dictate defensively, the points piled up fast. Even after LeBron missed two wide-open threes on the same trip, the onslaught didn't stop. As a screener, he knocked down a 15-footer. As the ball handler, he drilled an 18-footer. Off the ball, he collapsed five blue jerseys and kicked to Chalmers for a wide-open three. On a post-up, he jabbed and buried another jumper, barking at Lance Stephenson as the Pacers called timeout to slow the bleeding.

Indiana had no answers for the MVP, and Hibbert wasn't solving the riddle. A 3–2 lead and another trip to the Finals, once shaky in March, was suddenly one win away.

"That's what I came here for, to be able to compete for a championship each and every year," LeBron said. "I'm one step away from doing it once again. It's not promised. It's not promised at all. I made a tough decision. Obviously, I think we all know the story. I envisioned something that was bigger as far as a team...and we've got an opportunity as a team, once again, for the third year straight to make a trip to the NBA Finals."

But LeBron was the only Heat player seemingly with a pulse in game six, a complete second half letdown as the Pacers pounced in the third quarter, to take their own 13-point lead into the fourth quarter behind a raucous home crowd.

"It was total domination by the Pacers in the third," LeBron said.

"They just flat-out beat us in every facet of the game. They just outclassed us in that quarter," elaborated Spo.

Haslem, coming off his best game in game four, scored zero points, Bosh struggled going 1 for 8 from the floor, while Wade and Chalmers only hit three field goals apiece.

Spo, sensing the dire straits, attempted a LeBron lineup with four bench players to varying degrees of results.

With the game slipping away, LeBron was whistled for a dubious charge on Hibbert — who had leapt inside the restricted area with his arms draped over LeBron under the guise of 'verticality.' Furious, LeBron sprinted downcourt in disgust and drew a technical. David Fizdale, just as baffled, picked one up too. The Pacers cashed in with two free throws and a Hibbert layup seconds later, pushing the lead back to 13 and effectively shutting the door. Riley, usually statuesque, shook his head and Mourning, ever his co-pilot, put his head in his hands in bamboozlement.

As the game wound down, LeBron sat next to his longtime trainer, Mike Mancias, patting him on the knee as if to say *we got this back at home.*

Even though the stakes of the series were not lost on the Heat, they did not seem like a team that sensed an inordinate amount of danger. Playing as poorly as they did in game six was unlikely to happen in game seven, at home, nonetheless.

Dan Le Batard wrote:

> *This entire season, excellent though it was, didn't feel anything like the first two of this experiment. Miami winning was a droning excellence, the championship a foregone conclusion, an expectation. There weren't surprises or confusions or doubts or fears. But tonight we go right back to the us-against-the-world that made the Heat, for the last three years, the most interesting and rallied around team in the history of South Florida sports. The critics, quiet all year, hiding, are perched and ready to pounce, buzzards waiting for someone else to take care of the kill so they can dine. They crowed in Year 1; they fled in Year 2. At about midnight tonight, they will either be spooked by South Florida's roar, or they will feed with gluttonous delight.*

A sold out, all white-adorned crowd welcomed the defending champs and the feisty upstarts for game seven. And early on, the upstarts prevented them from having anything to cheer for, taking a solemn 21-19 lead after one quarter and, for the first time since game six in Boston the year before, a true sense of jeopardy of the Heat as presently constituted.

That feeling was quickly doused as the Heat scored nearly every possession to start the second quarter (LeBron jumper and free throws, Ray Allen three, Birdman paint shot, another Ray Allen three, another LeBron jumper) and Indiana could only muster five points in the last five minutes of the half to face an almost unthinkable 52-37 halftime deficit.

"It's hard to believe somebody's ever better than LeBron," Pacers big man Tyler Hansborough said to his younger brother, Ben, on the bench.

The lead grew to 21 after three quarters and the Pacers were toast; they had played the best game of their season in a do or die situation at home in game six, the tank was now empty, and the *championship DNA* wasn't there to save them.

Paul George, who had been so revered for his play in the series and overall growth in one short season, went 2 for 9 for seven points to go along with three turnovers and eventually fouling out with 7:43 to go. Hibbert, who allegedly gave the Heat fits, had zero blocks and also had five fouls, contributing to the Heat's large advantage in free throw makes and attempts.

Wade, still on balky knees, matched his playoff high with 21 and Ray Allen knocked down three threes, all in the second quarter. The Heat not playing anywhere near their best game and winning going away to advance to the Finals sent a striking message to the Pacers, who had believed they were on equal footing as the champs.

"The great thing is we're a young team and we are past the building stage," George said. "This is really our first year tasting success. The rate we are going, we see championships soon."

"Everybody in this country knows who the Indiana Pacers are now," Vogel said. "And we represent all the right things—class, character, hard work, old-school basketball, playing the game the right way. We represented our franchise, our city and our state extremely, extremely well, and we have a lot to be proud of."

"We didn't like the Pacers," Bosh wrote later. "And they didn't like us. But to be honest, their trash talk didn't do anything but get us even more hype. Because we despised these guys. And, if I'm being straight with you, we didn't love their fans either."

While the Pacers of course had taken the series to seven, it may have been a little self-congratulatory: they never led the series, and three of their four losses were by double digits including a crucial home game three with the proverbial momentum swung to their side. They certainly felt like they belonged after the 2012 series, even though that was without Bosh or Allen, possibly warranting the perceived next step.

The Pacers, like the Bulls, prided themselves on being a blue-collar, no-frills team in contrast to the Heat's perceived flash. In practice, that meant slow, grinding games and often disjointed offense. Yet the Heat went 4-0 against those teams in the playoffs, a fact that never got the credit it deserved. Miami might not have chosen to play that way, but they adjusted well enough never to let it derail a series.

"Everything that happened in the first six games didn't mean anything to us," Wade said succinctly. "It was about tonight. It was about Game 7. It was about finding a way to win here at home."

"It's just a privilege to be with this great team, great teammates, and we have another opportunity to go back to where we are," Bosh said. "You never really want to get it out of the way too much. Game 7s don't happen too often. We enjoyed it and now we have to move on."

And moving on now meant facing the team that could have been standing between the Heat and 30 wins in a row: the veteran San Antonio Spurs.

Chapter 18 - Yellow Ropes

The Spurs had dropped both regular season meetings with Miami — first on a Bosh game-winner in Texas, then in Miami when San Antonio rested four starters. A true clash of full rosters never materialized. Even the Heat's 120-98 blowout the year before came with an asterisk: Wade was sidelined, the Spurs' lineup looked different, and a wild 39-12 third quarter flipped a 15-point San Antonio lead into a double-digit deficit.

San Antonio was well-respected, having won four championships in an eight-year span, all with different roster iterations around their transcendent future Hall of Famer Tim Duncan. Losing to the eight seed Grizzlies in 2011 (ultimately paving the way for Dallas to come out of the West) and blowing a 2-0 lead against Oklahoma City in the 2012 Western Conference Finals had forced coach Gregg Popovich and general manager RC Buford to retool the team on the fly, looking to a new horizon rather than to their storied past. It resulted in the Spurs finishing with the third-best record in the league and rolling over the wounded former preseason NBA title contender Los Angeles Lakers in four routine games. Sweeping through the Grizzlies in the Western Conference Finals meant the Spurs would have a full ten days off before starting the NBA Finals.

This matchup also invited the inevitable eye rolling talk of *dynasties* and *legacies*; one team having accomplished their *legacy* over the span of fifteen seasons, the Heat, now in their third, had to deliver to be considered a *legacy* and a *dynasty,* whatever that actually meant. The Spurs obviously hadn't won championships every season, even with a two-time MVP in Duncan in the mid-2000s. In fact, the dynastic Spurs had lost in the first round twice in four seasons (once to an 8 seed), and blown multiple series leads including in two Western Conference Finals. Stunningly, those results were always forgotten when discussing their *legacy*. Almost as if an insane double standard was placed on certain teams. For example, the Mavericks, after winning the 2011 crown, didn't win a game in the 2012 playoffs and didn't qualify for the 2013 playoffs. No one discredited the title or, more applicably, discredited Nowitzki, even though in the four seasons before the title he had been a member of one playoff series win.

ESPN, obviously, wanted to ask all the unquantifiable questions in the lead up to what certainly could be one of the best Finals.

What does Miami need to accomplish to justify the Big Three hype? their panelists were asked in a "breakdown" before game one. Thankfully, Kevin Arnovitz, not one for hyperbole or narrative spinning, got the first go.

"I think it's unfair to demand a team justify the public attention it generated," he wrote, seemingly both calm and annoyed. "Only a few teams a decade win multiple titles, which means it's a rarified accomplishment, no matter how high the expectations."

A breath of fresh air for sure, only to be followed up by narrative fiend and Dallas Mavericks fanboy Marc Stein: "Honestly? Unless the Heat shock the world and rebound emphatically from the pounding they took from Indy to blow San Antonio away—which I don't see happening—this group can't. Not even if it wins it all."

The dynasty and legacy talk felt trite, boring, and wholly unimaginative — especially considering who was on the floor. There was a four-time MVP at the apex of his game; a banged-up Wade, still capable of channeling his mid-2000s alter ego, *Flash*; and Bosh, whose game matched up much better against the Spurs. On the other side stood Tim Duncan, a future Hall of Famer who had seemingly found the fountain of youth after knee issues had nearly ended his career. There was Manu Ginobili, a diamond-in-the-rough turned legend, whose herky-jerky style and all-around game made him a constant problem off the bench. And finally, Tony Parker — a quick, crafty, true point guard who was easily the best floor general the Heat had faced in a series. "Tony Parker is the kind of blurring, efficient point guard who has plagued Miami in the past," wrote Chris Mannix, "and, unlike Oklahoma City last year, the Spurs won't be intimidated by the moment."

The great Rob Mahoney, previewing the Finals for *Sports Illustrated*, wrote about a factor few bothered to take into consideration:

> *Lost in the micro-analysis of the Heat's up-and-down Eastern Conference finals was the fact that Miami had compromised its small-ball style and changed its lineup structure out of necessity against Indiana—a concession that deprived the Heat of optimal spacing and sapped their scrambling defense of its effectiveness.*

Miami would be able to go back to the way *they* wanted to play without conceding crucial keys such as offensive rebounds and paint points. San Antonio would make you pay, to be sure, but in completely different ways than Indiana, and their offense was *not* the archaic slog the Pacers trotted out. The Spurs didn't even have the same offense that made their *legacy*. What was once an old school, static post-up offense was now a frenzy of passing, cutting, screening, fake screens, and threes. Defenses that weren't committed to defending for the entire shot clock got capitulated in no time. In essence, the Heat and Spurs didn't play all that differently offensively, it was defensively that was going to be jarring, what with the Heat's hyper aggressive trapping defense and the Spurs' much more conventional drop defense and aversion to switching.

Despite Wade and Chalmers being good defenders, the challenge Parker presented was completely new and sprouted the thought within some corners that LeBron would defend Parker, at least in certain scenarios.

"Varying the coverage is the best way to defend Parker," Kevin Arnovitz wrote about the possibility of LeBron defending him. "Sometimes that means throwing size and strength at him; other times it means quickness. The Heat will want to blitz Parker on pick-and-rolls, and they should—but not always because Parker is unstoppable when he knows what's coming."

Aside from the x's and o's, one thing was abundantly clear: the Heat, if not limping, was wavering into the Finals, not fully healthy and not firing on cylinders. The Spurs, meanwhile, absolutely were.

Despite that, Wade and LeBron were working out hard the night before game one at body & soul near LeBron's Coconut Grove home. Mixing in boxing, pushing weighted sleds, and grueling core workouts (a LeBron specialty), Wade motivated himself between sets, shouting, "I need three!" every chance he got, referring to a third championship.

"Road to a championship!" LeBron gasped from the floor after the final core workout.

"The biggest thing is mental focus," Wade said to a documentary film crew in the gym as he left, "and what we need to do, and that's win four more games. It's going to be hard, so tonight we started that process, tomorrow the basketball begins."

Game one lived up to all the hype. Chalmers got in the passing lane on the first possession leading to the patented Heat fastbreak, ending in a Wade two handed jam. The Heat clearly was enjoying a more free flowing style and made 18 of its first 30 shots. They got out to a five-point lead around a minute to go in the first quarter which was promptly erased by two Spurs jumpers.

Cole hit a 3 to put Miami up nine in the second quarter, the Spurs quickly got that down to two and trailed by just three at half. As well as Miami was playing, they couldn't shake the veteran Spurs and took the three-point lead into the deciding fourth quarter.

Former LeBron teammate Danny Green drilled a three on the weak side as Mike Miller was tagging Duncan on his screen to give the Spurs an 88-81 lead with just over two minutes remaining.

But this was the Heat, they'd come back all during the win streak in February and March. And they started quickly chipping away, first with a tough LeBron lefty layup driving past Duncan and then three free throws from Ray Allen when Green took him out right in front of the Miami bench. Cutting an eight-point lead to three in two possessions never hurts.

LeBron and Duncan traded free throws and all that was left for Miami to have a shot at winning game one and holding serve was one single defensive stop. The Spurs put Parker through a pair of screens to get LeBron off him as a defender and then to get Bosh switched onto him late in the clock.

For all the heat Bosh took, pardon the pun, he was as good a big man defender switched onto smaller, quicker guards as there was in the league. Parker couldn't shake him, driving to the baseline and right into LeBron, who made a seamless switch onto Parker with only four on the shot clock. Parker started to dribble back to the wing, slipping onto one knee. He glanced up at the shot clock, reverse pivoted as LeBron flew by to his left to contest without fouling, and calmly hit a kissing runner off the glass and in.

"Just gets it off in time… and he *banks* it in!" exclaimed Mike Breen on the ABC broadcast. "What a shot from Parker!"

The bank shot was so close to the shot clock horn, it took multiple looks on the broadcast to find an angle that definitively showed the ball off of Parker's fingertips before the red light on the backboard glared.

Down four with only five seconds left is nearly an impossible mountain to climb and Wade missing a quick layup was the final indignity.

"With one crazy shot from Tony Parker in Game One of the finals, our home court advantage vaporized," said Bosh.

"Obviously, Tony is the engine behind everything, so we just have to do a better job," Wade said. "As the series goes on, we'll make adjustments. We'll get to see where we can be better at defensively. Give them credit. They came in and didn't shoot the ball very well, but they stuck with it."

The game was instantly a Finals classic.

"We got a little bit lucky in Game 1," Parker said sheepishly. "Sometimes that's what it takes to win games."

"This is a hell of a game to play because both teams are so good offensively and defensively," Bosh said. "You can't have any letdowns."

Parker's shot was hardly a letdown, defended brilliantly by both Bosh and LeBron, just a case of incredible clutch shot making. The bogged down offense for most of the fourth quarter was the bigger culprit, much more of a letdown.

"In the fourth quarter, we had some mental mistakes," LeBron said. "And it's only a couple of teams you can't have mistakes against, especially in the fourth. And San Antonio is definitely the No. 1 team."

"I thought we were a little fatigued honestly in the fourth quarter," Wade said. "Looking around, we looked like a team that came off a seven-game series."

And the truth of it was, this was also a seven-game series; a close game one loss counted as one in the loss column, but there were other games to salvage the series.

In game two, the Heat looked like the 27-game win streak team again, except for LeBron for large portions of the game. He started the game a dismal 3 for 13 from the field, buoyed by good starts by his running mates Bosh and Wade, who scored six and four, respectively, in the opening frame.

The pace and space that had been covered in cobwebs in the Chicago and Indiana series reappeared in full force.

"With defenders who must stay home on shooters, the already otherworldly talents of LeBron James and Dwyane Wade are magnified all the more," wrote Jared Wade of *Bleacher Report*.

"The defenders guarding players like Ray Allen, Mike Miller and Shane Battier are constantly put to the test when the Heat's two dynamic penetrators make their moves. Do they sag off and help thwart the imminent threat of the drive? Or do they worry more about the drive and kick that could lead to three points instead of the two James and Wade may score at the rim?"

The Heat, even with Wade or Bosh or both on the bench, put multiple shooters on the floor, moved the queen on the chessboard, LeBron, all around, and forced the Spurs to make calculated gambles every time down the floor.

In game two, the Spurs played all the wrong hands. Well, the Heat was actually down 62-61 with less than four minutes left in the third quarter after Green slinked along the baseline for a rare layup. But with a three shooter lineup combined with LeBron and the Birdman, the Heat started to pull away, generating open threes by Miller and Allen or layups in tight from LeBron rolling as a screen or Chalmers as the ball handler.

"We were much more efficient offensively," Spo told ABC's Doris Burke between quarters.

When LeBron started to take the ball handling over in the fourth, he was met with a familiar Spurs tactic that had been used against him going back to the 2007 Finals: San Antonio went under every ball screen on LeBron, daring him to shoot jump shots. It was jarring to see the MVP be given seven or more feet, dribbling above the three-point line and a Spurs defender slipping below a screen near the free throw line. LeBron clearly wasn't comfortable, if he wanted to pass up jumpers, he would be driving into not only his primary defender stationed and ready, but the screen defender and the whole weakside ready to slide over.

One way to combat that was to get stops and push the ball the other way (the pace in the pace and space), or as they did to open up a fifteen-point lead, get a stop, push the ball, and get LeBron in a quick cross match on the post. San Antonio, naturally, sent help from the free throw line, and the MVP found Mike Miller wide open in the corner for a three.

Chalmers' aggressiveness could not be understated either. He wasn't just there to get a screen from LeBron and quickly pass out; he probed deep into the lane and hit a series of layups and floaters, some against the Spurs' best defender, Kawhi Leonard.

While the unique lineup played to almost all of LeBron's strengths, it was sacrificing some on the defensive end with three average defenders that weren't above average switching defensively in Allen, Miller, and the Birdman. But that didn't mean the activity level dropped. And it was on defense where LeBron produced one of the best highlights of his career and nuked any momentum or sense of a comeback the Spurs may have had.

Parker, now all too familiar with the Heat's high hedge strategy against him in the pick and roll, slid a nice pocket pass between Miller and Chalmers to big man Tiago Splitter who caught the ball at the free throw line with no one between him and the hoop. LeBron slid over from the short corner, squarely in the restricted area, directly under the rim. Splitter had gathered and was rising for a one-handed dunk from between the circles. LeBron calmly out jumped Splitter and rejected the dunk attempt with the right hand.

"Oh, what a block from James!" Mike Breen shouted. "*Throws* it back at Splitter who was ready to dunk! One of the great blocks you will ever see."

LeBron lingered on the baseline mean mugging at the crowd as the Heat sprinted the other way. He probably thought the Heat would score quickly, only to run down and set a late ball screen for Chalmers. But in yet another exhibition of his all-around greatness and ability to read the floor, he caught the ball, glanced at the weakside, then back at Bosh cutting behind him, only to rip a cross court pass to Ray Allen for another wide open three as Green lunged ever so slightly to try to beat what he thought was a pass to the thundering Bosh.

San Antonio could only tip the cap, suffering their worst defeat of the entire playoffs, 103-84.

"In the second half they just run us over," the Spurs' Manu Ginobili said. "We didn't move the ball at all. Their pressure really got us on our heels."

"We didn't play well. We didn't shoot well. I know I played awfully," Duncan said. "Whatever it may be, they responded better than us. So hopefully we can look forward to this Game 3 and regain some of our composure."

Chalmers, who had been buried behind the clunky vets Carlos Arroyo and Mike Bibby in 2011, had once again stolen the show in an NBA Finals game, offsetting quieter than normal nights (on the stat sheet, at least) from Bosh, Wade, and LeBron. The bench, also, delivered in a big way, with Miller and Allen hitting three threes each and Birdman going for 9 points and 4 rebounds (and five fouls) in just 14 minutes.

It was only one game, the adage for the NBA playoffs ringing true: whether by one or one hundred, one playoff win counted as one. And of course, it was unlikely both Parker and Duncan would struggle as much as they did (combining to shoot under 30% from the floor with six turnovers).

Game three, on the surface, looked like game one and the first two and a half quarters of game two: two good teams exchanging body blows and the judges scoring it extremely close. The Spurs stretched a six-point halftime lead to 15 by the end of the third, the anemic Heat offense showing itself once again with a 19 point quarter, six by LeBron in the final minute.

The Heat still had a puncher's chance, but the Spurs snuffed it out immediately, scoring on their first six possessions of the fourth quarter. Four of those buckets were threes — two each from Gary Neal and Danny Green — slamming the door before Miami could even think comeback.

"Those guys shot incredibly," Duncan said understatedly. "Gave us the breathing room when we needed it."

The night ended with the Spurs setting a new NBA record for three pointers in a Finals game and handing the Heat the third-largest loss in Finals history, 113-77.

"We got what we deserved," Spo said. "I didn't even recognize the team that was out there tonight," he added harshly.

"They came out in the third quarter, and they kicked our butt pretty good, and frustration started to set in," Wade admitted.

Miami, hardened by the collapse in 2011 and the pressure that followed them until they broke through as champions, never let one game define them. They stayed even, never too high after a win or too low after a loss. This would be no different.

The stakes now matched the sliding doors moments of the Big 3 era: the 2–1 hole in Indiana, the 3–2 deficit in Boston, even the 1–0 start against Oklahoma City in the 2012 Finals. Once again, they were on the road, trailing in a series, with a loss that would all but end their season.

The *South Florida Sun-Sentinel* wrote of how the coaching staff felt with the series nearly halfway over:

"I was despondent," Heat head coach Erik Spoelstra. "I was beside myself." So he went back to his hotel suite to break down some game film. Video coordinator Dan Craig was there too. About 20 minutes later, there was a knock at the door. There stood Heat president Pat Riley with three bottles of wine and an offering of help. 'So we gave him a laptop and he helped us break down film in a role reversal from 2006,' said Spoelstra, a Heat assistant coach under Riley back then. "It was one of the most special moments in my professional career."

"I repeated what I did after our tough loss in Round 2: I got in the car and got myself a burger," said Bosh. "And in Texas, you don't go to McDonalds. You get Whataburger. Bacon Cheeseburger. Fries."

And, as the Heat had done each time, the bell was answered in game four. It has largely been forgotten because of how the series would ultimately end, but it was likely the best game the Big 3 collectively played together given the circumstances, opponent, and stage.

"It was on our shoulders," LeBron said. "We had to figure out how to win the game for us and play at the highest level. When all three of us are clicking, we're very tough to beat."

"We knew if we lose that game, this team is going to be really, really tough to beat three times in a row," said Bosh rhetorically.

The Heat withstood an early 10-3 deficit replete with Neal and Green three pointers (who said one game has no impact on the next?) and Bosh shook off a cool start to actually lead after the first quarter, behind 11 points from LeBron and 10 from Wade.

What looked like a runaway win for the Heat quickly unraveled, as the veteran Spurs erased a 10-point deficit midway through the second quarter and tied the game by halftime. But by the time the fourth quarter arrived, so did vintage *Flash*.

With LeBron taking a fourth quarter breather, Wade looked every part the player that in 2008 and 2009 was firmly in the conversation for best player in the league. He hit his patented midrange jumpers, push shots in the lane, jumped passing lanes and then euro stepped over Gary Neal for a dunk and sneered running back on defense.

"They're too good in these situations," marveled Jeff Van Gundy on the ABC broadcast.

A byproduct of Wade going supernova was it bought LeBron more time to rest. Wade hunted mismatches, getting Duncan in isolation up top and drilling a long two, then getting Diaw switched onto him and finding Bosh near the rim. It seemed contagious: soon after, Toronto Bosh arrived, facing up and stepping back right over Duncan.

LeBron finally re-entered just past the halfway point of the fourth, but that didn't stop Wade from continuing his marvelous effort, cutting hard on a Ray Allen drive and finishing over Duncan to stretch the lead to 15.

With the game virtually decided and the Heat in the mode of milking down the clock, LeBron likely set the stage for his performances in the remainder of the series, knocking down three jump shots in quasi garbage time.

When the horn sounded, what had emerged was not only a Heat win to even the series, but one of the best combined performances by the Big 3. Combining for 75 points, 30 rebounds, 10 steals, and five blocks, together outscoring the entire Spurs' starting five. It was likely Bosh's best game in a month and probably Wade's best game in three.

"It was all about myself, Chris and LeBron coming out and leading this team to a victory," Wade said.

"The thing we talked about is we all have to make an impact in this game, somehow, some way."

"Wade did what the Spanish settlers who colonized Florida could not when he found the Fountain of Youth," wrote *Bleacher Report*'s Daniel Keller.

"When Bosh, Wade and James score the way they did tonight and shoot it the way they did tonight, a team is going to have a difficult time if you help them like we did," Spurs coach Gregg Popovich said.

"When those guys are playing like that, you better be playing a perfect game."

The Spurs hadn't played a perfect game in the series, nor had the Heat. Both teams had ridden hot quarters and halves to each of their two wins apiece. But with the win, Miami guaranteed themselves at least one more home game in the 2-3-2 Finals format.

The lingering question was, for both teams, which team could sustain the highest amount of consistency the longest? All four games had virtually been decided by one team having a prolonged run, alternating by team each game.

Game five started like the others in the series, tied at 17 apiece when LeBron drilled a three pointer with 4:45 in the first quarter. The Heat, trying to avoid the scenario of winning two do or die games at home, would find themselves down 13 only four minutes and forty-five seconds later. A Spurs flurry was exacerbated by the Heat trying to decide which they liked better, missing bad shots or turning the ball over. But, as the Heat had done so often all up and down their schedule, clawed back and only trailed by one late in the third. Before you could blink, the game was headed to the fourth quarter and the Spurs were back up by 12.

Decent games from the Big 3 (66 points combined) couldn't overcome all the Spurs starters in double figures on an overwhelming 64% from the floor.

"They just absolutely outplayed us," Spo said, clearly exasperated. "At times they were just picking one guy out at a time and going at us mano-a-mano. That's got to change."

It couldn't change in just the next game; it had to change in both. Otherwise, a season tracking toward history would end — if not as bitterly as 2011, then only slightly less so.

"This is the position we're in and the most important game is Game 6," LeBron said. "We can't worry about a Game 7, we have to worry about Game 6."

"We're going to see if we're a better ballclub and if we're better prepared for this moment," Wade added, alluding to the last time Miami trailed in Finals 3-2. If it was any consolation, the Lakers only three years before had come back from down 3-2 to win the Finals, claiming victories in the final two games at home against the prideful Celtics.

"It may be shallow, it may be narrow-minded and it may be unfair," wrote Brian Windhorst. "But it is also reality and there's little use talking around it.

"The next three days will define these three years for the Miami Heat."

Tom Haberstroh felt it was likely the burden LeBron had carried for the duration of the playoffs was beginning to catch up with him, showing signs of exhaustion in game five that were abnormal and weren't seen in the regular season.

"When James struggles in the Finals, the general public immediately points to psychological factors to explain his dropoff," wrote Haberstroh "He is mentally weak. He shrinks under the pressure. He lacks Michael Jordan's killer instinct.

"But what if it has nothing to do with that? What if his body is failing him? What if it's a simple case of physical exhaustion?"

That may have been the case. What was undeniable, however, was that even if LeBron's play had dipped in the Finals, nearly the entire rest of the Heat roster's play had cratered entirely. The bench gave them next to nothing, Wade and Bosh had struggled even more mightily than LeBron with a much lesser load, and the defense that had caused so many opponents to wither under the pressure was too often forcing the Heat themselves to shrivel, capitulating to the ball movement of the Spurs.

Whatever the reasons for the Heat's inconsistency — after winning 27 in a row, they hadn't strung together two wins since the end of the Chicago series and the start of the Indiana series more than three weeks earlier — Windhorst wrote that none of it would matter. If the Heat lost the series, it would simply be branded as a choke job.

The 66 wins, the 27-game winning streak, the record field goal shooting, the MVP award, the Birdman, all of it will go to the fine print.

No, this isn't normal. Usually, it's the other way around. Usually the victor gets the spoils, at least on the public perception front. But the Heat are one of the greatest outlier teams in American professional sporting history. They live by a different set of rules, like it or not.

It may cause eye-rolling to bring it up again, but when James uttered the phrase "taking my talents to South Beach," it changed everything.

Game six was game six and nothing more, only a liar would tell himself. The Heat undoubtedly had played better at home in the playoffs, but the Spurs, on both ends, were obviously their toughest opponent; while defensively they weren't the bludgeoning, physical prototype of an Indiana or Chicago, they were almost more malleable and thus harder for Miami to tilt. Indiana and Chicago never truly seemed like a long-term problem for the Heat, more of an annoyance and a true dedication to playing a certain way for an entire series.

Offensively, however, San Antonio was in a class only occupied by the Heat. The ball movement, the shooting, the ball handling with Parker, it all was much harder to defend than bruising, plodding, 1990s sets. And more exhausting, too.

"I guarantee you the Spurs didn't book their hotel rooms for enough nights to get them through Game 7," said Ray Allen years later. "Teams do that sometimes as a way to pump themselves up: 'Let's check out of our hotels before Game Six because there's not going to be a Game Seven.'"

"Yup, it's another 'LeBron's legacy is at stake!' game," wrote Bill Simmons after the game five shellacking "We're up to like 12 for his career, and really, Game 6 against Boston should have ended the legacy stuff once and for all. But now we're here. Again.

"As always with LeBron, it's a little unfair. He has played an unfathomable amount of minutes since Christmas of 2011 — 138 of 148 regular-season games, 44 playoff games (and counting), plus everything in the 2012 Olympics to boot — and it's hard to remember another NBA team asking more from its best player. He's the Heat's leading scorer, rebounder and assist guy, their main creator, their best playmaker and their best defender. He plays four positions for them. He's averaged a whopping 42 minutes per game these last two postseasons — just an unconscionable workload considering everything they ask from him, and if you don't think we're seeing the side effects lately, you're crazy."

"They've lived in the fishbowl of pressure for three years," Tim Reynolds said. "And yes, they've never faced anything quite like this. But at the same time, they're not going to be phased by win or go home."

BROTHERHOOD was the only message on Spo's pre-game whiteboard.

The Heat played probably their most cohesive, smooth offensive quarter of the series in the first quarter of game six. Chalmers scored 10 points in the frame including two threes, Battier, long ago buried on the bench, banked in a three of his own. He had been shooting so poorly, Spo hadn't even bothered to play him in game seven of the Indiana series.

"Worst slump of my career after having the best shooting year of my entire career," Battier admitted. "So broke...I'd never been that bad for that long, ever."

Bill Simmons later recalled running into Battier during the Finals. He asked him, "You alright?" Battier just shook his head. "I don't know, man." Simmons pressed: "What are they telling you about not playing?" Battier's answer was blunt: "They're not telling me anything." Simmons laughed and asked, "Can I even say that on TV?" Battier shot back, "I don't care."

Battier had seemingly found the issue to his shooting woes: every time he shot, the ball drifted right.

"In golf and all a sudden you're slicing the ball to the right, you aim it more left," he said matter of factly. "I'm just going to shoot left a good four inches...I was trying to hit the left side of the rim."

It seemed to be working.

LeBron added five points early. The only problem was, San Antonio wasn't budging. Duncan was superb, 12 points on six shots, and San Antonio only trailed by two.

"We're on pace now for the game to be about in the 120s," marveled Mike Breen at the efficiency of both teams.

Neither Bosh nor Birdman had any luck slowing Duncan in the second quarter. He put on a classic low-post clinic, carving out deep position and dropping in soft shots around the paint. By halftime, he had already notched the most first-half points of his Finals career. A fortunate bounce with under two minutes left sparked a 6–0 Spurs run, and the Heat, scoreless for the final 4:30, went into the break trailing.

"We need to hold the fort," was Spo's halftime message. "Regardless of what happens."

A six-point lead wasn't alone going to do in the Heat. But as Jeff Van Gundy mentioned as the second half began, the Heat had no fast break points because of the Spurs' efficiency offensively, shooting 58%.

After Wade had knocked knees in the first half, the Heat started Ray Allen in his place, putting three shooters around LeBron and Bosh. The hope surely was to open up the floor a smidge more and flip the script by putting some pressure on the San Antonio defense.

But the Heat looked more like the second quarter Heat than the first quarter, and faced a deadly ten-point deficit heading into the fourth quarter of what was looking like their second shocking Finals loss in three seasons.

"We need our best defensive quarter of the playoffs to take us home," a clearly concerned Spo told Doris Burke between quarters.

A nervous "Let's go Heat" chant broke out as the fourth quarter began and LeBron collapsed the defense to find Chalmers for a corner three.

Spo was sending out the lineup that had completely changed Miami's fortunes in game two, LeBron and Chalmers with Birdman and two dead eye shooters in Allen and Miller. LeBron loved the lineups that gave him the most shooting and less condensed floors; it showed as he got right to the rim via a semi transition drag screen to cut the Spurs lead in half in two possessions. How long could Popovich leave Duncan on the bench without suffering on both ends? "Splitter is not nearly the rim protector that Duncan is," Van Gundy said succinctly.

Splitter quickly scored under the hoop, possibly buying Duncan a few more seconds on the pine. As Splitter scored, Miller's shoe got stepped on from behind. He picked up the shoe and ran down the sideline, throwing it to the Heat bench and running around in only socks on his left foot. He trotted across the free throw line to the opposite wing, his defender either discounting his threat playing in one shoe or intentionally trying to get the ball out of LeBron's hands left him to defend next to Diaw at the top of the key. LeBron with no hesitation ripped a pass to Miller, who of course knocked down the three.

Popovich probably let the Heat off the hook by taking a timeout immediately. As the ABC broadcast went to break highlighting Miller's big possession, Breen marveled, "On one sneaker! Not going to affect his shooting stroke, how about this?! One on, one off, count it!"

"Shoes are overrated!" Van Gundy added.

"I don't think it matters what the dude has on," smirked Battier later. "No shoe, no problem."

It felt like the shot in the arm the Heat needed.

LeBron answered a Splitter one handed banker with a dunk as the roll man and then recovered a Chalmers air ball for another dunk. The lead was three, and the raucous Miami crowd was back and engaged. Moments later, LeBron took Leonard to the post and scored a left-handed scoop.

"The power of shooting gives James more space on the floor in that back-in move," Van Gundy explained.

Wade and Bosh were still planted firmly on the Heat bench, but the shooting lineup may have been the secret sauce to get Miami back in the game and have a chance.

The Heat nearly paid for a blown box-out when an offensive rebound kicked out to Danny Green on the wing, but he missed the open look. On the next trip, as Duncan shaded over to help against LeBron isolating Parker, LeBron slipped a pass to Birdman ducking in along the baseline on Ginobili. The foul that followed sent him to the line for free throws.

LeBron wasn't only creating everything offensively; on the very next possession he snuck all the way off Parker on the wing to block Duncan who would have had an uncontested layup. This time, as opposed to the game two rejection of Splitter, LeBron didn't loiter at the other end, flexing, as the kids say. He got the ball in semi transition, screaming around another drag screen to meet Duncan deep in the paint. Unbothered, he used a textbook step through move to tie the game. A ten-point deficit had evaporated in just over five minutes.

"What a defensive play by LeBron James!" marveled Van Gundy, insinuating at the play that had led to the points.

Danny Green, who had hit an ungodly 30 three pointers in the first five games (on an astronomical 56%) missed a corner three. In the scramble for the rebound, Miller and Duncan ended up in the stands and Miami, while playing an even four-on-four, had San Antonio in uncomfortable crossmatches, and found more money in the couch as Allen drove baseline for a reverse layup and the token Popovich timeout to stop the bleeding.

Out of the timeout, Spo swapped Birdman for Bosh, giving Miami more defensive versatility and an extra shooting threat. The floor opened up, and LeBron went straight to the post against Diaw, knowing help wouldn't come. And if it did, four shooters waited on the weak side. No help came—easy layup.

"They (the Spurs) can't be paralyzed by the shooting," Van Gundy said.

Bosh and Chalmers forced a turnover out of the pick and roll in vintage Miami fashion, length meeting ferocity in trapping a pet Spurs action.

Wade checked in at the 3:48 mark for Miller in what may have been more a need to get Miller a blow than a need for Wade to be in the game.

But he quickly made an impact, altering what would have been a Parker open shot and then snaring a rebound on a Duncan miss, sweeping across the lane.

Parker drilled a top of the key three right over LeBron after a solid Miami defensive possession, tying the game in dramatic fashion. Before the deadeye shot, Parker had knocked down one single three in the series.

With under a minute and a half to go, it was time for the vaunted clutch offense that Haberstroh had so glowingly researched to rear its head and get to a game seven.

Instead, everything unraveled.

Chalmers turned it over in the key, Parker hit a short reverse pivot shot, LeBron turned it over deep in the paint, Ginobili knocked down two free throws, and LeBron turned it over again trying to force the issue.

"As soon as that happens it's like 'ahhhhhhhhhhhh' you hear this collective groan and you're reliving 2011," admitted Bosh.

Moments earlier, it looked like Miami was going to grind out a season-saving win and force game seven. Instead, players stared at each other in disbelief as Ginobili split free throws to put San Antonio up 94–89 with 28.2 seconds left.

Cameras caught LeBron in the final huddle of regulation, his face betraying a mix of dejection and nerves. Leads had been erased before, but never in a game like this. The only path forward was perfection for the final 28.2 seconds.

More than a dozen yellow plaid security folks were kneeling on the Heat baseline with a yellow rope in tow, preparing for the inevitable Spurs championship trophy presentation. "That's the worst thing a home team could ever see," bemoaned Eric Reid on the local broadcast.

"Your heart is sinking," he added later.

"It shifted from not very hopeful to dismal," said Bosh.

"This can't be happening, we can't go down like this," Allen said to himself.

"I was stupefied, I was confused," said Le Batard.

"It was dark," Wade said, shaking his head.

"You feel a little doubt at that point," said LeBron. "But at the same time, as a competitor, you say, 'Okay, we got less than 30 seconds, we got an opportunity to make a game out of this.'"

LeBron got free for an open straightaway three that missed badly; while he had been spectacular in the fourth, all his points were on free throws and shots in close, the jumper had not been working.

The Spurs, ever a fundamentally sound team if there was one, had textbook boxouts below the free throw line. Leonard leapt for the rebound, but Wade somehow poked the ball out straight up in the air. Diaw, Ginobili, and Leonard all leapt again, but none were able to corral the ball. It ricocheted off Allen and squirted right to Miller who flipped to LeBron for another three. The line drive desperation shot went in.

After the Spurs' final timeout, the Heat brilliantly defended the inbounds, forcing Duncan to beat the inbounds violation by finding Leonard near the timeline, the Spurs' worst free throw shooter.

Bill Simmons wrote about the pressure cooker Leonard faced:

After Miller fouled Leonard with 19.4 seconds left, he strolled impassively to the free throw line, with Miami's rejuvenated crowd suffocating him with boos and screams. I remember thinking, Forget about making these free throws — I wonder if this kid is hitting the rim. Leonard sized up those freebies, the clatter bouncing off him, a Spurs collapse suddenly in play. How many current players could have nailed these specific free throws? Maybe 10 total? Leonard clanged the first one. Mayhem. He made the second one, and by the way, I will always respect Kawhi for making that second one. Three-point game.

"One thing I notice...you can feel shaking...sometimes the basket moves, sometimes you're moving," said Bosh. "My hand is shaking because the stadium is shaking and you're supposed to make it. That's tough. Our game plan if we can foul anybody the worst foul shooter is Kawhi Leonard at 69%. It just kind of worked out."

LeBron meandered around a stagger screen, coming back towards the Heat bench to line up a three to tie. Diaw and Parker both lunged to contest as Bosh shuffled towards the hoop, watching the arc of the ball. For a moment there were no Spurs within several feet of him, but LeBron's three was off, kicking off the rim then the backboard.

Bosh, the tallest player on the floor by several inches with Duncan on the bench, ripped the ball away from Ginobili, who fell to the floor.

"When LeBron took that deep three, I followed it my whole way to the basket," explained Bosh. "One of the earliest and most helpful pieces of advice I ever got on rebounding was, 'All you have to do is get there before the ball does.' And as I played more and got better, I became better at watching the flight of the ball, trying to drill it into the point that it's automatic. Sometimes, watching can be dangerous—you can take an elbow to the face pretty easily. But not this time; no one was boxing me out that play. So, I watched the ball, figured out where it was going, ran there, and grabbed it... it didn't feel like traffic to me."

Leonard, Parker, and Green all converged on Bosh, who calmly looked to pass the ball out behind the three point line. He didn't have to look far. Ray Allen was back peddling to the corner right in Bosh's line of sight.

"I saw him right there the whole time," said Bosh. "There was nobody else to pass it to but him."

Allen caught the ball as his back foot crossed behind the three point line and almost instantly released a low, penetrating three.

"When he released it, I remember being under the rim," remembered Wade, "I was like, 'Oh my god, it's going in.'"

"*BANG!*" exclaimed Breen.

Boris Diaw tried to inbound the ball, but was stopped by referee Joey Crawford. They were going to review the play to ensure Allen had been behind the three point line. Popovich, as per usual, was incensed.

"You can't do that!" he bellowed.

The stoppage gave the Spurs a chance to draw up a full-court play, but it also let the Heat settle their defense, knowing there would be no substitutions or timeouts left for either side.

The sequence unfolded so quickly that the referees' pause became a gift—enough time for replays to roll and for everyone to process what had just happened. Out of nowhere, Allen had conjured a season-saving three, only after Bosh had slipped into the lane untouched to snatch the rebound.

The shot itself was remarkable, but Allen's instincts made it unforgettable. Instead of sprinting blindly to the corner, he backpedaled into Bosh's line of sight, set his feet, and released with Parker draped over him—defending as tightly as he could without fouling. It was breathtaking.

"Once the ball came off the rim, I just knew to get to the three-point line," Allen said. "We needed a three. Two points isn't going to cut it. So, my mental checklist is really to have my legs ready and underneath me so when the ball comes, if it comes, I was ready to go in the air."

"Nobody in NBA history was better prepared for this moment," remarked Simmons.

The Spurs' home arena was filled with fans, partying and watching game six on the jumbotron. What was elation at James' miss turned into a symphony of 20,000 groans and oh no's.

The only path forward was perfection for the final 28.2 seconds.

San Antonio had their chance to win the series at the horn, but a full court dash by Parker turned into a tough fadeaway from the baseline over LeBron that fell harmlessly short.

"Get those motherfucking ropes out of here!" Allen shouted to the security on the baseline as the Heat ran to the bench.

"Ray never swears, and when he made that shot, he looked over at the ushers and said get that blankin' tape outta here," remembered Eric Reid.

No, the Heat hadn't won the Finals, much less game six yet. A highly emotional overtime was still on deck.

"What a rollercoaster ride here in the fourth quarter!" remarked Breen as cameras showed LeBron, reinvigorated, slapping hands on the bench.

As much momentum or second life Allen's shot had given the Heat, it didn't immediately transfer to the overtime as the Heat missed a pair of contested midrange shots. But after a cross-match had Bosh guarding Parker, LeBron secured a rebound and found Bosh leaking out behind the Spurs' trotting transition defense for a twisting reverse layup while being fouled by Ginobili.

Miami looked to be making a concerted effort to run off ball actions with LeBron initiating, seemingly saving him for his defense on Parker. Allen curled around a free throw line screen for a short jumper. When LeBron did get a favorable matchup with the slower Diaw on him, Miami cleared out all to the weak side. As he drove, Spurs began to bleed into the paint. He kicked to Wade who drove baseline and flipped back to LeBron who quickly made a short floater to take the lead 101-100.

The Heat ratcheted up the temperature on their defense, almost fighting each other to guard Parker. Bosh altered a Leonard shot and then Allen blocked a Parker heave to beat the shot clock.

Bosh, inside a minute to go, tipped a Parker shot on a switch. LeBron ended up with the ball, but the Heat possession to put all the pressure on the Spurs came up empty, a clanked long two from Wade with 12 seconds left.

After everything that had unfolded, could the Heat really still lose? The wild swings—from leading late, to down five with 28.2 seconds left, to somehow forcing overtime—made it feel possible.

Popovich kept his timeout, trusting his veterans. Ginobili attacked Allen, barreling into the paint. Allen, never known as a stopper but always a willing defender, stripped Parker clean and came up with the ball on the baseline. Fouled on the play, one of the game's great free throw shooters suddenly had the chance to seal it and push the Finals to a deciding Game 7.

Chalmers shook his fist with 1.9 seconds left knowing what was coming.

Allen sank both. 103-100 Miami. While Allen's corner three wasn't literally the coup de grace for San Antonio, the free throws may well have been.

One more stop was all that was left now. While Spo had said the Heat needed their best defensive quarter of the playoffs in the fourth, what they really needed was their best defensive possession of the playoffs. Popovich, a master of the marker, was sure to draw up a play that would get a decent enough look to tie the game.

The set was a decoy screen by Splitter for Green coming towards the ball, only to flip the screen and have Green go back over it, all the way across the court from Duncan inbounding, right up along the Spurs bench. Allen got slightly hung up by a moving screen by Splitter (rarely called in last moment situations), but Bosh recognized the play quickly, sprinting to meet Green in the corner.

"Blocked by Bosh! Game over!" Breen roared. "There'll be a game seven!"

Bosh hopped, fists in the air in triumph.

"It took every second, it took every inch of wingspan to win that game," said Battier.

"You can never, ever, *ever* give up," Pat Riley said glowingly later.

"The Miami Heat not ready for their season to end," said Breen, attempting to narrate a whirlwind of a game that was hard to process in real time. "Chris Bosh with some extraordinary plays at both ends of the floor."

The game was an instant classic, the stakes palpable throughout. "It's by far the best game I've ever been a part of," LeBron said.

"You know when people are witnessing something historic, then claim they never realized the importance until after the fact?" wrote Bill Simmons for *Grantland*, trying himself to digest what he had witnessed live. "With Game 6 of the 2013 NBA Finals, you knew. You knew the entire time. The first 47 minutes and 31.8 seconds had already earned Game 6 a lifetime of NBA TV replays. But what happened next? That's what made it stupendous."

The key figures had made massive plays, from Duncan and Parker, to LeBron, Bosh, and of course Allen.

Allen would get the credit deserved for the astronomical shot to send the game to overtime, underscoring that he also had half the Heat points in overtime.

"There's never been a greater NBA shot," Simmons opined. "With all due respect to Jordan's iconic jumper against the '98 Jazz, Allen's shot had similar clutchness, bigger stakes and a higher degree of difficulty. If you or I caught that pass as we were backpedaling, then launched a desperation 3 with someone running at us, we'd screw up every time."

"When that ball left his hand, I'm like *that's good...*I go *oh shit* that's all I could say," said Battier. "At that point, you're like we're a team of destiny."

"It's the greatest shot ever," summed up Zach Lowe. "It's why they signed Ray Allen. It's not an accident he hit that shot."

"If you put in the work, the ball's always gonna come to you, and you have to be ready to answer the bell," said Allen. "That shot was the culmination of everything that I did in my career."

The shot would also overshadow how crucial Bosh had been on both ends, his ability to switch and defend Parker had flipped several critical possessions, while also being the primary defender of Duncan, who had tortured the Heat, mostly in the first half.

Who could forget Miller, not only hitting two threes (the shoeless one in the fourth forever underrated in NBA history) but securing several clutch rebounds including the offensive board leading to LeBron's three to get the Heat within two under 20 seconds to play.

Chalmers had 20 points on 7 for 11 shooting, playing the entire fourth quarter and overtime and running through God knows how many screens chasing around Ginobili and Green.

Battier, who had struggled mightily all playoffs, knocked down three threes in 13 minutes.

And then there was LeBron. It takes something extraordinary for any athlete struggling all night to dig deeper and conjure greatness out of nowhere. That's exactly what he did. After three forgettable quarters, he turned into a menace in the fourth — scoring or assisting on every point of the Heat's run that wiped out the 10-point deficit.

"He just made plays. I don't think there's any two ways to put it," Duncan said. "We were in the right position to close it out and he found a way to put his team over the top and we just didn't make enough plays to do that."

He defended Parker for most of the fourth and overtime, along with Bosh virtually erasing the Spurs' most dynamic threat (only six points in the last 17 minutes of the game).

"Ultimately, this is why LeBron is held to such a high standard," wrote Paul Flannery for *SB Nation*, "because he reached a level that few players have ever been able to match."

"He played like he was in Akron in high school," marveled Jalen Rose on the postgame show.

"LeBron's fourth quarter, for about nine minutes there, and I was at Boston game six last year, that's the best I've ever seen him play," Bill Simmons added.

"What LeBron James did in the fourth quarter ... holy hell," wrote Zach Lowe for *Grantland*. "All non-Spurs fans should be glad he came through like that, even though he was indeed in attack mode almost from the opening tip, because the volume on the 'WHAT IS LEBRON'S LEGACY!!!???' talk can shift down a couple of notches."

"We seen the championship board already out there, the yellow tape. And you know, that's why you play the game to the final buzzer," James said. "And that's what we did tonight. We gave it everything that we had and more."

The Heat had truly escaped. But for the Spurs, it felt like they'd let the title slip straight through their fingers, much of it self-inflicted. Some players looked stunned, even hollow, trying to process what had just unraveled. For a team as professional and steady as San Antonio, the thought of a championship had been so close — especially with under a minute left — that losing it now was almost unthinkable.

"It's a tough moment. We were a few seconds away from winning the championship and we let it go," Ginobili said, visibly upset. "A couple rebounds we didn't catch, a tough three by Ray and a couple missed free throws. It's a very tough moment."

"I have no clue how we're going to be re-energized," he added. "I'm devastated. But we have to. There's no Game 8 afterwards. We're going to have to play our best game, even better than today. Shoot better, better defense, less turnovers in my case, but, yeah, there's no secret recipe for bouncing back."

"I thought that was the worst loss in 25 years," Simmons said on the postgame show, zero punches pulled. "You can't come closer to winning a title and not win the title... this game, you win 99 out of 100 times."

"I have never seen a Spurs team play with that lack of composure and that lack of poise," an exasperated Michael Wilbon added.

How either team would respond after such an emotionally charged, physically draining Game 6 — where the game, series, and season all swung in an instant — was impossible to predict.

At dinner after the game, Bosh said he couldn't even speak. "I was in a daze for 24 hours," he said.

"You're somewhere in this euphoric state of dissociation between mind and body, but you can still feel a little of both," he tried to explain later.

"I walked into the locker room, and Mike Miller goes, 'There he is,'" recalled Ray Allen. "We'd all be in here packing up our shit if it wasn't for you."

The two days off were either a chance to reset or a torturous loop of replaying game six.

"I don't know if the Spurs can recover from this," Magic Johnson said grimly. "When you've got the championship in your hand, on the road, you gotta seize the moment."

San Antonio knew heartbreak. They'd lost to Derek Fisher's 0.4 miracle in 2004, then watched Dirk Nowitzki force overtime in game seven of the 2006 West Finals before Dallas finished it off on the Spurs' floor. Cruel as it sounded, the Spurs had been here before.

Duncan said the team went to dinner and would be ready for game seven.

Bosh said, "Kids are the best medicine cause they don't care anything about the game." He said the butterflies were gone after having fought them off for game six.

LeBron reportedly had tried to calm his mind watching SpongeBob with his kids.

The Heat was favored, for whatever that was worth. The Spurs, however, were 4-0 following a loss in the postseason.

The First Take blowhards, of course, picked the Spurs to win the title in game seven.

"If there is a team that has the ability to overcome such a collapse, it's the San Antonio Spurs," proclaimed Stephen A. Smith.

"I have resolution, I have conviction, I remain completely confident in my pick," Bayless blowed hard, "that the Spurs tonight will play a similar game to game six... except this time, my Spurs will make the championship plays down the stretch that will win them their fifth ring."

LeBron would not be braving the South Florida streets on a bike to arrive for game seven, but rather a black Porsche convertible.

Right before tip off, Mike Breen twisted the knife in the Spurs, but only speaking the truth: "That championship was right there, oh they were so close, a *crushing* defeat. So, the question is, how do they bounce back? Emotionally and on the basketball court?"

"It's not fatal nor final," the always succinct Van Gundy said.

Immediately, nerves didn't seem to be an issue, playing too loose may have been: Chalmers threw a lazy pass that was stolen and Duncan tried passing out of a double team quickly right into Chalmers' hands to start the game.

But Duncan looked like the first half Duncan of game six, tipping in a shot and then jumping another lazy pass for an uncontested dunk.

The Spurs opened up a quick 11-4 lead, but the Heat stayed the course. Battier, who had been so poor in the playoffs, hit two threes.

"After I hit the first two, I said, *oh boy...* this could be my Picasso," remembered Battier.

Andersen, so crucial in the shooting lineups with LeBron, put back a Chalmers miss.

The second quarter was a clinic in "ragged" basketball, as Breen said, both teams scoring, but the play was disjointed by a tight whistle and seemingly a Spurs trip to the line every trip down the floor. Battier hit another three, Parker and Duncan got to the line and scored easily. But the Spurs were only biding their time before the game bent to an unstoppable truth: LeBron.

The story was well-known six years later, but in LeBron's first Finals appearance in 2007, San Antonio had stifled the shaky young star by daring him to shoot, sagging way off and making him beat them with the jump shot. In no uncertain terms, it went poorly for LeBron, averaging a pedestrian 22 points on 35% shooting from the floor, and making a total of four threes in the four-game sweep.

San Antonio had gone back to the well in these Finals, laying far off LeBron once again, and up to that point, winning much of the battle. LeBron had been hesitant to shoot open jumpers, and when he did shoot, looked out of rhythm and uncomfortable. It was crazy coming from an MVP who not only was at the top of his game but had shot career highs from the floor *and* three point range during the season.

Lee Jenkins wrote:

> *Before Game 7, Miami assistant David Fizdale showed James cut-ups of the San Antonio defense leaving him alone near the free-throw line. Then coaches underlined his sterling percentages in that area this season. "Even the best have self-doubt at times when what they're doing isn't working," James says. "You need a reminder." He does not study hot zones, but he does watch old tapes. He found one that was taken last summer in his high-school gym, at St. Vincent-St. Mary, when he was burnishing his J. "Why would you abandon this thing*

As magnificent as he had been in the fourth quarter of game six, everything was deep in the paint, driving, rolling, rebounding, and posting up. He had made three shots outside the paint in game five and six.

So, when, on a stalled possession, LeBron dribbled into a straightaway three with his defender, Green, nearly six feet off of him, it felt like another Spurs win on the possession. LeBron drilled it.

A few minutes later, Allen found LeBron in the corner. A quick pass fake led to a wide open three. Nothing but net.

"They're daring him to shoot, but he's hit two," announced Breen.

LeBron did his final work of the half on the offensive glass, boxing out Parker for a tip in off a Wade missed jumper.

The Heat clung to a two point halftime lead after Wade knocked down a jumper over Leonard with under a second left in the half to cap off a 7 for 12 first half from the field.

"Just being aggressive," he told ABC's Doris Burke at the half.

The Spurs cut the Heat lead down to a single point, but the process may have belied the result; Bosh found LeBron for an uncontested corner three and soon thereafter, LeBron found Wade in a broken transition play for a dunk. LeBron, now taking the Spurs' open invitation to shoot uncontested threes, hit two more.

"Five threes, and no one remotely in the same area on any," said Van Gundy. "These are like practice shots."

LeBron, once again taking the Spurs' game plan and twisting it against them, drilled a long two.

As hot as LeBron was, and as much as both teams had settled in for the game seven bar fight, the Heat trailed by three with 46 seconds left in the third. But between tough layups from Neal and Parker, Battier hit a three off a Chalmers skip pass and then Chalmers beat the buzzer dribbling into, and banking, a long straight away three.

"Never afraid to take the big shot," Breen said of Chalmers.

One quarter left, one point apart. Neither team blinked. The lifeline Miami had snatched in game six hadn't broken San Antonio's will. Game seven was a pressure cooker at its finest.

LeBron, Wade, and Battier were the Heat's offense in the fourth. Battier hit a corner three to start the fourth, and LeBron and Wade alternated hitting tough midrange shots.

Battier's sixth three of the game gave the Heat a six-point cushion nearing the three minute mark, but the ageless Duncan quickly converted a three point play to cut the lead in half.

"Bosh can't believe it," Breen said of his fifth foul.

"I can't either," Van Gundy admitted.

Undeterred, Miami, out of a timeout, ran a nice curl action for Wade off a LeBron pindown to reassert the lead at five.

"Gorgeous bounce pass from Battier!" remarked Breen.

LeBron and Duncan exchanged misses before Kawhi Leonard hit his first three of the game with exactly two minutes to go.

The Heat walked the ball up, both teams visibly tired and not wanting to be the one to make the back-breaking and championship-defining mistake.

"Wade looks absolutely exhausted out there!" remarked Breen as the game ground to a near halt.

The Heat ran a halfhearted action, swinging the ball down the sideline in front of the Heat bench before Chalmers attacked late in the clock and inexplicably was fouled by Duncan.

The ever-confident Chalmers front rimmed both free throws.

Leonard missed a three on the ensuing possession on what looked originally like a busted defensive coverage by the Heat, only for Battier to sprint back into the picture and contest the three, which fell harmlessly short and bounded out.

Miami, undeniably, had dodged two bullets.

Wade couldn't get a mid range jumper to fall, and the LeBron rebound and kick out to the red hot Battier also yielded nothing.

The lead was only two now with under a minute left, reminiscent of two nights earlier.

LeBron gambled and failed at stealing a pass to Green near the timeline forcing Bosh to scramble to guard Green and Battier to try to defend the future Hall of Famer Duncan, well-sealed behind him on the left block. The Spurs quickly and wisely got the ball to their beloved center. Against the smaller Battier, Duncan took one dribble to the middle and then stretched up for a half hook as Battier reached to try to deflect the ball.

Duncan's shot was a little strong, caroming straight back. Battier, still scrambling to defend the behemoth, had a good body on a box out, forcing Duncan to try to tip it back in with one hand over the leaping Battier.

"I'm 215 pounds and 6-foot-8, so obviously I'm giving up major weight and height to Duncan," Battier said. "So, I was just praying that he missed it."

"The tip no good! And Bosh the rebound!" Breen said on the call.

Duncan was visibly upset, a rarity for the stoic MVP. He slapped the floor in disgust as he settled in a defensive stance.

"A point-blank miss by Duncan, and then the follow," a perplexed Van Gundy commented as Miami took a timeout.

Duncan leaned, hands on knees, head down in heartbreak.

He'd been brilliant all series, especially in games six and seven, which made the misery on his face all the more crushing. During the timeout he buried his head in his hands, frustration pouring out of him.

Could San Antonio pull off what Miami had just two nights earlier?

It wasn't impossible. Miami passed on a 2-for-1, running clock while LeBron waited for a Chalmers screen. For maybe the first time all series, the Spurs went over the screen, Leonard tossing Chalmers aside as Parker hedged high on LeBron

The hedge only bumped LeBron off his intended path slightly, acting more as a screen of Parker's own teammate. Parker retreated to Chalmers, giving LeBron ample air space over the recovering Leonard to square up and rise just off the elbow.

"James pulls up... puts it in! Four-point lead!" Breen exclaimed.

As the solid white-out Miami crowd went into delirium, LeBron slapped hands on the way back to the bench, one of the biggest shots of his career, if not the biggest.

"I know it wasn't the magnitude of MJ hitting that shot in '98, but I definitely thought about him," LeBron said later to *Sports Illustrated*. "'It was an MJ moment.' He paused as a turn of phrase came to mind. 'It was an LJ moment.'"

"Good shot!" Mike Miller bellowed at LeBron, offering a high five.

"When he hit that shot, I knew we were going to win," Bosh said of the kill shot.

Ginobili threw the ball away on the ensuing play, right to LeBron to likely seal a championship.

For all his good measure, and truly a diamond in the rough as a second round pick for San Antonio, Ginobili was horrendous in games six and seven with 12 turnovers.

LeBron, as he almost always did in big playoff moments, knocked home the two free throws.

Ginobili air-balled a three right to Wade, who would get a chance at a rousing ovation if he could put down free throws of his own.

The first hit the front rim and spun in, making the game a three-possession game with a mere 16.3 seconds left and one sole timeout for San Antonio.

They would never get to use that timeout, as Wade missed the second free throw and Chalmers collected the offensive rebound after a tip out from Battier.

The Spurs elected not to foul, conceding the game, and championship.

Fans jumped up and down.

"That's the great thing about a close game in game seven, is to win it at the end, there's this *explosion*," said a beaming Pat Riley.

"The exhilaration that you feel is just incredible," added Mickey Arison, now a three-time champion as owner of the Heat.

Wade hopped around under the hoop before joining LeBron in seeking out the broken Duncan.

"Congratulations!" a beaming Popovich said as he hugged LeBron. "That's a fuckin' way to end it."

He planted a kiss on Wade in congratulations.

"What a wonderful display of sportsmanship and class from Gregg Popovich and the San Antonio Spurs," remarked Breen.

Wide angle TV cameras, much as they had with Bosh, caught Duncan plodding into the losing visitors' locker room, confetti stuck to the sweat on his forehead.

As the trophy was wheeled out, for real this time, and the yellow ropes fenced in the home team, LeBron wanted his mother, Gloria, in on the action.

"Mom, come on, come inside," he demanded.

"This is the hardest series we ever had to play," Wade, adorned in a championship hat, admitted to Doris Burke. "But we are a resilient team, and we did whatever it took."

As LeBron was presented the Finals MVP trophy for the second straight season, he was asked by Burke, "You are constantly faced with the din of noise from the outside, scrutiny and pressure. How, when everybody is coming at you, do you keep your head and perform at the level that you do?"

"I'm LeBron James, from Akron, Ohio, from the inner city," he said. "I'm not even supposed to be here. That's enough. Every night I walk into the locker room, I see a No. 6 with James on the back, I'm blessed. So, what everybody says about me off the court, don't matter. I ain't got no worries."

The crowd howled with delight.

The locker room celebration was more muted than 2012, for the simple fact of the sheer exhaustion.

Wade sat on the ground, trophy between his legs, talking to everyone and no one in particular: "That San Antonio Spurs team was a hell of a team. We had to give everything we had, and we did it. I ain't got nothin' left."

"They gave us everything they could," Battier said.

After the champagne had settled and the noise faded, Spo gathered the team around one final marker of their playoff journey: a black replica trophy, each win checked off in ink. The Bulls and Pacers were marked in red, a nod to the blood-and-grit series they fought through. The Spurs were marked in silver, a sign of the standard they represented and the respect they commanded.

"The vision that I had when I decided to come here is all coming true," LeBron said at the winner's podium.

LeBron and Wade partied into the night, Wade complaining of his arm getting sore from holding an oversized champagne bottle too long.

The Heat was back-to-back champions. What in March seemed like an inevitability turned into a miracle.

"Nobody's ever gone to the cliff in a series in the finals and actually won a series like that," said Bill Simmons.

But they were holding the trophy, nonetheless.

And just like 2012, it was a team effort. LeBron deservedly took most of the spotlight, especially after his heroics in the fourth quarter of game six and his dominance in game seven. But without the ripple of contributions from everyone else, the Heat almost certainly wouldn't have repeated as champions.

Mike Miller, benched and unbenched and re-benched, had eight points and seven rebounds in the most minutes he played in the playoffs, 30, in game six. "Erik Spoelstra's move to insert him into the starting lineup changed the series and rendered Tiago Splitter irrelevant," wrote the great Zach Lowe.

Shane Battier, benched virtually the entire playoffs, hit nine three pointers in games six and seven. "The two three pointers that I missed, I didn't shoot to the left," he said of game seven. He had also defended Duncan on the series' crucial possession.

Heat owner Mickey Arison had had a feeling. "I know Shane. When he starts hitting threes, he doesn't stop," he told Pat Riley between games six and seven. "I knew he would do it," Arison told *USA TODAY* Sports. "I knew it. That's what happened last year, and it happened again."

"He was outstanding," Spo said. "There's something about that guy. He has championship DNA. He's got it. He's won at every single level. As the series went on and the moments became more important, he had a bigger factor. That's not a coincidence."

"I believe in the basketball gods," Battier said. "I felt that they owed me big time. I had a bunch of shots in San Antonio that went in and out. So, when that banker went in, I said you know what, they owe me. It was the start of a pretty good streak there.

"Honestly, I felt good the last couple of games. And I made a couple of threes last game, and so I felt really confident tonight. I knew that our starters were going to be pretty tired after Game 6. It was an emotionally and physically draining game. I only played 12 minutes so I felt great."

Andersen had been such an energy jolt in the early rounds that he found himself firmly in the LeBron plus shooting lineup that turned game six.

Chalmers, though he missed key free throws, always played his best in the biggest games; he had three of his best games of the playoffs in three of the Heat's four Finals wins, including the banked three in game seven.

Ray Allen, the consummate pro, was asked to hold down the fort as an almost 38-year-old in the Finals. He never took possessions off, was always ready, and delivered the biggest play in Miami Heat, and maybe NBA, history in game six.

Wade's sacrifice was loud, obvious, the handing of the throne to LeBron. Bosh's was quieter, heavier. He gave up the post, absorbed the blame, and fought men bigger than him every night. Yet he was always where he needed to be—sliding over, switching out, boxing out, saving possessions. Game six was his proof, game seven his paradox: a scoreless night, but fingerprints everywhere.

He stayed underappreciated in the moment, destined to be fully seen only when his career was over. Because nothing in Miami worked without him. LeBron was the engine. Wade the accelerator. But Bosh? Bosh was the fuel, the hinge, the keystone of Spo's grand design—a small, switchable machine that reshaped the league.

"Lots of big men can space the floor, though only a few do so at Bosh's level, and those that do cannot defend from the rim to the midcourt line with Bosh's speed and disruptive long arms," Zach Lowe wrote glowingly.

"Bosh did everything for Miami's defense," analyzed Drew Garrison of *SB Nation*. "From playing a physical game against

Duncan to moving fluently and intelligently off-ball, Bosh was locked in."

And there was Wade. Damaged, battered, whatever word fit, it applied. The bone bruises had stolen much of his breathtaking lift, threatening to conquer him entirely. But Wade was never a one-note player. He leaned on guile, grit, and timing to summon his two best games in the playoffs—four and seven—when his team needed them most.

A lesser star might have bristled at sitting nearly an entire fourth quarter of an elimination game, as Wade did in game six. He didn't flinch. No complaints, no drama. Just humility.

Before game seven, his knee had to be drained. Eight hours of treatment just to suit up. And when the war was over and champagne sprayed, he poured some on the knee itself—a toast to the body that barely held up, but still delivered.

"He seems to always bring it when they need it the most," said Jalen Rose.

"Dwyane Wade has become the greatest unselfish superstar we have seen, ever," declared Magic Johnson.

And, of course, there was LeBron.

"A word about LeBron," Zach Lowe wrote. "It's over now. The noise needs to stop.

"He might be the game's best elimination-game player since Bill Russell," he continued, "and maybe the best ever... He's faced more big-stage moments than any player on earth over the last two seasons, and he's risen to all of them."

It was hard to imagine that in just almost exactly two calendar years, a meek LeBron that had bowed out of the Finals, untaping his wrists with hardly a mark on the Finals had transformed into *this guy*, dictating entire championship rounds in a tour de force rarely seen, against an organization that thought they had him completely figured out.

"If you still hate LeBron you really need a life coach...," tweeted Andre Iguodala of the Denver Nuggets. "And I'll sponsor you..."

"James remains on the NBA's mountaintop," wrote *Bleacher Report*'s Jimmy Spencer, "the king of the league despite the criticism and pressure that comes with being an active legend in a game overly analyzed in a way Michael Jordan, Larry Bird and Magic Johnson never knew.

"So much for shrinking in the moment," he continued.

"The narrative has fully been reversed. No one can take away James' two titles, and no one will forget his 32-point triple-double in Game 6 or his 37 points in Game 7."

He had done it all offensively, capped, of course, by the five three pointers in game seven, but he had also hounded Parker, as he had Derrick Rose, in key moments, showing that a man his size also had the quickness and mobility of a man much smaller.

"One of the best all-around games I've ever seen in a game seven from LeBron James," Bill Simmons mused.

"For reasons that are both his and the sports media's fault — and yes, this is my obligatory reference to The Decision — his basketball achievements and abilities are never appreciated for the cartoonish implausibilities that they actually represent," Gene Demby of NPR opined.

"There are many who give LeBron the type of credit that the best player in the world deserves, but there are so many more who do not," Dan Grunfeld of *SB Nation* wrote. "That's unfortunate, not because LeBron is perfect and immune to criticism (this is far from the truth), but rather because the storylines and narratives that focus on critiquing and evaluating all things LeBron often drown out the more meaningful reality: that LeBron James is one of the greatest basketball players we will ever have the privilege of watching. To be fair, most people readily acknowledge LeBron's incredible talent, but with all the noise created by the many 'click-worthy' LeBron stories that are concocted out there, do we take ample time to appreciate just how great this guy really is?"

In the fourth quarters of the final two games, Miami had ratcheted up the heat, pun intended, scoring an astounding 120.5 points per 100 possessions, while only allowing 84.1, an astronomical net rating of 36.4. Haberstroh had been correct months ago: the Heat in the clutch was otherworldly, and proved it on the largest and most pressure-filled stage.

Once upon a time, the Heat were the villains. But not anymore. Struggle has a way of softening edges, of turning arrogance into resilience. To fight, fall, and rise again makes a team feel more human, and in triumph, more respected. Miami hadn't just won—they had endured, escaped, and survived. And in that survival, they were no longer the villain but the worthy champion.

"Congrats to the heat," tweeted Dirk Nowitzki. "LeBron is the best player on the planet. Off to bed for a few more hours."

A championship, as much as talent took the limelight, was decided on the margins. The proverbial grain of rice tipping the scales was never more true than in a seven game Finals series.

"Each opponent that has been put in the way of James and his Heat teammates have brought their very best game and it's not been enough in the last two years," a column in CBS Miami wrote. "It's a testament to the vision of Heat president Pat Riley, the coaching of Erik Spoelstra, and the unmatchable talent of the best player in the game."

LeBron, only days after the exhausting game seven win, was watching a movie with his sons when he got word the Chicago Blackhawks had scored two goals in 17 seconds to take a late lead in Game 6 of the Stanley Cup Finals. He forced his boys to pause the movie and switch to the hockey final.

"I immediately pressed pause and got in trouble with my kids," he said. "And I turned to the end of the game and saw what had happened."

"When I saw them hoisting that Stanley Cup trophy, I was able to be like, 'I know exactly what that feeling's all about.'"

"It's something that I want again," he added. "Because the time goes fast. We won it Thursday night, and we've already had the parade, and now it's like, what do you do? It's the summer. For me, I'm obsessed with success. I want that feeling again."

How could he, and the Heat, top the 2012-13 season? The winning streak had been a historical appetizer to one of the best Finals ever, culminating in the championship. A third in a row, of course, would be sweet, but could it possibly bear the same weight as this did?

Chapter 19 - Three-peat?

The three-peat talk was inevitable. NBA cameras asked LeBron in the summer if he was thinking about a three-peat. Did they really expect him to say no?

"You think about it, sure," Bosh said. "We're all basketball fans. Of course we want to three-peat. But the way to do that is to take it one day at a time. This season is different from last season."

"After we won last year, I thought I'd care more about the fact that we had won back-to-back," Battier admitted. "But I really didn't. I mean, the fact that we won back-to-back is cool. But it's not this euphoria, just joining this club. History is nice, but when you're going through the grind, you don't appreciate history."

"I just want this thing to keep going," a beaming Pat Riley said. "I'm at an age right now where I'm ready to, you know, fly off somewhere. But I'm not going to, because the good lord has blessed me with a team that's allowed me to grab onto his coattails, for as long as they want to be together."

The team would stay together virtually unchanged; Ray Allen opted into the second year of his contract and the Birdman Chris Andersen re-signed. But, to shave down on salary, the Heat made a move many saw coming, but a very unpopular one in the locker room: applying the amnesty clause on Mike Miller which would take his remaining $12.8 million salary off their books and save them almost $17 million dollars from luxury tax payments.

Miller had been injured, benched, and inconsistent during his three years in Miami, but he had shown up in the biggest moments for the Heat. "Everybody loves Mike," Jonathan Abrams of *Grantland* wrote a year and a half after the Heat cut him in a glowing piece on how Miller was the fulcrum of every locker room he was in.

The Heat had announced during the Finals they wouldn't cut Miller, only to reverse course a month later.

"Believe me, I get all that stuff," he told Abrams later. "I learned that for 15 years. The thing that was tough was that we had the chance to do something seriously special. Even if it was waving a towel, I wasn't there to do it. That's tough."

"I don't think we can replace it," Bosh said. "Hopefully we can make up ground because what he brought to the team is going to be difficult to replace. I just hate that he's going to be picked up by another team, to defend against him now, we had a great time with him, and he was a huge part of the team and of our locker room and it's going to be difficult moving forward without him."

While giving the Heat some serious savings against the tax, it also shortened their bench and took a shooter and a passable defender off a team that needed both to succeed. Spo had learned to keep his playoff rotations tight, an adage of "play eight, trust seven" which saw Norris Cole, Rashard Lewis, Udonis Haslem, and even Battier relegated to the bench for long stretches of the playoffs.

The Heat would, on paper, bolster their frontcourt with the signing of former number one overall pick Greg Oden, who hadn't played in three full seasons but was attempting an NBA comeback. Oden was a massive human (the Heat truly lacked those), but the addition was hopeful at best.

"The Oden signing qualifies as more of a 'Why not?' move rather than a slam dunk, but it adds another undeniable level of intrigue to a team that was already the league's most fascinating," Ben Golliver of *Sports Illustrated* wrote.

The offseason would not be the whirlwind that the 2012 offseason had been. There was no Olympics, no endless press tour after finally conquering the championship demons. The pressure was on to three-peat, sure, but there would be nothing remotely like the pressure coming off losing the Finals or the pressure of coming out of a 3-2 Finals hole with under 30 seconds left.

Bosh and his family embarked on a worldwide tour, including Morocco, Spain, Montenegro, India, and Italy. "I'm glad we did it, I got to take my family and see some cool and unique things," he said.

But, in a rarity only really matched by Linsanity and the Dwight Howard trade (which fizzled out in nearly a week), the Heat took a backseat to not one, but two teams during the offseason.

The Brooklyn Nets, in an attempt at legitimization, had made a splashy move for three Heat foes: Kevin Garnett, Paul Pierce, and Jason Terry. The explicit goal was to dethrone the Heat, because, hey, the Celtics had done that so well in the gentleman's sweep of 2011 and blowing a 3-2 lead to the virtually Bosh-less Heat in 2012.

"Who wants a piece of them?" asked the *Sports Illustrated* cover, which quickly brought back memories of the Dwight Howard/Steve Nash cover the year before.

"Garnett's health is key, and there are just a ton of guys here on the wrong side of 30," Zach Lowe wrote. "Brooklyn is going to be very, very good, but we have to see how healthy they are in the spring; whether Jason Kidd (with a huge assist from assistant coach Lawrence Frank) can juggle this rotation; and whether Miami's speed overwhelms this verryyyy sloowwwww group if the two meet in the playoffs."

LeBron was nonplussed. "Ray got killed for leaving Boston and now these guys are leaving Boston?"

While one rival was being created out of thin air, a different rival re-emerged. The Pacers were frothing at the mouth having lost to Miami two playoffs in a row. They openly announced they likely would have won the Eastern Conference Finals if they had home court advantage and explicitly stated their goal was to get the top seed, secure that home court advantage, and finally beat the Heat.

There had been iterations of challengers to the Heat since the summer of 2010: Boston, Orlando, Chicago, New York, and then Indiana, and now Brooklyn. The Heat generally disregarded all challengers as non-threatening. Though they bemoaned the incessant media attention, they always became jealous that another team or player was getting more than them, a feeling that no team deserved the same or similar attention without having paid the price they had.

"Members of the Heat chuckle at the irony of it all: They are fresh off their second consecutive championship, a massive accomplishment, and yet it feels as if they are less of a 'story' now than they've been at any time since their high school smoke machine pep rally in July 2010," Lowe wrote for *Grantland*. "The hate has dissipated, and the curiosity has shifted elsewhere. The

Heat seem like a known commodity — a small-ball machine built to engineer rim attacks and 3-pointers, proud practitioners of a blitzing defense that is stylistically unique. They've found their identity."

"It was true in July 2010, and it's true now: If all three of Miami's stars are healthy, both of mind and body, nobody is going to beat this team four times in seven tries in May and June," wrote Lowe in a different *Grantland* piece previewing the 2013-14 season. "But that 'if healthy' stipulation has happened exactly zero times since the Heat threw that little pep rally for themselves — DOS MINUTOS! — in July 2010. LeBron James fell apart in the 2011 Finals, Chris Bosh battled injuries through the 2012 playoffs, and Dwyane Wade has dealt with serious knee issues in each of the last two seasons."

Bill Simmons, talking to Lowe in an annual exercise ranking the watchability of each team, said, "My only fear: They never added that one hungry-for-a-title veteran who might keep them focused during the dog days this season... It's tough to stay motivated/healthy/happy after playing 310 games over 32 months, which is really what we're asking from the Heat here. Our recent three-peat history in the regular season isn't great... but I worry about their day-to-day intensity... Not including the preseason, they've played 313 games together in the past three seasons — 246 regular-season games, 49 playoff games and 18 Finals games. That's basically four seasons in three."

A prevailing thought was Miami would take it easy in the regular season, knowing and having experienced the grind of three wall to wall seasons. Everything coming from the Heat refuted that.

"Once you try to shortcut this league," Spo said, "it has a way of paying you back for that — dearly. When you start to devalue the regular season, that sends you down the wrong path."

The Heat would get to value the regular season right out of the gate, facing old foe Derrick Rose and the Bulls on ring night. The bench buoyed the Heat, shooting a sizzling 64% as a unit and hitting 8 threes as the Heat handled Chicago, 107-95. It was a crowning moment, literally, for LeBron and his 2013 year; he had finally tied the knot with Savannah in what he called his second favorite city in the world, San Diego. The ceremony was intensely private, with giant tents shielding guests and no paparazzi in sight. Still, LeBron loved retelling one detail: the would-be wedding crashers who gave themselves away by calling someone on the guest list by their legal name instead of the nickname everyone else knew them by.

Playing in Philadelphia 24 hours later, the Heat found themselves down 23-2 midway through the first quarter. LeBron hit a short shot nearly five minutes into the game for the Heat's first basket. The Heat, not devaluing the regular season already, clawed back to trail by a deuce at the half, and then, after Ray Allen hit four threes in the last 1:43 of the third quarter, remarkably led by nine going into the final frame.

The offensive output ground to a halt, however, and the Sixers won, 114-110. The rollercoaster game was at once troubling and incredible: how a team could struggle so mightily in the first six minutes of a game, so thoroughly dominate the next two quarters, and then fizzle in the fourth and eventually lose to an inferior team was breathtaking in its polarity.

"The second game that year against Philadelphia…Philly was bad, they were doing the process…oh man that's a bad loss," remembers Battier.

It of course didn't help that Wade sat out the game with his balky knees and Sixers rookie Michael Carter-Williams drilled four three pointers (in the ten years after that game, he never made four threes in a game and only made three threes in a game five times in that decade span).

The Heat would get a day off before the heavily anticipated matchup with the new-look Nets in Brooklyn.

The long-awaited game lived up to the hype, Brooklyn storming out to another large lead against the lethargic Heat, only to see their 12 point lead with under three minutes left shrink to two on a Chalmers three with 18 seconds left and then one after a LeBron corner three. Down three, Bosh made the front end of a trip to the free throw line and needed to miss the second to give the Heat a chance at a tip in offensive rebound. He made the free throw.

Much was made of the Heat losing two in a row for the first time since nearly a month before the 27 game win streak.

The Heat was unbothered. While they weren't going to devalue the regular season, they weren't going to overreact either. Nonchalance was the mood in the locker room more than anything.

"It was a good game," LeBron said. "Both teams wanted to win, but they came out with a little bit more sense of urgency from the start, and in the third quarter, and that's kind of what dug us a hole."

"It's the second home opener we've played on the road," Bosh said, trying to hide a smile. "We got caught blindsided again."

The Heat got back on track, winning three in a row before a wild one point home loss to Boston featuring two missed free throws by Wade with .6 seconds left that led to a Jeff Green corner three over LeBron on a great inbounds play design by newly christened head coach Brad Stevens. LeBron slightly got lost on the winning play, but the fact the Heat lost a game it led by four with 2 seconds left was a little more jarring than losing road home openers.

But, as the Heat had done the previous three seasons, a winning streak ensued, this time a ten gamer.

Sitting at 16-5, the Heat hit the road to take on the 18-3 Pacers, still frothing at the mouth to unseat the Heat.

Miami looked unfazed, scoring on their final eight possessions of the first quarter against the vaunted Indiana defense to lead by 11 after the first quarter. But as was the Heat recipe of righting the ship slowly, the Pacers scratched back into the game and a smothering third quarter flipped the game. Indiana won 90-84.

"It was fun, a real intense game," Pacers forward Paul George said. "Both teams were playing at a high level. You could see an urgency to win this game tonight."

Indiana ~~loose cannon~~ guard Lance Stephenson had said before the game that it felt like a championship match. Wade and Bosh stopped short of rolling their eyes at the thought of that, politely downplaying the claims from Stephenson.

"I thought we brought it tonight," LeBron said. "We know they're a very good defensive team. I thought they hit some tough shots, and they attacked the rim real well but even though they had us down by 10 rebounds, I thought we rebounded well and we battled."

The Heat went on another winning streak, this time a tidy six, which included a rubber match in Miami versus Indiana. Behind 71 points from Bosh, Wade, and LeBron, the Heat flipped an 11-point halftime deficit into a 94-90 win. (No one from the Heat had mentioned anything about it feeling like a championship match.)

"It shows we're a team that's been there before," Wade said. "No matter what the score is, we always feel we have an opportunity to win the game."

"It was a good win," LeBron added. "Good, good, quality win against a very good team on our home floor. We had to overcome a lot."

The Heat Big 3 had played very well, but a concern in the foundation was looming for the Pacers: their bench was a horrible matchup versus the Heat, and particularly the Heat bench. The Pacers four bench players that saw action combined for twenty points, but the level of physicality and defense dropped off a cliff when Hibbert and David West were replaced with Ian Mahinmi and Luis Scola.

Not only was the Heat not devaluing the regular season, on its face at least, their level of concern with Indiana and the rest of the East was limited, even with Wade missing game after game after game in an attempt to save his knees for the inevitable postseason run.

The maintenance program, as Spo called it, was probably necessary. But there also seemed to be a sense, at least from LeBron and Bosh, of frustration; not knowing if Wade was going to play any given night turned from an annoyance to a burden.

Annoyance also boiled to the surface when the Heat embarked on a holiday road trip, starting on Christmas Day in Los Angeles against the battered Lakers. Historically, the defending champions get a home Christmas game, something LeBron, as calculated in his words to the media as any superstar in sports, made sure to mention.

"Growing up, I thought that was a rule," he said. "I don't know if it was a rule, but I just thought that was like given. I don't remember ever, besides, I guess, I don't know if I've ever seen M.J. play on the road on Christmas. Maybe in the Garden, maybe."

Wade had been vocal in a meeting a month prior with Adam Silver addressing the discrepancy. Silver, ever a player placate, had tried to ease the frustration by quipping if the Heat won another championship, he would ensure they were home on Christmas Day 2014.

"Great incentive, huh?" LeBron scoffed.

If a road trip over the holidays wasn't enough, the Heat, LeBron in particular, was disgusted at the Adidas sleeved jerseys unveiled for the game, complaining of the tightness around the arms when shooting.

The Heat sleepwalked through the ultimate 101-95 win over the Lakers, sans Kobe Bryant, highlighted by several fast break dunks and Lakers firecracker Nick Young scoring 20 quick points off the bench.

The Heat took three of four on the West Coast trip and were sitting at a respectable 27-8 before a wild six game road trip up and down the Eastern seaboard presented itself through the middle of January, culminating on Martin Luther King, Jr. Day in Atlanta.

A stodgy second half doomed the Heat in Madison Square Garden versus the Knicks in the first game of the swing; LeBron and Wade combined for 55 of the Heat's 92 points, but Wade missed six free throws and Bosh contributed a paltry six points in the loss to a resurgent, but ultimately still bad Knicks team.

The Heat faced a back-to-back against their new rival, the Nets, in a nationally televised game. The NBA tried to juice the spectacle by slapping nicknames—real or forced—on the back of every jersey. The gimmick, filled with half-baked initials, drew more eye rolls than excitement.

Luckily, the game needed no extra sizzle.

Joe Johnson scored 22 of the Nets' 33 points in the opening quarter, missing a single shot in the frame. But somehow the Heat only trailed by one, bolstered by LeBron's 16 points.

The Heat could only muster 32 points total over the next two quarters, but roared back with a big fourth quarter, retaking the lead off a Norris Cole three with around two minutes to go.

Miami could never grow the lead and LeBron split a pair of free throws to tie the game with 40 seconds left. Brooklyn, in an all too familiar NBA late game tactic, took the clock down, isolating Joe Johnson on Bosh at the top. LeBron came from the wing, off of Pierce, to force Johnson right and into a tough shot fading away near the elbow. The shot caromed long, with the Heat unable to corral the rebound with a big numbers advantage in the paint. Pierce got his chance against LeBron to win the game, creating good separation just off to the left side of the arc, but spinning out the potential game tying three.

Just what a contrived rivalry needed: overtime!

But the drama seemed to never get to peak as LeBron got caught flinging the forearm into wiry defender Shaun Livingston and fouled out for the first time in a regular season game since

2008. Norris Cole stuck a long two over Livingston to send the game to double overtime.

Any hope for more drama was dashed as Miami couldn't muster a point in the second overtime until less than 20 seconds left, succumbing for the second time to their "rivals".

A Brooklyn hangover couldn't be the excuse in the Heat's next contest, five nights later in Washington, D.C. where an 11-10 Wizards first quarter lead somehow ballooned to a 43-18 advantage at the quarter buzzer.

The ceremonial champions' trip to the White House had given them no extra fervor. The Heat righted the ship, but the hole was too deep.

"They was playing at another speed," LeBron said. "They was playing at, like, 15 and we was playing at, like, seven. Don't even gonna give us that much of a credit. We was playing at, like, five."

Wade was back from taking the game off in Brooklyn, what amounted to nearly a week off, but only managed 8 points on 4 for 11 shooting.

Wade's absences and occasional listless play didn't help, but the bigger issue was the team's energy. It was always going to be hard to summon June-level urgency for January road games, fair enough. Still, this Heat team often looked slow, tired, and uninspired. Some around the team pointed to Mike Miller's departure as part of the drop-off, and maybe that was true. Add in the grind of 82 games, Wade's maintenance program, and injuries to Battier, Chalmers, and Andersen that kept the rotation in flux, and there just wasn't a single game or moment—nearly halfway into the season—that felt like the fire-breathing dragon of the two years prior.

The Heat went 2-1 on the remainder of the road trip, and welcomed a four game homestand, originally scheduled as a pre-All Star litmus test facing Boston, the Lakers, San Antonio and Oklahoma City.

Winning the first two games to set up a much-anticipated Finals rematch, Wade returned from missing four straight games to come off the bench. The game was hyped and circled on nearly every NBA calendar since the schedule release, but the game was a dud, Wade's return notwithstanding.

Never trailing and getting remarkable efficiency from the starting lineup that featured Ray Allen in place of Wade, the game felt much more like a late January, Sunday afternoon game than it did a rematch of one of the best NBA Finals in memory.

"Did that feel like The Finals? No, it did not feel like The Finals," Spo said before even getting a question in his postgame remarks.

If the Spurs rematch was the most anticipated game on the Heat schedule, the matchup with the Thunder three nights later couldn't have been lower than second. Kevin Durant was working on what would become an MVP campaign and OKC was rolling, sporting the best record in the highly competitive Western Conference and riding an impressive eight game winning streak.

The Heat bolted out of the gate to an 18-2 lead, replete with Wade and LeBron jumpers, Chalmers and Bosh three pointers, and Chalmers getting into the paint at will.

Even with All-Star guard Russell Westbrook out, the Thunder weathered the storm, getting ten three pointers from their bench and 17 points from Durant in the third quarter and a couple minutes of the fourth en route to a 112-95 beatdown of the champs.

"They were ready for us to come in and play," Durant said. "They hit some tough shots early on, a few 3's, and we didn't panic. We just tried to stay together and that's what we did. Our bench was great in getting us back in that game."

"There's no running away from it," Spo said. "Other than the first eight minutes of the game they outclassed us tonight. They absolutely deserved this win."

"We played well to start the game," added LeBron. "We played well all the way until like the second quarter. From that point on they did what they want to do."

Troubling signs were either popping up or exposing themselves more and more; the bench was wholly undependable night to night, the defense was not nearly as sharp or lethal as it had been only 365 days earlier, and the Wade conundrum hovered over the team on a daily basis.

But, as they had done at the sight of trouble going all the way back to 2010, they started winning and winning a lot, taking six out of seven before a rematch in Oklahoma City.

While Miami had a complete team effort in the first quarter of the first matchup with the Thunder, this first quarter was all LeBron, going 8 for 10 from the floor and getting the Heat up 34-17 after one. This time around, there was no let up. Wade scored three baskets in the second to keep the lead while LeBron rested, then they combined for 14 in the third to head to the final frame with an eleven point cushion.

Wade and Bosh took their turn in the fourth playing a marvelous two-man game, Bosh drilling a pair of threes and a long two.

With under six minutes left, LeBron got Serge Ibaka switched onto him on the left wing. With no rim protection, he easily drove by going right and punched a one-handed dunk over Ibaka while tumbling to the ground.

LeBron didn't get up from the baseline as the Thunder inbounded the ball and ran the other way.

"Is that blood?" asked Kevin Harlan on the TNT broadcast as the cameras showed LeBron in the fetal position on the other baseline.

LeBron had been hit in the nose by Ibaka, breaking his nose in the same swift movement as the poster dunk. No foul called. He walked off with a stack of towels below his nose.

Bosh and Wade finished off the 103-81 drubbing.

LeBron sat in his locker after the game with a towel draped over his head, the rest of the team in hushed awe at what they had witnessed.

"I'm like everybody else, you're used to seeing him like Superman, get up and sprint back even after tough hits and tough falls," Spo said. "So, we knew something was up."

The game was an exclamation point on a six game Western road trip that saw the Heat win five of the games. The Big 3 had tallied the same output as the entire Thunder team, 81 points, in one of their most complete games, offensively and defensively, of the whole season.

Three nights later, the Heat suffocated the Bulls, 93-79 behind 51 from Bosh and Wade as LeBron watched in a gray suit from the bench.

He returned four nights later in a rare three games in a week stretch for the Heat, facing the pesky Knicks. The Heat wore black throwback jerseys and LeBron, completing the look, donned a black carbon fiber mask protecting the broken and tender nose.

While the mask got all the attention, LeBron's performance in his first game in a week was as menacing as the mask. "He played like a Batman," Bosh said of the 13 for 19 performance.

LeBron wasn't in love with the mask saying, "As much as I don't like it, I have to figure out how to make it work."

Wade culminated a strong February with a 10 for 13 outing and was nearly as good against Orlando the next game going 10 for 14 from the floor as the Heat win streak reached seven.

"Defensively we're flying around and we're communicating," LeBron said. "And offensively, obviously we're playing at a high level."

The streak seemed to breathe the first sense of joy into the team all season, which in turn bore fruits on the floor.

Wade's hot February and 20 for 27 shooting in the last two games would get completely overshadowed, first by LeBron's mask (which the NBA mandated he dump after the Knicks game) and then by a career-high 61 points versus the lowly Bobcats, a game in which Wade sat for his maintenance program.

LeBron had 24 at halftime, then added a gaudy 25 in the third quarter alone. Sixty felt reachable.

"He was in a great groove, obviously," Spo said. "The rim looked like an ocean for him."

"Once he sniffed 60, we knew he was going for it," Battier said. "And the amazing part is the efficiency. Good Lord. Sixty-one on 33 shots, that's Wilt Chamberlain-esque. That's pretty amazing. Incredible performance."

LeBron scored a driving layup right at the outset of the fourth to crack 50 and added a long jumper thirty seconds later.

He made two more layups in the middle of the third to eclipse 57 points, a new career-high. He made a running, twisting bank shot to get to 59 and moments later knocked in two free throws to set the Heat franchise record, exiting to a standing ovation.

"I was happy I was able to make a few plays to help us win," LeBron said, with no hint of irony in his voice.

There would be no repeat of March 2013; the Heat promptly dropped three straight on the road, including the second in the rematch series with the Spurs. To the outside eye, only four games remained on the Heat schedule of any consequence: two each against Brooklyn (both in Miami) and Indiana.

The third matchup with Brooklyn was probably the most well-played of the three to that point, Brooklyn holding a four-point lead before a Bosh three point play with 30 seconds to go. Chalmers did a good job forcing Nets guard Deron Williams into a tough stepback jumper and Miami had a chance to win the game after Wade collected the rebound.

"Bosh has to get it inbounds," Mike Breen announced on the ABC broadcast. The comment may have seemed innocuous when Bosh threw the ball into LeBron who was rolling towards the hoop after setting a flare screen for Allen. But Shaun Livingston, who had drawn the offensive foul to disqualify LeBron in the last matchup, got his long arm just in the way to knock the ball away toward the baseline. The Heat never got a shot up.

"We do need to execute down the stretch," Wade said. "We need to be able to at least get the ball up to the rim, so we're going to have to work on that a little bit. We've got something to work on as a team. That's not a bad thing."

As much goodwill as the winning streak had bought themselves, losing four out of five dampened the mood around the Heat even more.

"Losing four of five," LeBron said, "that's pretty bad."

"It's competition," said Spo. "It's survival of the strongest right now...We still feel confident about our game. We just need to put it together."

The losses to Brooklyn weren't alarming so much as they were interesting. The Nets, even having won all three matchups, weren't going to win the title. But the ways in which they matched up with the Heat was unique. While slow and wholly unimaginative offensively and defensively, virtually the entire roster was veterans who could create good shots one on one or weren't afraid of the Heat, or both. As well as the Nets played the Heat, the same couldn't be said for the rest of their schedule; they would finish the season one game up on the seventh place Charlotte Hornets.

All season, the Heat struggled to summon urgency for ordinary regular-season games. They still played well most nights—years of trial, error, and pressure had forged them into a battle-tested group—but the hysteria around them had cooled. Losses that once would have triggered DEFCON 1 headlines were now brushed aside with a shrug: we'll see in the playoffs.

The Pacers took a different approach. From day one, they made it clear they were chasing home court, the last step they believed they needed to finally dethrone Miami. Their regular-season clashes carried weight, but for the Heat, the same mantra applied: we'll see in the playoffs.

But when it came to the Pacers, the Heat held the same belief they had through the Eastern Conference Finals a season ago: the Pacers wanted to play a certain way and they had fallen into their trap all too often, exacerbated by what they felt was a generous, and unique, way of officiating the plodding Roy Hibbert.

That frustration was evident when LeBron was whistled for one of the rarest fouls possible in the NBA: the offensive *flagrant* foul.

Early in the fourth quarter in Indiana, LeBron cut hard from the opposite wing behind Paul George who had moved off him to defend Rashard Lewis at the top of the key. LeBron caught the ball at full speed, took one dribble, gathered at the dotted line and rose up, met by Hibbert whose feet were clearly on the charge circle line and certainly wasn't giving his beloved verticality as his arms were at 45-degree angles into LeBron.

LeBron drifted and brought the ball across from right to left in the air, catching Hibbert's chin as both tumbled to the floor.

The ensuing review and call, to a guy whose nose had been broken in Oklahoma City without even a foul called, was curious.

"It is what it is, they ref the game, we play it," LeBron said, clearly perturbed.

The Heat offense sputtered in the fourth quarter and a last second game winning attempt by Bosh was an airball.

"Unfortunately, that was what I diagramed," Spo said. "It probably wasn't the best call. It might have been a little too gunslinger on my part. I just wanted an open shot."

The Heat didn't play its best game as LeBron and Wade were the only players in double figures but also had six turnovers a piece. Five wins out of six, all in blowout fashion, didn't move the needle much either way.

A late season scheduling gift from the gods (for the networks and the fans, at least) was Brooklyn and Indiana both visiting Miami in the same week early in April. But still without Wade, who hadn't played since the last Indiana game with a hamstring injury, the game lacked pop and fizzle. That is, until the final play of the game.

Up to that point, as had been the previous three tilts, the game was tight. Joe Johnson squeezed a floater over LeBron to beat the shot clock with a minute left in the game and give Brooklyn a four point lead. The answer came in the form of a LeBron and one following a timeout. Deron Williams found Plumlee for a tough two as Bosh came over to defend the basket after Williams had gotten by Chalmers from the top of the key. LeBron routinely found Bosh rolling down the lane for an uncontested dunk to pull the deficit back to just a single point. Joe Johnson couldn't shake Rashard Lewis from the wing and threw up a prayer that only hit the backboard, Miami controlling the rebound with ten seconds left and Spo not calling timeout.

The Heat had a mini fast break and LeBron slid a pass to Lewis cutting wide from the free throw line extended. Lewis went under the hoop, quickly meeting three Nets defenders as he picked up his dribble with six seconds to go. But LeBron was following the play and Lewis spotted him galloping to the rim and flicked a pass to him as he jump stopped and rose up with two hands.

Nets rookie center Mason Plumlee had recovered onto Lewis and quickly flipped around to try to defend the dunk attempt. He got some ball and a lot of LeBron's wrist and hand as no saving whistle came.

LeBron was incensed. Replays showed Plumlee virtually interlocking fingers with LeBron's right hand. "He grabbed my right hand," LeBron said. "He didn't do it on purpose, but he got my right hand."

It was accepted that refs generally swallowed their whistles at incidental contact late in games, but if a dunk attempt to win a game was going to get the treatment of looking the other way, what was the contingency plan then?

"My initial thought was to just foul and make him earn it at the free-throw line," Plumlee admitted.

"It was a foul from my vantage point," Spo said, resigned. "But what can you do?"

"That's just basketball," Nets coach Jason Kidd said. "You have the best player in the world going against a rookie and we got lucky."

Much was made of the Nets sweeping the season series with the Heat. Brooklyn won three of the games by a single point, becoming the third team in NBA history to have that many narrowest-of-margin wins over an opponent in the same regular season and the first team ever to do so without playing more than four times. The Heat, congruently, had suffered their last three losses all by a single point. While the season sweep was interesting on its face, it meant nothing in terms of playoff seeding or home court advantage. Miami seemed more frustrated at officiating and another deep rotation player having a career night against them, this time Marcus Thornton who shot 6 for 8 from the field.

The schedule did the Heat no favors, playing a game the next night in Memphis against the Grizzlies who desperately needed wins for their playoff seeding hopes.

Obviously without Wade, LeBron scored 37 points with 6 rebounds and 5 assists, but it wasn't enough against a fully healthy Memphis team (Miami was starting Toney Douglas and giving minutes to little used, but effective, young center Justin Hamilton).

The matchup with the Pacers loomed large, even with the season now on its last legs: the first seed was still up for grabs with the Pacers holding a paltry one game lead over the Heat with four games to go. The final head-to-head would be worth that one game in the standings for whoever won it.

Wade-less again, the Heat pounced and strangled the Pacers in the middle quarters, coasting to a 98-86 win and drawing even in the standings.

"This is not the biggest game we've played in our four years together," LeBron said after his 36 point night. "It's always great to have competitive games like this in the regular season. I mean, we've played Game 7 in the Finals before. It doesn't get no bigger than that."

The Pacers didn't fully say the loss was demoralizing, there were still three games on the schedule, but their tone and body language were that of a team seeing its season long goal flash before its eyes.

"We're still a good basketball team," Pacers coach Frank Vogel said. "I think we're taking steps to get ready."

The next night in Atlanta, the Heat face planted, dropping a game against a desperate Hawks team that clinched the East's eight seed. Wade returned and was solid, 24 points on just 14 shots. But the ground that had been gained in the playoff race 24 hours earlier was now evaporated.

"It was good, better than I can envision," Wade said. "When you're out so long, you're just thinking of getting your wind back. I think the best thing that happened was the first play of the game, getting that block and then LeBron kind of holding up and letting me get the first dunk. From there, I kind of was into the game."

The second half doomed the Heat much as it had the Pacers the day before.

"Needless to say, that was a tough second half," Spo said. "We couldn't get it going on either side of the court. It's disappointing to have this type of performance on the road."

In a not so surprising move, Spo elected to sit LeBron and Bosh for the final two games of the season as opposed to putting the foot down on the gas to secure the top seed; Miami was ceding the top spot to Indiana.

Which may not have been a terrible decision. Indiana stormed out of the gates with a lofty goal and lots of ambition, starting the season 16-1. But they had fallen back to earth late in the season, finishing the campaign a paltry 6-9, losing to teams headed for the offseason and in dogfights against playoff teams. The back half of the once so promising season had been filled with drama, infighting, and public airing of grievances, not to mention a ridiculous R&B group style photoshoot in *GQ*, complete with jeans, track jackets, and towels around shoulders.

"This is the Heat's point of view," wrote Michael Dunlap of fansided after the Heat punted the final two games of the regular season. "They see a team that is struggling to find their identity. They see a team without a go-to guy. They see their previous version of kryptonite (Roy Hibbert) as a shell of his former self without any confidence at all. They're figuratively betting for themselves by betting against the Pacers."

Miami, to their credit, never gave attention to what other teams they might face were doing; they truly were a take care of their own business outfit. So sweeping the overmatched Charlotte Bobcats while the Pacers gutted out a seven game series against the newly minted eight seed Hawks should have drawn shrugs. But *how* the series went was eyebrow raising for the entire league.

The Hawks were without their steady force in the middle, versatile big man Al Horford. In his place, Atlanta staged Pero Antic, a first year Macedonian center rocking a shaved head and full beard. Stationed behind the three point line, and letting threes fly with abandon, Indiana was forced to pull Hibbert away from the basket which allowed the skilled Hawks players all sorts of runways to the hoop. It was becoming obvious, painfully for Indiana, that a Hibbert unable to glue himself next to the rim was a Hibbert unable to impact the game, on both ends (no one was confusing Hibbert's hands for Jerry Rice or his post moves for Hakeem the Dream).

Though eventually overmatched and succumbing in seven games, the Hawks had ripped the scab open on the Pacers, something the Heat had discovered almost too late one postseason earlier.

As the Pacers tussled with another team with quick guards and a pair of frontcourt bigs that could match up with West and Hibbert, the playoff series almost spoken into existence since July of 2013 was now a reality: Brooklyn versus Miami.

Chapter 20 - Nuisances

Unfettered by the season sweep at the hands of the Nets (gasp!), the Heat rolled, using a massive third quarter run and balanced play up and down the roster to take game one, 107-86. Showing little if any signs of rust after eight days off, Wade, LeBron, Bosh, Chalmers, and Ray Allen all scored in double digits and the Heat shot nearly 57% from the floor.

"It was great that we were able to come out the way we did after being off eight days," LeBron said. "We got a lot of work in. We had eight days off of not playing a basketball game, but Spo got us in the gym. (We) got each other in the gym. We made each other accountable throughout the layoff and it proved tonight."

"It's fun when you win the game and you can at least for a night do whatever it is you do, have some dinner, chill at home and exhale a little bit," Bosh said. "When you lose, you can't sleep, your stomach hurts and it's not a very good situation." He didn't have to worry about that, the Heat hadn't lost now in three weeks.

That time frame would continue as the Heat had little trouble in game two, getting another quintet of double digit scoring outputs from Wade, LeBron, Bosh, Chalmers, and Allen on nearly 52% shooting. "That's what our team is all about," LeBron said. "We don't really care who scores."

"As the game wore on we started picking up the pace," Allen said. "We started to getting how we play basketball."

Bosh, who had long admitted Garnett was his favorite player growing up and somewhat intimidated by him the first season in

Miami, had no trouble with him now, a strong 18 point, 3 block performance to take a 2-0 series lead.

In a desperate spot, down in the series with little to glean from the first two games, the Nets responded with an all out assault from three point range, hitting 15 threes as a team on 60% from deep, burying the Heat in a decisive third quarter.

Much was made of Pierce asking for the assignment of guarding LeBron in game three, and Pierce, never one to miss a chance to toot his own horn, talking about the level of leadership and the fearlessness his team exhibited.

"We're not scared of them," Pierce boasted on the heels of his 14-point game. "You know you've got to have that type of mental [approach] when you're going against a juggernaut," he said. "When you go against the best...a lot of series are won on fear factor, or the non-belief. When you have that non-belief, then you have no chance.

"What I try to do in this locker room and with my teammates is just try give them belief—that we can beat this team. They're not unbeatable. You've got to have that mental [approach] if you're trying to get over that mountain that you're trying to climb.

"Tonight was the type of urgency we're going to need for the rest of the series."

LeBron, as diplomatically as he could, downplayed the Nets' win and any threat he felt they presented: "I've been part of a lot of series and understand that the series is never won in two games or in three games," he said. "Words don't win the game, you've got to go out and play. Why should there be a fear factor, it's just basketball. We're not trying to win a war here, it's just basketball. We're all grown men, who cares about who is fearing who. We've never been a team that talks, we don't get into that. We've never been a bulletin board team. We just want to play the right way and give ourselves a chance to win."

LeBron, though he talked to the media twice a day on game days and was generally more at ease than he had been the first year in Miami, still rarely gave any comment that could be considered to rock the boat. He knew acutely how quickly his words could and would become the headline. So as a great politician, he said just enough and downplayed almost every attempt at a side swipe. But privately, he, and the team, openly mocked the efforts of other teams, not just Pierce and the Nets, of talking about the Heat and how unfearful they all were. Maybe it was real, but all the fearless teams in the East hadn't managed to beat them in a playoff series; even in the tight series, the intrepid and courageous teams found a way to always bow out to Miami.

It is generally accepted that the hardest game to win of a playoff series is a road game three when leading 2-0, simply for the statistical probability of coming back from a 3-0 deficit, which has never been accomplished in the NBA, is too daunting. The team leading is playing with house money, after all. So, it was no surprise the Nets not only won, but played their best game of the season against the Heat, the regular season sweep notwithstanding.

So, it was only fitting LeBron would play one of his best games of the season in game four, routinely putting Pierce and whoever else the Nets dared put on him in the torture chamber right around the basket with a series of post ups, duck ins, and drives to the rim. He had 12 points in the opening quarter, many directly against Pierce who picked up two fouls. Joe Johnson,

Alan Anderson, and Mirza Teletovic fared no better than Pierce, all getting a great look at LeBron's 25 first half points on an astounding 9 for 13 from the floor.

LeBron underplayed his dominance in the first half, simply calling it "attack mode" when asked by Rachel Nichols at the halftime interview.

The second half was much like the first, LeBron using every method to get to the rim against the helpless Nets: spinning around Livingston, driving around Pierce, going through Garnett's body, taking Anderson and Teletovic off the dribble at will. Tied at 92 with under three minutes left, Joe Johnson and Pierce became the targets as LeBron spun around Johnson deep in the paint and finished over a hapless Pierce, fearful of picking up yet another foul.

Sitting at 48 points when Johnson badly missed an almost meaningless heave, LeBron gathered the rebound and expected the game to end, with only 2.5 seconds left. But unbeknownst as to why, Deron Williams fouled with 1.6 left in the game and the Heat up 101-96. LeBron had a chance at the coveted 50 points. He swished the first free throw, and rimmed out the second, an audible groan from the crowd who wanted to see history if they couldn't see their Nets tie the series up.

When asked on the floor after the game about the miss, an embarrassed grin came over LeBron. "At the same time that I'm in the moment, I understand history," he said to Nichols. "To put up 50 in a playoff game that've been pretty cool. But I understand a win is what's most important."

The Nets had found out what almost every other playoff opponent the Heat had faced through four postseasons had also found out: the Heat has LeBron, and you don't.

"He was what was needed on the road and that's what makes him the best player in the game," Spo said.

The series, for all intents and purposes, was over. Eight teams had come back from a 3-1 deficit in the playoffs in NBA history, only two in the previous 15 seasons. Brooklyn could say all the right things, but they simply did not present the challenge a San Antonio, or, in theory even an Indiana, presented.

If the series was over, no one told the Nets.

Riding a hot third quarter, the Nets took a nine point lead into the fourth in Miami. Whereas the original 2011 playoff version of the Heat would have stalled out offensively, leaning on tedious and antiquated offball action to end up in an isolation situation late in the clock, this version was fine-tuned. They started the fourth with a simple side pick and roll, getting the Nets in rotation and swinging the ball around the perimeter to Rashard Lewis for a lightly contested corner three. Moments later, Wade got the ball to LeBron out of a double team for a wide open three.

But Pierce and Johnson, proud and battle-tested, didn't let up, taking turns scoring from the left side of the floor, with Pierce forcing a Spo timeout after drilling a tough corner three right in front of the Heat bench to extend the lead back to nine.

Bosh momentarily stopped the run with what was now becoming a patented corner three. But Johnson was relentless. Iso Joe kept hitting tough iso shot after tough iso shot, almost all with LeBron firmly attached.

The Heat trailed by eight with under three minutes to go, the proposition of a return to a rowdy Barclays Center in Brooklyn looking more and more likely.

Wade found LeBron in semi transition for a wide open three and then scored on a fallaway on the baseline on the next Heat possession to cut the eight point lead to three. LeBron then finally got the better of Johnson, blocking a short jumper and getting fouled, putting home both free throws.

Somehow only trailing by one with 43.2 seconds left, the Heat, in what would seem mind-blowing in 2011, again ran a simple LeBron/Chalmers pick and roll, getting the Nets' Williams and Pierce confused if it was a switch or a stay. Williams tripped over Pierce, who had done a great job getting through the screen and in front of LeBron. Seeing the numbers mismatch on the weak side, LeBron quickly shoveled a one-handed pass to Chalmers fading to the top of the key, undefended. Livingston, defending Allen on the weak side wing, made a picture-perfect closeout move, shuffling his feet and trying to close the gap on Chalmers while also not entirely leaving Allen wide open. Chalmers rose up to attempt a lead-stealing three. Except he didn't. He made a great pass in the air out of a shooting motion to the now open Allen on the wing, who took a step left into the corner and let fly.

"Ray Allen'll take the three for the lead, *it's in*!" thundered Brian Anderson on the TNT broadcast. "Ray Allen *again*!"

Two more Allen free throws put the Heat up five with 21.6 seconds to go, which felt safe until a Nets offense rebound yielded a Johnson corner three with 11.4 left.

LeBron split a pair of free throws after being intentionally fouled. Brooklyn still had a chance to win or send the game to overtime and ultimately send the series back to New York. But Johnson, trying to make something out of absolutely nothing with only seconds remaining, initially had the ball slapped at by

Allen and then knocked away right before the buzzer sounded by LeBron, who leapt on the TNT to the delirium of the Heat crowd.

"Miami has done it!" said Anderson.

"For us, it was just about getting stops," Wade said. "We knew offensively that we needed to execute, but we knew we weren't going to win the game unless we got some stops."

The Big 3, in yet another big moment, had been sterling, combining for 73 points, and all making enormous plays in the decisive fourth quarter.

Indiana would extinguish the Wizards the next night, setting up the rematch they had been craving, and with the homecourt they had intentionally sought out at the beginning of the season to get.

As hot as the Pacers began the season, and as tight as the four regular season matchups were, the prevailing sentiment among those predicting the series was unchanged; it was almost unanimous in picking the Heat to win the series.

"I don't know if the Pacers make the Heat uncomfortable so much as they feel comfortable playing Miami," wrote Amin Elhassan.

The Pacers certainly didn't instill confidence to an outsider, no matter how hard they portrayed it. The complete face plant in the second half of the game left a lot to be desired from a team wanting to be taken seriously, and it wasn't a bridge too far to think the Heat punting the final handful of games of the season was only how the Pacers secured home court advantage.

Regardless of how it was attained, the Pacers did not waste it in game one, jumping out to a 7-0 lead in the first two minutes, a ten point cushion at the half and opening an 18 point lead midway through the third in a relatively easy game one win.

Fifty-two combined points from Wade and LeBron were mostly in an attempt to get back in the game. All Pacers starters scored over 15 points on very good efficiency and Hibbert, George and point guard George Hill combined for 27 free throw attempts, more than the entire Heat.

"There's nothing to celebrate. It's not like we won a championship. It's one game," Hill said. "Yes, it was good, but if we come out and lay an egg on Tuesday, this game doesn't mean anything."

"We've been complacent many times. We just can't get complacent," George added. "We've got to stay humbled off this win and come in with the same mind-set that we have to get another one."

Some in the media were in panic mode.

"For Miami to advance, it's going to take yet another superhuman effort from LeBron James," wrote Bill Simmons. "Maybe even a super-duperhuman effort. The Heat spent four years riding on LeBron, Wade, defense, Bosh and 3s, in that order ... and right now, they can only count on LeBron from game to game. That's pretty sobering."

For much of game two it looked like the Pacers did have the same mindset as the game ground to a disjointed halt, no superhuman efforts to be found. But trailing by one in the fourth, Wade and LeBron flipped the game; in now three straight playoff series, the defensive juggernauts still couldn't manage an answer to stop them in the biggest moments.

LeBron cut behind Paul George for a layup to take the lead very early in the fourth, then collapsed the entire defense on a rudimentary pick and roll and pitched out to Cole for a wide-open corner three. Wade snaked into the key and hit a short fallaway over Hibbert. He then kicked out to LeBron at the top of the key when Paul George attempted to double him as Hibbert came over from the baseline to do the same. LeBron finished a nice give and go with Andersen as the slow-footed Hibbert couldn't get to the basket in time. He added two more free throws and standard out of bounds play shot corner jump shot when George once again died on an off-ball screen. Wade got a tip dunk after a LeBron steal and missed layup to give the Heat a five-point lead with under three minutes to go.

The Pacers conjuring any late game heroics was unlikely; the Heat had seen the door slivered open to start the fourth and kept tapping it more and more open.

Wade abused Hill and Stephenson in the midrange to keep the game at arm's length and then cut down the baseline for a reverse jam to ice the game with 21.6 seconds left. Pacers on the bench threw their arms in disgust; Wade and LeBron had scored all but three points in the fourth, stealing the coveted home court advantage right out of Indiana's greedy paws.

"That's why they're the hundred-million-dollar guys," Cole said, who scored the only other three points for the Heat. "They're unstoppable. They make the game easy for everyone else when they're in attack mode."

The Hibbert conundrum had once again reared its ugly head for Indiana: they were too undersized to not play him but playing him yielded nothing when the Heat decided to not wrestle in the mud and play lineups that stretched Indiana's defense further and further from the paint. Time and time again, Andersen in the short corner (the birdcage, the Heat called it) and Bosh flexed out several steps above the three point line, producing clear runways for LeBron or Wade to cut down the lane or get a head of steam and get defenders scrambling from far away. Though a noisy and oft times unreliable measure, the Heat was an astounding +25 in the 29 minutes Andersen was on the floor.

Exacerbating the defensive issues, George was inefficient and the lowly Pacers bench, now devoid of any pop or fizzle with the insertion of Stephenson to the starting five, produced a meager nine points.

"We were winning the whole night," lamented George Hill. "We controlled the whole game until the last couple minutes."

"It's about who can sustain runs, you know, who can get defensive stops?" LeBron said. "Who can not turn the ball over and who can get great shots? I think we did that in the fourth."

As fragile as Indiana had been during the second half of their season, that was all forgotten when they stormed out to a 17-4 lead in Miami in game three and opened up a 37-22 lead halfway through the second quarter, prompting a resting LeBron to sub back in the game.

He and Wade again got to quick work, assisted by five Pacers turnovers, and two Wade floaters had almost completely wiped the 15 points lead, a 40-38 Indiana lead at the half.

The house of horrors continued for Hibbert as Miami went to favoring a Wade/Haslem side pick and roll and exploiting Hibbert's comfort standing at the rim as opposed to defending the action; Wade got a series of short floaters and then when Indiana decided to just switch the action, Chalmers got free for a layup. LeBron and Wade both made threes in the final 1:20 of the third, and what was once a 15-point deficit was now a seven point cushion at home against a team that was clearly devoid of answers. LeBron and Wade had the same amount of points, 22, as the entire Pacers team in the third quarter.

Wade didn't slow down, drilling another three from the top and, against a Hibbertless lineup, picking on another plodding big man, Ian Mahinmi for a nice floater.

But even as Indiana inched back into the game behind some shaky calls and timely bench shooting, an all-too-familiar face emerged for Miami: *Jesus*. The Pacers, curiously deciding to have powerful big man David West defend Ray Allen (an "unenviable task" said Jeff Van Gundy), paid a dear price. Allen got West trying to jump a pindown from Bosh, fading to the corner for a wide open three. The Heat ran the same action the next possession, this time West doing an admirable job of staying with Allen coming off the screen. But CJ Watson lost his man, Cole, for a layup, started by Allen's gravity as a shooter and complemented by Hibbert being glued near the corner on Bosh. The cat and mouse game would continue for Hibbert soon after, choosing to try to wall off a thundering LeBron, leaving Bosh wide open in the corner. While the shot caromed softly off, LeBron outmuscled Stephenson and George for the rebound and the putback.

The game plan was scarily simple for Miami: attack Indiana's big men, but not in the old school manner of driving right at them. No, no. Get them forced into defending off-ball actions (like West chasing around Allen) or in tight pick and roll situations where LeBron or Wade or even Allen could react faster than they could move. Allen got Hibbert immediately indecisive to draw two free throws.

And then the worst-case scenario started unraveling: the Pacers started losing Allen, first in transition for a walk-up angle three and then Stephenson with his back literally turned to Allen in the corner who drilled another three to balloon the lead to 11. He would hit another three from the same corner moments later when Stephenson, out of control as was not unnormal, was on the floor at the other end and Indiana couldn't defend LeBron, Bosh, and Allen all on the same side of the court in transition.

LeBron and Wade, and even Cole, had turned the tides, Allen had gotten the ship to cruising speed, 4 for 4 from three in the fourth and a tough loss for Indiana to swallow.

"When they made a run," Lance Stephenson said, "we never responded." Stephenson wasn't good in game three, nor was George. And the offensive struggles were putting more pressure on the rickety defense than it could seem to handle.

The Pacers seemed to be falling back on the same kind of canned responses, while ignoring the underlying themes: the Heat wasn't going to allow for the Indiana defense to dictate the flow by sitting in shell defense and playing to their strengths, and consequently the Pacers weren't built any other way, already with a failing bench and dollar star versions of the starting five.

Miami continued capitulating the vaunted defense, force feeding Bosh early and often in game four. Bosh had struggled finding his role and his rhythm, scoring 9 points per game in the series and striving visibly to get comfortable. So, in yet another way to skin a cat, the Heat got him the ball for quasi open jumpers around the key as Indiana once again resisted coming all the way away from the paint to defend. He had eight points in the first 2 minutes of the game, and by the time Indiana had caught its bearings, LeBron had begun to punish anyone and everyone off switches, starting with Hibbert, then attacking West and George Hill.

The Pacers could never recover, falling behind 3-1 in the series. Bosh, Wade, and LeBron combined for their best game of the series with 72 points and all but wrested the series away for good.

Vogel used an odd big brother little brother example to try to urge the faltering Pacers. "He's got to make a decision at some point in his life, that no matter what, we're not going to lose this fight anymore," Vogel said, the Pacers of course symbolizing the little brother. "We're at that point."

"They won this game at the free-throw line," George said, ignoring the glaring x's and o's Miami was exploiting at will.

"The Pacers are at risk of becoming one of those teams people remember as a character in another team's story," Zach Lowe wrote in *Grantland*, "the underdog full of aspiration that tests a champion, pushes it to be legendary, and fades into a victim's role on that other team's highlight reel."

"From Puffed Chests to Sagging Hopes" was the headline in the *New York Times*.

"We don't want to come back for Game 6," LeBron said. "We love our fans, obviously. We love being in Miami, but we want to try to close it out. But we're going to have to work for it. It's not going to be easy, not against this team."

It wouldn't be easy when LeBron curiously got into early foul trouble, limiting him to just 24 minutes, and Paul George played one of his best games of the playoffs, with 37 points on finally an efficient 15 for 28 from the floor.

Despite nine three pointers from Lewis and Allen, the Heat could never get over the hump and so many minutes in a high stakes game without a full throttle LeBron was untenable.

"We still had enough opportunities to come away with a win," Spo emphasized. "We just couldn't get over the hump."

Indiana had staved off death, but it took LeBron's worst game in about 1,000 days and George's best in weeks. The way the series was rolling, the likelihood of both of those repeating seemed next to none.

The Pacers started 4 for 6 from the floor and enjoyed a very early 9-2 lead. They scored four more points the rest of the quarter, trailed 60-34 at the half, and, in one final indignity, bowed out meekly, 117-92.

"It was just one of those games that we want to play from beginning to end," Bosh said. "Here on our home court, we wanted to make a statement."

"For the entirety of the regular season, the supremacy of the Miami Heat in the Eastern Conference was brought into serious question by the Indiana Pacers," the ESPN game story read.

"Then came the playoffs.

"And the question was answered—emphatically."

"It's bitterly disappointing to fall short of our goals," Pacers coach Frank Vogel said. "It's bitterly disappointing to lose to this team three years in a row. But we're competing against the Michael Jordan of our era, the Chicago Bulls of our era, and you have to tip your hats to them for the way they played this whole series."

The Pacers had to feel after game five as if they were playing with stolen money; the way the series had unfurled was reminiscent of their season at large: heady, controlled, focused and dominant in game one, and then less and less and less so as the series went on, bordering on embarrassing antics. It was somewhat fitting that the season-long goal of home court advantage never came to fruition, the long-cautioned trap of playing for one specific result. Atlanta and Washington, and to be fair, the Heat the previous playoffs, had pulled at the threads of the Indiana philosophy, and it finally, mercifully, completely unraveled for good.

David West had been asked before the game if Indiana and Miami were on the same level as equals. "They've won championships," he said. "No, we're not equal."

The Heat joined the 60s Celtics and the 80s Lakers as the only teams to advance to four straight NBA Finals, an accomplishment not lost on them in the euphoria of their 14th playoff series victory since 2011.

"I'm blessed. Very blessed. Very humbled," James said. "And we won't take this opportunity for granted. It's an unbelievable franchise, it's an unbelievable group. And we know we still have work to do, but we won't take this for granted. We're going to four straight Finals, and we will never take this for granted."

Awaiting them, as it just had to be, were the dynastic San Antonio Spurs.

Chapter 21 - Game 8

USA Today's Adi Joseph wrote: "The Spurs have been the best team in the NBA all season. They have unprecedented depth, with no one averaging 30 minutes a game in the regular season, and they play with a natural grace through ball movement that makes them one of the most beautiful-to-watch teams in the NBA. That's a product of coach Gregg Popovich, who is the very best in the business."

The matchup was intriguing, and not simply for the low hanging fruit of *vengeance* and *three-peat* and *legacies* and *dynasties.*

San Antonio had bolstered its depth since the 2013 Finals, adding respected wing Marco Belinelli and bringing back Tiago Splitter and Manu Ginobili, who had enjoyed a Hall of Fame career but was abhorrent in the final two games of the Finals. They stormed through the regular season 62-20 ("the Spurs made sure to rest key players heavily too and still ended up with the NBA's best record," Tom Ziller previewed in *SB Nation*).

They were similar as the prior year's version in much the same way: an offense that was uniquely built to punish a defense for an entire shot clock, with constant attacking closeouts and swinging the ball all around the floor, usually one pass ahead of a scrambling defender. Defensively, they weren't anything spectacular, just solid, in the right spot, with capable defenders all over the roster.

Parker struggling through an injury was a concern, especially after the damage he had created in the first five games of the Finals. "I was initially leaning toward San Antonio in 7, but I'm spooked by Tony Parker's mysterious ankle injury," wrote Lee Jenkins in *Sports Illustrated.*

The Heat found answers in the nick of time in 2013, but there were some blind spots now. Where Battier and Miller had taken turns in games six and seven with one anvil smash three pointer at a time, Miller was now gone and Battier just wasn't a reliable contributor anymore, try as he might. Wade had been a breath of fresh air against Indiana, but San Antonio in 2013 had lived on the bet that he would not beat them regularly from the midrange.

Prognosticators were well split on who would lift the trophy; the series felt like it would be as evenly matched as the 2013 version, save for a few advantages on the fringes.

"It's kinda like picking right back up where we left off," Chris Bosh said. "This is Game 8."

The contrast between game one of the Finals and the Eastern Conference Finals that had just wrapped up was like watching two different sports, one a slow, monotonous ground game, the other a whippy, snappy, furiously paced chess match. The temperature was also vastly different; San Antonio was claiming an electrical failure for the power that ran the A/C for the entire building. The arena felt like a sauna, hot and damp and inescapable. Fans were using whatever they could find to fan themselves.

"Man, it feels like playing in my old high school gym," Bosh said to Ray Allen, "there's no air moving in here."

"The closer I get to the court, the closer it gets to 90 degrees," reported Doris Burke on ABC.

Early on, the temperature and the heat didn't seem to bother either team.

Bosh scored five points in the first minute, Wade looked as spry as he had in the Eastern Conference Finals, and San Antonio got three three pointers from Ginobili in the opening frame.

Ray Allen hit three threes of his own in the second quarter and added two assists as the back-and-forth game stood at 54-49 at the hot break.

The climate inside the AT&T Center couldn't be ignored. LeBron asked for colder water, multiple players had cold towels over their heads and shoulders, and ABC even threw up a graphic showing the outside temperatures in San Antonio and Miami being lower than the inside temperature of the game. Pat Riley, ever the mind-game player, didn't even bother to remove his suit coat.

Rashard Lewis took the baton from Allen in the third, connecting on a pair of threes. Wade, who seemed more willing and slightly more able to make threes, hit a wing three in front of Popovich and LeBron hit two of his own, one off a long offensive rebound and the other over Kawhi Leonard with only seconds remaining in the fourth to give the Heat a six point cushion. But, the ever present and focused Spurs got a layup at the quarter buzzer, a beautiful find by Parker to Splitter who slipped a drag screen and made a tough reverse layup with LeBron and Bosh squeezing in.

"This is awesome," an NBA scout muttered, clearly not talking about the A/C.

Bosh said it felt like it was game 8, and the play definitely felt like a sequel of the seven gamer from 2013, down to boneheaded Spurs turnovers (nine in the third quarter) and the fluid offense.

He and Splitter swapped baskets to start the fourth quarter, and Chalmers, who was becoming increasingly unplayable, drove wildly into Ginobili for his fifth foul.

The Heat was having problems figuring out how to defend Splitter since he was the screener in so many Spurs offensive sets. The aggressive high trapping to take away the driving threat of Parker was leaving the Heat scrambling on the back end, with Splitter getting clean catches and a beat or two to either pass out of the paint or go up for short shots, which he was electing. Duncan subbing in was no consolation prize.

Bosh stepped on the sideline in front of the Spurs' bench, wiping away a three pointer on a nice feed from Cole. He got a mismatch on the next possession and got two of the three points back down low. After a LeBron steal, Bosh hit an angle three over Duncan, also drawing a foul to the incredulity of Duncan. Bosh drilled the free throw, giving the Heat its largest lead of the night.

LeBron missed back-to-back corner jumpers, on the latter signaling to the Heat bench he needed a blow. "Cramping type of situation?" Van Gundy wondered aloud.

A Duncan layup cut the Heat lead down to two, and Spo mercifully called a timeout, LeBron walking gingerly to the bench. Mike Mancias, his longtime trainer, quickly came over. "I don't think I've ever seen LeBron James look that tired during the course of a game," remarked Breen.

It appeared the Heat could manage a few minutes with LeBron subbed out. Wade hit a mid-range jumper to re-establish the lead to four. But then Wade got caught trying to help on a potential Duncan post entry and left Green open for a corner three, then in transition, Green slinked to the wing unguarded to hit another three and give the Spurs the lead. "Uncage the bird!" exclaimed Van Gundy as Andersen knotted the game back up, with a nice reverse layup on Duncan.

LeBron re-entered, along with Bosh and Chalmers, at the 4:30 mark to close out the game. He wasted no time taking Diaw off the dribble for a layup to get Miami back within two. But it didn't appear he would be closing out the game. As soon as he landed on the floor, he hopped around gingerly and immediately signaled to the Heat bench. Spo and Fizdale were out on the floor gesticulating and screaming for the Heat to foul.

"James couldn't even make it down the floor," Breen said on the broadcast as LeBron, on the opposite baseline, attempted to massage his left quad. He dragged his left leg back to the scorer's table before James Jones and trainer Jay Sabol escorted him to the first chair on the Heat bench.

As the cameras tried to capture LeBron, it was impossible to miss Spo standing, hands on hips, his powder blue dress shirt drenched, seeping into his maroon necktie.

The Heat could only manage one more field goal the rest of the game, a Chalmers three, as the Spurs rode what had to be an emotional wave coupled with Danny Green catching his early 2013 Finals form and Kawhi Leonard, a below average but improving jump shooter, hitting two threes as the Spurs ran away with game one, 110-95.

"After I came out of the game, they kind of took off," LeBron said. "And it was frustrating sitting out and not be able to help our team."

The story of the game inevitably would be the busted A/C, and more specifically, LeBron's cramping, and how could it not be? Viewers were inundated, appropriately so, with cuts to fans trying to fan themselves with programs, foam fingers, and t-shirts, and just as much video of the players, jerseys drenched and dark, pounding liquids or placing cold towels on head and shoulders.

LeBron, miraculously, had been out of the critical spotlight for what felt like years now. That couldn't hold forever. *Jordan wouldn't cramp up! Tough it out! Drink some water!* Were the hilarious, original takes all too many had, of course the Venn Diagram of those who had never suffered cramps in a sports setting and those tweeting such things being one circle.

"I know I'm the easiest target that we have in sports, I'm aware of it," LeBron said in the days following the game one cramping. "I really am. I believe it."

Of course, the tried and true *"why was* he *the only one cramping"* morass appeared.

"There are definitely, quote-unquote, 'crampers,'" said Dr. Marci Goolsby, a sports medicine physician at New York's Hospital for Special Surgery. "Not that I know if LeBron is one of those people…It is a bit of a puzzle sometimes to try to figure it out. It's just some people may be more susceptible.

"Unfortunately, once it starts, it can be really hard to try to get rid of," she continued. "You can try to get their fluids up. You can try to hydrate them quickly. But sometimes, once the muscle cramps, it's hard to get rid of. And it's incredibly painful.

"But you mostly just have to wait for it to pass," she finished. "And then the muscle is tight afterward, and it doesn't take much to get it to cramp again."

Almost anyone who *has* cramped up can attest. Very easy to ignore all of that when pointing at an athlete cramping up hundreds of miles away.

"Toughness might let players play through pain," wrote Joseph Stromberg for *Vox*. "But it doesn't let anyone deal with muscle contractions so extreme that they don't let you bend your knee."

"I was going to try to give it a go and Spo said, 'No,'" James said. "It sucks at this point in time in the season."

"Suggesting that James had been 'asking out' by raising his hand and requiring the help of a trainer misunderstands the situation," a sensitive Ian Crouch wrote in the *New Yorker*. "It feels silly to even have to say this, but his leg cramps, which he has suffered from during hot games in the past, are not some signal weakness, of a physical manifestation of the purported psychological flaws that keep James from being a perfect basketball players at all times.

"Those of us watching at home, wedged comfortably between the couch cushions, with one eye on the television and one hand poised to post our latest snarky observation, may have benefitted from pausing for a moment to wonder what it might feel like to try to play professional basketball while suffering from painful, involuntary leg spasms. He's a great player on two legs, but couldn't have been much help to his team on one."

Tom Haberstroh, as he had all season and really since he showed up in Miami in 2010, had an excellent piece in ESPN about salt being the best conduit for cramping. Using Heat big man Justin Hamilton's experience with severe cramping and water intake doing nothing, he highlighted the need for salt, especially in situations where salt was being lost through sweat.

"A body short of salt, or sodium chloride, won't deliver the water efficiently to the muscles," Haberstroh wrote. Even though

LeBron was taking sodium cramping pills, that was likely too little too late.

"The rationale is good," a Sanford doctor told Haberstroh of James taking cramping pills. "But what amount of sodium? Those salt pills might contain 600 milligrams of sodium, but he might need a thousand or tens of thousands of milligrams. Often times, it's not enough. The salt pill is often nowhere near enough once the cramps occur."

Crampgate aside, what was lost was the Spurs' masterful performance down the stretch.

"Forget LeBron James's cramps: The Spurs shot the lights out in the fourth quarter of NBA Finals Game 1," was the headline in the *Washington Post*.

And it was spot on. The Spurs missed two shots *total* in the fourth quarter, made all their three pointers, and forced four Heat turnovers.

The A/C failure could be blamed, sure, but Miami led going into the fourth quarter and trailed by a mere two points when LeBron exited for good with 3:59 left. Getting outscored 16-3 in the final four minutes, regardless of who was on the floor, wasn't going to get it done, not against these Spurs.

"That was one of the greatest fourth quarter offensive executions in the history of the Finals," Breen said.

And it was a tough one to let slip, because Rashard Lewis, a new starter, had played well, Ray Allen had been excellent in the second half and the Heat got solid games up and down their starting lineup; Bosh had 18 points and 9 rebounds on just 11 shots, Wade apparently was having a good knee day and had 19 points, LeBron of course with a routine 25 points. Chalmers was atrocious, but that was to be expected at this point and had been since midway through the Brooklyn series.

The Spurs vowed that after a two-day break, the A/C in the AT&T Center would be fully functional. "The AC system has been tested, is fully operational and will continue to be monitored," the team said in a statement. "The upcoming events at the AT&T Center, including the Romeo Santos concert tonight, the Stars game on Saturday night and Game 2 of the NBA Finals on Sunday, will go on as scheduled. We apologize for the conditions in the arena during last night's game."

"I want the AC to come back, I want to play the real Miami Heat, the two-time champs, with LeBron back," Tony Parker said. "I hope it's not bad. And I hope he's going to be 100 percent on Sunday. Because as a competitor you want to play against the best, and that's how I feel."

"Right now, the air conditioning working just fine!" Mike Breen welcomed the national audience on ABC to game two.

LeBron said he wasn't necessarily back to normal, but felt better. He missed his first three shots before a thunderous driving dunk. Bosh was aggressive early, hitting his first three shots. But the Heat could not corral the Spurs defensively. The entire quarter seemed like the Heat was in scramble mode, always one step behind the Spurs' ball movement, even on interior passes (mostly to Duncan). The Spurs were constantly in motion, driving, kicking, and attacking frantic Miami closeouts in rapid succession. Duncan had 11 points on 5 for 6 shooting in the first frame, and San Antonio as a team picked right up where it left off in game one, shooting nearly 58% from the floor as a team, taking a 26-19 first quarter lead.

After just a two point first quarter, LeBron roared back into playoff mode with 11 in the second and Miami tied the game up before the break.

The Heat withstood the Spurs' 52% shooting in the third by having their own Spurs-esque quarter as a team, shooting a robust 76.5%, led by LeBron's gaudy 6 for 7 in the third, hitting five straight jumpers in just over a two minute span. "For me, once I get into a good groove, I feel like everything is going to go in," he explained.

But the Spurs would not let go that easily, scoring a flurry of 14 points after LeBron's barrage to take a one point lead into the fourth.

Diaw took advantage of a repeat sin by Wade, helping on a drive one pass away, to nail a three and tie the game at 90 with 4:39 to go. Every possession felt immense, if the Spurs were on defense, the thundering chorus of *DE-FENSE* and if on offense *LET'S GO SPURS*. But Miami didn't flinch.

"This is terrific Miami defense right now," Van Gundy remarked. "We're seeing them cover the initial pick and roll, and x out of the help and get out to the three point line."

"Game two hanging in the balance," Breen said as the clock ticked inside three minutes. Andersen would score on a tough reverse layup seconds later to give the Heat a whimsy two point lead that would disappear moments later when Parker hit a three over Bosh who was very late contesting.

It was hard to tell who was more displeased: Spo who immediately called timeout or LeBron who slammed the ball in disgust, some form of *are you kidding me* being shouted out.

"A nip and tuck game," Breen called it.

The Heat continued its stellar defense, losing out on a review that clearly looked like LeBron had stripped the ball off Parker's leg, but securing a rebound off a Ginobili heave. Sensing the enormity of the moment, LeBron did what he had done literally his entire career: found the open guy.

Parker, in a vain attempt to not get switched onto LeBron, virtually screened his own guy, Leonard, as LeBron came careening downhill near the elbow. Seeing the blown coverage, Duncan slid three or four steps off Bosh in the corner to get to the front of the rim. LeBron maybe noticed it a split second late, but pinged the ball to that corner. Bosh caught, gathered, and drilled it. The renaissance that began in earnest in the 2012 Eastern Conference Finals was coming full circle.

"LeBron was so criticized in Indiana in game five, when he drove, made the same play to win the game," an exasperated Doug Collins said after the game. "Bosh missed the shot, but all everybody talked about was 'LeBron should have shot the ball, he should have shot the ball'. Well, you know what, tonight the guy's got 35 points, he drives, gives the ball up... he always makes the right play, the unselfish play."

Ginobili tried to bait the refs on a touch foul then lasered a wild one-handed pass off Duncan and out of bounds. LeBron then fouled out Leonard and split the free throws, the Heat clinging to a three point edge.

Then, as Miami milked the clock, Bosh showed off the complete repertoire, crossing Duncan over on the wing and a nice one-handed bounce pass to an unguarded Wade for two.

A Ginobili three at the buzzer didn't even affect those with money on the game (Heat +4.5 was the line) and it all felt like 2013 again. Game nine?

Duncan was excellent but had inflicted most of his damage in the opening quarter. Bosh had more than equaled him, and his fourth quarter was exhibit A for what he could still do. No, he wasn't Toronto Bosh. He hardly had any post-ups in the game. But he was the defensive anchor, able to switch onto Parker or Ginobili while also banging with Duncan and Splitter, while also being a stretch shooter and, at the end, a savvy creator.

LeBron may have said he wasn't back to normal, but it sure seemed like it. Thirty-five points and ten rebounds in 37 minutes would have checked the LeBron back to normal box with ease. The only other player with a 35 point, 10 rebound game on over 64% from the field in the Finals was a certain guy named Shaq. Rare company, but not even a top ten or fifteen LeBron game of his career.

"What happened on Thursday was Thursday," he said. "My whole focus was how I was going to try to help this team even this up and just try to make some plays."

"Down the end there they executed really well," Duncan said. "LeBron made some great passes and guys made open shots. We had the same result in the first game. They kind of flipped it in this one."

"The best player on the floor took over," Mark Jackson summed it up.

The Heat had to feel pretty good with a split in San Antonio. Wade hadn't played particularly well in either game, Ray Allen had been very good in game one and a ghost in game two, and Chalmers was, as Ethan Strauss opined, "either injured or in one of his worst slumps".

Chapter 22 - Extinguished

The NBA rolling out the new 2-2-1-1-1 format was an odd development, and either side had its merits. The team with the home court advantage now would get three of the first five games at home, but a game six would be on the road. It all depended on who you talked to, but it was certain San Antonio was happy to not face the series possibly ending in Miami, as Oklahoma City had in 2012.

It felt like another long, classic series was unfolding.

That is, until the Spurs absolutely body-bagged the Heat in the first quarter of game three.

"You're on top of the world, you think you're gonna do the thing, you're up 1-1 with home court advantage, and we got *smoked,*" laughs Bosh.

Not often does a team shoot nearly 53% from the floor in a quarter, only turn the ball over three times, and find itself down 16, but Miami sure did.

Whatever the Heat may have found in the second half of game two defensively was not applicable in the first quarter of game three. Aside from putting the Spurs on the free throw line 13 times, the Heat almost literally couldn't force the Spurs to miss. Uncontested layups, contested layups, uncontested threes, contested threes, it didn't matter. The Spurs shot an unworldly 13 for 15 from the floor (86.7%) and Kawhi Leonard, who had made six field goals in the first two games, was five for five with three three pointers, with most coming right over LeBron.

Ginobili even rattled in a banked three to beat the first quarter buzzer for good measure.

"A sizzling first quarter from San Antonio," said Mike Breen, "who now own the two best shooting quarters in NBA Finals history."

The Spurs cooled off considerably in the second quarter only connecting on 12 of 18 shots, to take a monstrous 71-50 halftime lead, the largest halftime lead by a road team in the Finals in almost 20 years. It would make sense that the Spurs also topped the previous best for shooting percentage by a team in a half in Finals history.

And make no mistake, Miami had played well offensively, shooting almost 56% from the floor themselves, and 50% from three. But that wouldn't and couldn't match the Spurs. The Heat trimmed the lead to 11 going into the fourth, but the Spurs tightened the screws and pulled away, 111-92.

"We just moved the ball, and every shot went in," Ginobili surmised.

The Spurs "came out at a different gear than what we were playing at, and it just seemed we were on our heels the most part of the first half," Spo said.

Was it a fluke? Between what the Spurs had done to the Heat in games three and five in 2013 and in certain quarters of these Finals, it was hard to say it was fluke. Unrepeatable? Possibly, at those mind-blowing efficiency clips.

"Versus the Spurs, any minor mistake, they will make you pay," LeBron said on the day off between games.

The Heat limited those mistakes early in game four, but almost a worse scenario unfolded: the offense couldn't score, barely inching over the five point mark midway through the first quarter. Bosh and LeBron combined for 11 points, but San Antonio, while not at the record-setting levels of game three, chugged along offensively and grabbed rebound after rebound on Miami clanks.

Following up a 16 point first quarter with a 19 point second, the Heat found themselves once again in a huge halftime hole, this time 55-36. The possibility of mounting a comeback to square the series felt out of reach with how the offense was performing.

LeBron tried single handedly to get the Heat back in the game, scoring 19 of the 21 Heat points, including every basket from 8:53 on after a Chalmers layup. But, as they had done all series, the Spurs machine roared on, with no answer from the Heat at large. Inside, outside, upside down, the Spurs capitulated the Heat repeatedly. Down 20+ much of the final quarter, ABC didn't even attempt the customary between-quarter interview with Spo.

A trio of garbage time threes by James Jones made the final score closer than it felt, 107-86.

"They smashed us," LeBron admitted. "Two straight home games got off to awful starts. They came in and were much better than us in these last two games. It's just that simple."

"They played great, and I can honestly say I don't think any of us were expecting this type of performance," Spo added.

Some on the Heat talked of being in a position to make history, that at best felt like a pipe dream. Defensively they had no answers for the Spurs constant movement and pinpoint passing. Whereas San Antonio had literally handed games to the Heat in 2013 with blunderous turnovers and very questionable decision-making, this was the master taking the student to task.

Yet, if there was a team to overcome a 3-1 Finals deficit for the first time ever, wouldn't it be this team? Bosh, Wade, and LeBron? This culture, this pride?

For more than a moment in game five back in San Antonio, it seemed like maybe, just maybe.

LeBron came out the most aggressive he had in any game of the series, exerting his will early and often, first with a transition dunk set up by Bosh and then a putback dunk in transition off a missed Wade floater. He hit a wing three then set up Bosh for a layup. Moments later, he got a transition and one. He beat the shot clock from about 30 feet over Patty Mills and hit two free throws, the finishing touches on a dominant 17 point quarter. Miami had their first real lead since the first quarter of game three, 29-22.

And then, as quickly as they had taken the lead, the Spurs flipped it as the Miami offense fell back into disarray, scoring a meager 11 points.

"There was one point in that second quarter where they just kind of collectively, you could see the spirit sag out of them," Bill Simmons said.

A calculated gamble by Spo had failed: he had inserted Ray Allen into the lineup over the dead man walking Chalmers. As soon as the benches were called upon, the Heat had only blanks left in the chamber.

"I thought LeBron did his A+ game in the first quarter," Simmons said at halftime. "That was everything he had in the tank; San Antonio withstood it and they he ran out of gas in the second quarter, I think they missed their chance."

Simmons then summed up what no one would say, but virtually everyone was thinking: "Unfortunately, I hate to say it, but he's on the 2010 Cavaliers again. This team, the supporting cast, just didn't show up."

Any chance of slipping up by the Spurs evaporated to none when the Heat didn't score for over four minutes of the fourth and the Spurs, behind frantic ball of energy Patty Mills, turned a 12 point lead into a 20 point lead as Miami tried combatting Spurs three pointers with two pointers, a futile exercise.

Miami wouldn't quit, but for all intents and purposes, the game, and the series, were over.

Bosh, Wade, and LeBron got some pride baskets in the fourth, and Michael Beasley, the summer free agent signing, was dusted off to score nine points.

"We had a great first quarter, but from that point on they were the better team, and that's why they're the champions in 2014," said LeBron.

"The Spurs turned the Heat from proud champions into helpless victims," wrote Zach Lowe. "It was astonishing. It was, frankly, a little bit uncomfortable. You felt pity for Miami. They had no answers. The Spurs had figured out Miami's frenzied defense, and the team had no fallback plan."

The Spurs rightfully soaked it in. The 2013 Finals had been such a gut-wrenching defeat it was miraculous they hadn't caved in, let alone waltzed through the regular season with the best record and won a staggering 12 playoff games by 15+ points.

"It makes last year OK," Duncan said.

The entire Heat organization congratulated the Spurs, showing the level of respect the latter had from the former.

"Man, if I'm gonna get beat, it's by you guys," congratulated Chris Bosh. "I can respect that."

San Antonio had long been branded as boring, a slow, methodical, fundamental team, revolving around their talented big men, first David Robinson, then Tim Duncan. But the Spurs had evolved, a fast, yet still fundamental team, with a new approach to NBA basketball that had swung largely to more isolation, more shot creation off the dribble, and more pick and rolls. San Antonio had managed to create absurdly open shots, both inside and out, using the pick and roll as the means, but not the end.

"You showed the world how beautiful this game is," Adam Silver had said before handing the team the championship trophy.

Bosh, in the years that would follow, never beat around the bush:

"We lost to a very, very good team."

"They beat us, and you tip your cap."

"They mopped us up easy."

"We got smoked."

"It was a classic beatdown."

But for the Heat, this wasn't 2011. Players weren't falling to their knees in agony, LeBron wasn't in a defensive shell telling the hating world they were still broke, and he wasn't.

"At some point you run out of things to keep the edge sharp," Battier admitted. "It's hard to climb back on that horse. they kicked our butt, and we all knew it."

No, the feeling in the loser's locker room was one almost no one in the organization had felt in those four years.

It was relief.

"The whole locker room was relieved," said Ethan Skolnick.

The season, undoubtedly, had been a grind. From the second game of the season when Wade sat out, to being on the road for the holidays, to the faux rivalry with the Pacers, all the way to the end being ground to dust by the Spurs.

Several Miami writers noted the team hadn't had fun all season, save for welcoming Mike Miller back to get his championship ring.

The Heat had laughed off TNT analyst and future Golden State Warriors coach Steve Kerr, who had told them before the season they wouldn't three-peat because of the mental strain required.

"I can't tell you how after that three-peat we were so done with each other and so mentally completely fatigued," he had said.

"I see why people were saying three-peating is hard. I get it now," Bosh said. "I get it. There's just so many other things you have to fight. The human psyche, the human condition. We're all human. And it was a long, tough season."

"Playing in four straight Finals is the NBA's version of running a marathon, doing a triathlon, scaling a 15,000-foot mountain and finishing a Tough Mudder in back-to-back months," Bill Simmons wrote in unpacking the series. "Wade, Bosh and James played five seasons in four when you incorporate those 87 playoff games; combined, they played over 10,000 more minutes than Duncan, Parker and Ginobili since 2010-11.

"And it's not just the physical toll — many times in the playoffs, they looked like they didn't have much fun playing together."

"I don't think anybody really enjoyed this season like in years past," Bosh told The Associated Press. "There was no, like, genuine joy all the time. It seemed like work. It was a job the whole year. Winning was just a relief. Losing was a cloud over us sometimes, and then we'd break out of it—and then go right back. But we got here. We had a chance. They were just better."

"We just weren't as sharp as we were last year," Battier admitted. And that would have been pretty difficult. He would announce his retirement soon after, saying "I've given everything I can to the game, and I don't have any more to give."

"Mixed emotions," LeBron said, the Spurs celebrating their championship audible behind him.

Meanwhile, his running mate Wade had re-emerged for periods in the Indiana series only to falter in a huge way at the back end of the Finals, looking a combination of old, hurt, and lost.

"Everything bottomed out during those last two Finals games," Simmons wrote, "the nadir of Wade's career, no question — when Wade got swallowed up in the paint over and over again, couldn't finish plays, kept turning the ball over, couldn't defend anyone and jogged around on defense with his spirit broken. I don't mean to sound harsh; this was genuinely disheartening to watch."

The relief of the season being over, and consequently, no title defense looming, contributed to a feeling not of finality, but of renaissance. Surely Bosh, Wade, and LeBron, who all had player options in their contracts, would be back. But the rest of the roster was going to be a lot of question marks, with the salary cap continually squeezing down on the Heat's flexibility, even if the proverbial Big 3 was to opt out and all take salary cuts.

LeBron claimed he wasn't thinking about all of that. Whether or not that was true, it still was only minutes after an arduous season had come to an end; getting LeBron to take the bait on a question like that was unproductive.

But Brian Windhorst felt LeBron was laying out bread crumbs: "LeBron was pissed and then he went into the press conference and he started talking about my team, he wasn't talking about the Heat and I was like *uh oh, uh oh.*"

He would address the media again two days later, looking tired and definitely ready for the offseason. As taxing as the season had been for the Heat, no one had shouldered more than LeBron, or been as consistent in doing so. He had been the constant for the Heat all season, and his impact was unmistakable.

He told the assembled media, mostly Miami area reporters, that he still hadn't given his future much thought and wouldn't until after a previously planned family vacation.

"Thinking about the future while I'm in the moment is something I've never done," LeBron insisted. Still, whispers about his next move were already in the air. During a preseason game against the Nets, TNT's Marv Albert noted on-air, "There is speculation that LeBron could end up considering a move back to Cleveland or LA."

Pat Riley, in his annual end-of-season press availability, made waves with his words, which seemed directed right at LeBron and the prospect of him possibly leaving. "I think everybody needs to get a grip," he said. "This stuff is hard. You have to stay together and find the guts. You don't find the door and run out of it."

Riley was applauded far and wide for his unminced soliloquy. How it would be received by LeBron and the rest of the team remained to be seen.

LeBron's decision to opt out on June 24th wasn't surprising. Any meaningful offseason moves for the Heat would have required restructuring the top contracts, beginning with his. And if he planned to leave in free agency, opting out was the first step toward that as well.

On June 27th, NBA "insider" Ric Bucher spun straw into gold with a scoop no one else had: "An agreement in principle on a deal that would send point guard Kyle Lowry from the Toronto Raptors to the Miami Heat is 'imminent,' a league source with direct knowledge of the negotiations said."

The reason no one else had the scoop was that it wasn't a scoop; it was bullshit plain and simple, which shouldn't have come as a surprise to anyone who had listened to Bucher for any amount of time.

The Big 3 met before vacation to lunch at the Soho Beach House, a hushed free agent summit, staked out by seemingly every Miami media member. "They were relaxed and laughing," reported the *Miami Herald*.

LeBron and his wife Savannah were spotted at a Beyonce/Jay-Z concert later that night, LeBron allegedly wearing a Miami Heat hat.

A few days later, Wade opted out of his contract, and 24 hours later, so too did Bosh.

"Pat Riley will soon have the chance to make the Miami Heat even better," wrote Tim Reynolds for the Associated Press.

"I don't think we've got to recruit Chris, Dwyane or LeBron," said Riley. "I'm not dropping rings on the table for those guys. They could drop their own."

"Privately, Heat management is not worried," Dan Le Batard wrote, a friend of Pat Riley's and a regular Heat water carrier.

"Privately, management would be blindsided by any of the three leaving. Privately, management says nothing has changed in the past week except for the volume of media noise."

Riley spent time with LeBron's mother, Gloria, at the summer wedding of LeBron's longtime trainer, Mike Mancias, but said he didn't broach the topic of free agency with her.

After free agency officially began on July 1st, LeBron and his team scheduled a meeting with Pat Riley in Las Vegas for the organization's second free agency pitch to him in four years, on July 9th. That same day, Chris Sheridan, formerly of ESPN and the AP, and Chris Broussard of ESPN, reported LeBron was leaning towards leaving Miami and returning to Cleveland.

Wade showed up to LeBron's basketball camp in Vegas on the 11th, and a long video surfaced of the two on the tarmac in the wee hours on Friday morning, before they both boarded the same plane bound for South Florida.

Bosh's phone buzzed in Africa with a text from LeBron, letting him know what the rest of the world would soon learn. Hours later, in his own words, LeBron would make it official:

I'm coming home.

Chapter 23 - El Fin

LeBron, as had been speculated for years and rumored for months, was going back to Cleveland. This time, instead of a made-for-TV spectacle, he announced it in a heartfelt essay with *Sports Illustrated* — a move equal parts sincere reflection and savvy PR.

"These past four years helped raise me into who I am," he wrote. "Without my time in Miami, I wouldn't be able to do what I'm doing today." He thanked Wade, Bosh, Haslem, and the rest of the Heat, making clear there was no bad blood. "Nothing will ever change what we accomplished. We are brothers for life."

And then came the line that drew a sharp contrast to 2010: *"I'm not having a press conference or a party. After this, it's time to get to work."*

As quickly and forcefully as the Big Three had come together and shook the league, it had lost its driving force.

"I knew that automatically made Cleveland the best team in the East," said Bosh. "We thought that was going to happen forever, four years boom done. You have to enjoy it while it's there."

"Obviously, the hit we took with LeBron leaving just crushed us," Riley said to *Bleacher Report*'s Ethan Skolnick "Everybody. It just did."

He and the Heat scrambled, stealing Bosh away from a deal with Houston, re-signing Wade to a bigger contract, and bringing back Andersen and Haslem to short deals. Ray Allen wasn't officially retired, but if he were to return for another season, it was widely expected to be with LeBron in Cleveland.

Allen was notably frustrated with the 2013-14 season, not for its untimely conclusion at the hands of the Spurs, but rather the process leading to it all. He felt the Heat needed to ease up and think big picture, something Spo and Riley were not inclined to do.

"It certainly was tough on all of us as players," Allen said. "Organizationally, I don't think they ever adjusted. Most of the guys, having gone to so many Finals, me being an older player, having played a lot of basketball the last five, six years, organizationally and coaching-wise they didn't adjust.

"With a team as old as we were, and with as much basketball as we'd played, we were still doing a million appearances," he continued. "We still were having all the practices, and doing all the things that typically wear you down by the end of the year," he said. "Just being on your feet so much. The team didn't learn how to manage our bodies better."

What he said likely had a lot of merit, and yet it was unlikely to influence Riley or Spo going forward, something Allen surely wasn't going to sign up for again.

Riley had signed veteran wings Josh McRoberts and Danny Granger before the LeBron announcement and, in what seemed like an overt attempt at placating LeBron, drafted UConn point guard Shabazz Napier, solid, yet very unspectacular moves. (LeBron had tweeted that his favorite player in college was Napier who had just led UConn on a riveting national championship run.)

There was a gut-punch disbelief in Miami — what was supposed to be a dynasty was over in just four years. The Finals loss stung, but now came a new chip on the Heat's shoulder: *we'll show them what we can do without LeBron.*

LeBron's move, though, was almost universally applauded. The delivery was simple, the message clear, and the situation undeniable: he was joining a young, hungry team with sky-high potential.

It was almost surreal. In four short years, the Big Three era had come and gone, and LeBron had gone from villain to revered. Back in 2010, he was painted as Robin to Wade's Batman, a second banana without the killer instinct. Simmons even wrote that he'd always finish with one fewer ring than Wade, a permanent demerit on his legacy. Instead, LeBron left Miami with two MVPs, two titles, and a resume proving the opposite: even his best couldn't always carry Wade across the line.

Wade, who had recruited LeBron and Bosh in the first place, understood.

"If that's what that man wants to do for his life then I support it," he said. "Everybody's going to win no matter what you do. If you stay here, we all win. If you go to Cleveland, Cleveland's going to win. You got to do what's best for LeBron. If this is what's best for LeBron James, Savannah James, Bryce and Bronny... if you looking for blessing from me, you got my blessing. I'm not going to hold you back.

"Was there a part of me that was a little pissed? Yeah, I'm human. I don't want to lose the best player in the game."

What once seemed like a throwaway line from his infamous Nike ad after *The Decision* now felt prophetic. Just weeks earlier, the assumption was simple: Miami would retool around LeBron and make another run.

"Should I be who you want me to be?" he asked in that spot, the screen fading to black.

In the days after LeBron's departure, word slowly seeped out — mostly from the Heat's side — about what really went down between the Finals and the *Sports Illustrated* letter.

The Heat brass flew to Las Vegas feeling like they'd been lured under false pretenses. Riley even had to ask if they could turn off the World Cup during his pitch to LeBron. At one point he considered wheeling in the championship trophies, but the vibe killed that idea fast. He brought along a bottle of Promise wine, the same label Maverick Carter had once gifted him, only to realize Carter wasn't even going to be there. That absence told Riley all he needed to know.

He still pressed on. Marc Stein reported Riley, "with a smile and a burst of his usual gumption," floated the idea of LeBron taking less than a max deal. The room met it with silence. Two days later, Riley got the call — LeBron on the line via Rich Paul, breaking the news.

"I was silent," Riley said. "My mind just went. And it was over. I was very angry when LeBron left. It was personal for me."

LeBron had already decided. He invited SI's Lee Jenkins into his Vegas suite to draft the letter, then boarded a jet with Wade back to Miami, editing it mid-flight. Wade didn't even know until they landed. "You can't ask Dwyane to carry that [secret]," Paul explained. "It would've put him in a terrible position."

Wade admitted later he was upset, though he had sensed the night before that the move was coming.

Shandel Richardson reported:

He could tell there was something different about his former teammate.

All it took was noticing James' body language.

"Yeah, I went to sleep knowing," Wade said Friday before his annual Fantasy Basketball Camp at the Westin Diplomat Hotel. "He called me the next day. But I knew then. Obviously he still had to say the final yay or nay, but I knew. I could tell."

"As his friend, I'm just supportive," said Wade, who made no recruiting pitches to James. "As crazy as that might sound, I'm supportive of my friends doing what makes them happy. Obviously, same thing with him in this situation. You've gotta do what makes you happy—selfishly do what makes you happy. The decision to go back home was that."

Riley took the whole process as a slap in the face.

"I had two to three days of tremendous anger. I was absolutely livid," he admitted. "My beautiful plan all of a sudden came crashing down."

"You leave Riley's side, and you are no longer his friend. Or you work for him for an eternity," Dan Le Batard explained. "I remember at the time how upset Pat Riley was... it felt a bit like Pat Riley was taken over to Vegas as a showpiece, as a chess piece."

But maybe the Riley-LeBron relationship was never what people thought.

"I don't think LeBron was ever really close to Riley... I question how close they ever were," said Brian Windhorst, who'd covered him since high school. "I like the story of how Riley put the rings out on the desk... but I don't think that's why he went to Miami. He went to Miami to play with Dwyane Wade and Bosh... Riley wasn't the guy that won him over. It was Dwyane Wade."

"It's a business and you can never forget that. That whole loyalty shit and 'we're a family'... fuck that," laughs Gabrielle Union, Dwyane Wade's wife.

It wasn't exactly bad blood, but there was a lingering awkwardness between LeBron and the Heat in the years that followed. His first return to Miami in Cavaliers yellow, on Christmas Day, felt strange, though the home crowd relished the Heat beating Cleveland to cap the holiday.

Publicly, everyone in the Heat orbit spoke warmly of LeBron, while carefully pivoting the focus to the present — translation: LeBron wasn't here anymore. Yet the unease lingered. Even at Bosh's Hall of Fame induction in 2021, which LeBron attended, he was conspicuously absent from the Heat's official photos on social media.

Nearly a decade later, Spo said players still ask him about LeBron's routines in Miami.

"Young players always want to know about his routine," he said. "When he would come in on a shootaround or practice, how long he would stay afterwards. The thing I always mention to young players coming in about building the right professional habits is that LeBron was dialed in to *everything*. Always one of the first in the building, never late for anything... a meeting, an airplane...

"His locker was pristine...the first time I saw him in the locker room, he was folding up his clothes and putting it perfectly in a pile."

"The sense that I got was not any anger or frustration with LeBron like there was with Pat," Jorge Sedano said of Spo's emotions with LeBron's departure. "It was more melancholy that it didn't last longer."

Meanwhile, Riley and LeBron never spoke again.

LeBron, through Wade, said he carried a hidden chip in Cleveland — sparked when someone in Miami told him leaving was the worst decision of his career. Most presumed it was Riley, though he denied it. LeBron never named names.

"That really can't be anyone but Riley," wrote Ethan Skolnick for the *Miami Herald*. "It certainly wasn't Dwyane Wade. It's not Erik Spoelstra's style, nor Andy Elisburg's, nor even Micky Arison's. And he and others — like Mario Chalmers and Udonis Haslem — remained close."

Still, Riley reached out before Game 7 of the 2016 Finals, as LeBron stood on the edge of history with the Cleveland Cavaliers. "I didn't want to send him anything that he could read before he hit the floor," Riley said. "As soon as he hit the floor, I sent a text to him. I said, 'Win this and be free.' He never got back to me with a response."

Chapter 24 - Villainous and Vulnerable

If you have made it this far, first of all, I thank you. And you might be a little bit sick in the head.

I have tried throughout this to not interject myself; as I mentioned in the foreword, I was hoping and aiming that this would be a commentary while also acknowledging it does trend a little encyclopedic at times.

Which brings us here and now. And to the question that sparked this entire undertaking:

What is the legacy of the 2010–2014 Miami Heat?

It can only be understood by looking at what came before and after.

The Big 3's rise was slow — building from 2008 to July 2010 — but the backlash came instantly. The outrage of The Decision, the pep rally, and the Heat's every move defined that first year. By the time it ended, the hype was already fading. And when LeBron left in 2014, it ended as suddenly as it began.

"Miami is a blur," said Maverick Carter.

"Definitely a blur," echoed Rich Paul.

There was no proper send-off. LeBron's "coming home" branding softened the edges, and it was easier to root for Cleveland than for Miami's glitz and rivals teaming up. The Heat quickly felt like they belonged to another era entirely.

Pat Riley believed the Big 3 could have stretched into a decade-long dynasty. Instead, as Miami came apart, Golden State was taking shape — a dynasty that seemed, at least on the surface, like everything Miami wasn't allowed to be.

Homegrown, celebrated, embraced. Whether that was entirely fair or not didn't matter; perception was reality.

"They started the trend and then the trend got more fascinating," said Dan Le Batard. "LeBron gets here, they do that pep rally, we think it's going to be easy for them. And then we saw that it wasn't any kind of easy. The reason people are still mad at Kevin Durant is because we saw how easy it was when he played on that team."

Gabrielle Union framed it simply: "It changed the NBA, and it gave a modicum of power to the players. And once they were successful at it... it became a blueprint."

Durant's move to Golden State drew criticism, but nothing close to *The Decision*. He was accused of teaming up with a rival, chasing rings, and taking the easy way out — the same charges once leveled at LeBron. But by 2016, the tone had shifted.

LeBron had already taken the arrows. He absorbed the vitriol, then forced the basketball world to reevaluate. Suddenly, the justifications that were unacceptable in 2010 — "doing what's best for him," "no loyalty in sports," "better basketball situation" — were shrugged off when Durant made the same choice.

Durant may have seemed humbler, but he followed LeBron's playbook almost step for step: mimicking his PR wins, copying his MVP speech cadence, even publishing his departure letter in essay form, just like LeBron had in 2014.

He got the benefit of the doubt. LeBron never did.

Aside from the LeBron-centric lookbacks, it's hard to imagine anyone in July 2010 thinking the Heat's run would last only four years. The Big 3 were in their primes and largely healthy. To frame those years as underwhelming is misleading.

They won 71.7% of their regular season games (a 58-win pace), reached four straight Finals, and won two titles. Only two teams ever beat them in the playoffs. That's an 87.5% series win rate. For all the noise about what they didn't do, what they did stacks up with or exceeds other dynasties. The Shaq-Kobe Lakers didn't win half the titles in their run. Neither did the Spurs. The Celtics love to argue they could have. Even Golden State's run—with Durant in the middle—produced three in five years.

It's undeniable that the Heat carried the heaviest expectations, the loudest criticism, and the most scrutiny of any four-year span in NBA history. Winning multiple championships through all of that can't be undersold.

The legacy debate—did they live up to it or not—is less interesting than the actual basketball.

On defense, the Heat played a frenzied, trapping, high-speed style that could and often did overwhelm opponents. They could switch and blitz seamlessly, fueling a transition attack that became a dunkathon. Yes, they were exposed at times against traditional bigs or on the offensive glass. But going small often neutralized those weaknesses. "Time will remember us as innovators," Shane Battier said.

Offensively, they transformed. What started as stagnant, awkward sets turned into a fluid system built around LeBron's versatility and Bosh's perimeter skills. By 2014, Miami could attack from anywhere: LeBron as post scorer, cutter, initiator, or even screener, surrounded by shooters. "We were really pleasant to watch," assistant coach Ron Rothstein said.

The balance was what made them special. Championship teams usually can't be great on only one side of the ball. Miami ranked top-six in offense and top-11 in defense each season, despite the physical toll of their system. "I don't know if the NBA is really built for a team to make the Finals four straight times," Bill Simmons said. "By that fourth year, you've been playing nine months a year for four straight years."

They weren't unbeatable, but they were a nightmare. Opponents needed elite shot-making, speed, or execution to have a chance, usually all three. Most nights, every arena treated them like villains. "Every arena wanted to kill these people," says Wosny Lambre. Teams could get hot, or catch Miami coasting, but only two ever managed to beat them across seven games.

"We were all bad, we were nice, we were cold, whatever you want to call us, we were it," Chris Bosh laughed.

"It was surreal...we got every team's best every night," Wade recalled. "We had to show everyone we were built for your best every night."

And the backbone of it all was sacrifice.

"The sacrifices that Shane made, that UD made, Juwan—you saw the sacrifices everybody made to be part of the team and help win," said Ray Allen.

Bosh took the biggest hit, constantly reminded he wasn't Toronto CB. "I thought I was going to be the leading scorer," he laughs now. Yet his evolution—spacing the floor, defending multiple positions, anchoring the system—was what unlocked it all. "He was the piece that made it all work," Wade said. "He started this wave of bigs shooting threes, playing on the perimeter...he was the piece me and Bron relied on."

Wade himself stepped back from being "the man." Nearly everyone sacrificed shots, money, and individual accolades for the greater good.

"Dwyane Wade took $3 million less, LeBron and Bosh took $1 million less," Gilbert Arenas explained. "Mike Miller turned down thirty; Haslem took that pay cut to make it all happen."

That kind of sacrifice set the tone. "The level of excellence those guys played with, tremendously professional," said assistant coach Ron Rothstein. Eric Reid put it more bluntly: "It was…San Antonio-esque, stars sacrificing to win. LeBron's sacrifice was leaving his hometown and taking on all the criticism. He took the brunt of the heat and the hate."

LeBron's teammates still talk about him in almost reverent tones. "He was the queen on the chessboard," Shane Battier said. "As a ball handler, post player, screener—he unlocked our versatility, which was our biggest strength. He's a Patton type; he likes to be out front and lead by example."

"Playing with him is unbelievable," Mike Miller said. "He's as good a teammate as he is a player. He lifts everybody in the locker room. Ultimate dude. The best."

"He did everything we needed and more," Udonis Haslem added. Bosh was just as direct: "When it was winning time, he stepped up."

Plenty of teams tried to copy the formula. Nearly all failed. The Lakers built around Dwight Howard and won zero playoff games. The Rockets took their shot at the Durant Warriors, only to blow a 3–2 lead and flame out soon after. Durant himself tried again with Kyrie Irving and James Harden in Brooklyn. That lasted 18 months and produced one playoff series win. The Clippers made their splash with Kawhi Leonard and Paul George—four years in, three series wins, and a front-row seat as LeBron's Lakers hoisted the trophy instead.

For all the handwringing about Miami "ruining basketball," teams still try to replicate the model. Most come up short. The Warriors were the lone exception, and even they broke the rules in their own way. "The hardest thing to do is to get a lot of talented guys to click like that," Bill Simmons said.

The four years in Miami are still judged against preconceptions. The Heat ruined basketball! False. The 2011 Finals loss defines LeBron forever! Also false, though it was formative.

"It gave me an opportunity to learn who I am as a person and how I'm going to go forward," LeBron admitted. "That shit burns me to this day." He still calls Dirk "the shit...one of my favorites of all time."

"I think he needed to go through all that to get to where he ultimately ended up," Rachel Nichols said.

"To be that close, to taste it, I didn't know basketball could give you that much pain," Bosh said. "We had to feel that pain; you have to know what's necessary to be successful and what you have to lose."

"We both needed that series to reinvent everything," Spoelstra admitted.

"It humbled us, it put us at our level, and it allowed us to focus on what was real and why we had got together," Wade added.

Bosh was even blunter: "Karma wouldn't have allowed us to win a championship because it wasn't pure for us. We didn't want to win for the right reason."

The Heat were going to win 75 games! False. A knee-jerk take on the roster's talent, nothing more. Winning that many games is nearly impossible, even for dynasties. Miami learned as much during the 27-game streak in 2013: the higher you climb, the heavier the legs get.

And Riley's vision of a ten-year dynasty? Maybe plausible in 2010. Maybe even in 2012. But that's not how the NBA works anymore. Teams don't last that long. The human element—the fatigue of seeing the same faces, running the same race—always sets in.

"They were just tired of each other," reporter Ethan Skolnick recalled. "We could sense it."

"Jokes weren't funny no more in the locker room," Wade said.

"It gets tougher and tougher to get your mind fresh," Bosh admitted. "You can't cheat the process."

This wasn't just championship fatigue, either. The Heat lived under the most suffocating microscope in NBA history. At first, maybe the theater of it all was fun. But after four years, and especially after the first two years of chaos, the only way out was to walk away.

"No team has ever gone through the kind of stuff that team went through," Skolnick said.

"Legitimate sports hate! It was insane!" Wosny Lambre laughed. "We couldn't have gotten that hate without the old heads stirring it up."

And no, LeBron wasn't destined to be Robin to Wade's Batman. In truth, Miami often won in spite of Wade's body breaking down. His balky knees left LeBron carrying the burden nightly, and by 2014 Wade admitted he'd even considered retirement. By the Finals, Wade's diminished form made the early debates feel absurd.

So what is the legacy of the Big 3? Maybe that's the wrong question. Maybe the real one is: how will they be remembered?

Bosh didn't hesitate: "The greatest atomic bomb the league has ever seen. It's just a blip...but it was a hell of a ride."

Mike Miller echoed: "Our team was just cool. We were all in, and we were either going to do it together or fail together."

"That team was a party for four years," Dan Le Batard said. "They were loud, spectacularly Miami in every way. It was fun! Fuck yeah, we had a good time."

"They didn't call them the Heatles for nothing," Ron Rothstein said. "It was a traveling circus."

Battier framed it differently: "You remember the streak, the four straight Finals... but between each milestone was a lifetime of work. Fighting the feeling that it could all come crashing down in a moment."

The Heat were a great team, yes, but more than that, they were a phenomenon. Miami, LeBron, villains. A perfect storm, lightning in a bottle, reshaping the NBA both by design and by accident.

"The first team to revolutionize the NBA as a business entity," said Zach Lowe.

"It was the big bang of the modern NBA," Lambre added. "Everything about the league today flows out of the Decision."

Binary narratives—two titles, two failures—miss the point. Their story was human. They were cast as villains, and LeBron leaned into it.

"There were so many different narratives of who I was, and I wasn't that person," he said. "And then I started to become that person because I was like, fuck it, if they're gonna make me wear the black hat, I might as well wear it. It's like a glitch in a computer when it goes from a glitch into a full-blown virus."

But wearing the black hat carried a cost.

"It was not fun at all," Bosh admitted. "You have to have a strong bond for those things not to get to you."

"It wasn't a joyous year to play basketball," Wade added quietly.

Forged in symbolic flames, the Heat transformed. Still burdened with expectations and constant criticism, their first season together became almost freeing. It couldn't get worse, and there were only two outcomes: win a title or see the experiment blown up.

Through the fire, and despite the villain label, something emerged that no one in July 2010 or May 2011 could have predicted: a sympathetic non-underdog.

"It's the best way to go to fame: famous, infamous, then more famous," said Le Batard. "We all saw how hard it was. The reason people are still mad at Kevin Durant is because we saw how easy it was when he played on that team. LeBron gets here, they do that pep rally, we think it's going to be easy for them. And then we saw that it wasn't any kind of easy...begrudgingly they end up taking our respect."

The human element bound the four-year run together. These weren't cartoon villains but real people under unprecedented scrutiny. From LeBron nervously announcing his decision at the Boys and Girls Club, to his shift in demeanor in 2012, to Wade and Bosh carrying the weight in their own ways, emotions were always at the surface.

How else could we have expected LeBron to react to the vitriol? Few stars would have met that storm meekly. He chose fight over flight, mocked for it, but eventually respected. By 2012 he was contrite, quieter, better. And when paired with the sport at its highest level, respect followed.

So what is the lasting memory of the Heat? They were flawed and talented, loved and loathed, champions and failures, all at once. More than anything, they made people feel.

"The NBA was leading ESPN!" Lambre remembered. "You can't beat the NFL for anything these days. People were so angry that these guys had the audacity to switch teams!"

"LeBron brought out this primal thing in people," said Tom Haberstroh. "He made you feel something," Wosny Lambre added. "He just struck a chord...there was no measured response to anything involving the Heat."

That kind of response is rare now. As of this writing, the Denver Nuggets are rolling to a championship in 2023, applauded but barely argued over. The Heat era hit differently. "I feel like we're still chasing the juice," Lambre admitted. "I've never felt like that before or since."

Why did the Heat make us feel? Because they were more relatable than we ever gave them credit for. Their vulnerability, their human messiness, their raw emotions — all set against a backdrop of superhuman expectations.

As Zach Lowe put it best: "They were fun because they were villainous and vulnerable."

About the Author

Chip Maude is a first-time author and avid sports fan. He and his wife, Mallory, have three cats: Theo, Tito, and Cleo.